# MILLIE CHAN'S KOSHER CHINESE COOKBOOK

# MILLIE CHAN'S
# KOSHER
# CHINESE
## COOKBOOK

HARMONY BOOKS
NEW YORK

Published by Harmony Books, a division of Crown Publishers, Inc., 201 East 50th Street, New York, New York 10022

HARMONY and colophon are trademarks of Crown Publishers, Inc.

Manufactured in the United States of America
Book design by John Fontana

Library of Congress Cataloging-in-Publication Data

Chan, Millie.
    Millie Chan's kosher Chinese cookbook / by Millie Chan.
      p.  cm.
      1. Cookery, Chinese. 2. Cookery, Jewish. I. Title. II. Title: Chinese kosher cookbook.
    TX724.5.C5C4622   1990
    641.5951'089924—dc20              89-15234
                                                 CIP

ISBN 0-517-57474-8

10  9  8  7  6  5  4  3  2  1

First Edition

TO FATHER, GRANDMOTHER AND FLORENCE LIN

# CONTENTS

# ACKNOWLEDGMENTS

There are many people I would like to thank, for without them this book would not have been written: Helen Nash, who introduced me to Jewish dietary laws. Rabbi Marc Angel, his wife, Gilda, and Judy Greenspan for giving them clarity; Judy was always there to talk, test and taste. My students for teaching me so much. Joy Mileaf for helping me create and test new recipes on hot summer days. Linda Epstein, who helped with the editing. Carol and Joe Reich for their encouragement, support, counseling and honesty during the many meals we cooked and shared together. Carol Wheeler, always cheerful, for her suggestions. And Elyse Feldman for her steady support. My deep gratitude goes to Florence Lin for being a generous, inspiring and encouraging teacher, mentor and colleague, as well as a dear friend. Finally, my husband, Lo-Yi, who has always been there and helped in more ways than I can say.

# MILLIE CHAN'S KOSHER CHINESE COOKBOOK

# INTRODUCTION

*I* can't remember when I didn't know how to cook! As in all Chinese families, food was very important in mine. It was even more so for us because my parents owned Chinese restaurants in San Antonio, Texas, where I was born. Many of our male relatives from our home village outside Canton came to help my parents in their businesses. Every night they cooked delicious home-style Cantonese dinners with many different dishes for my extended family. This is when I began to learn about Chinese cooking. My father, especially, loved to eat, and I can still picture him at the kitchen table, eating everything with gusto. I was encouraged to learn to cook when I was about seven or eight, and I loved it.

I also recall childhood trips to Arizona, where my mother had been born. I remember great cooking and eating vacations with my grandmother, an extraordinary Chinese cook. She had nine children, so an everyday meal meant cooking for at least eleven people. Often there were unexpected guests, and I still marvel at how easily she would cook a few more dishes to welcome them. All her meals were memorable, but I particularly remember the taste of her wonderful Cantonese dumplings.

When I married and had children of my own, cooking for my family became a very important part of my life. I experimented with Cantonese recipes, such as White-Cut Chicken (page 60), marinades for meats, and steamed dishes. I sought authentic tastes that I remembered from my childhood. The opportunity to teach came while I was taking classes at the China Institute. Florence Lin, the noted author and teacher, was my instructor; it was she who suggested that I teach with her at the institute.

As an American-born Chinese I am often asked by students in my Chinese kosher-cooking classes, "Are you Jewish?" I smile and say no. "Then how do you know about keeping kosher?" I learned about Jewish dietary laws, or *kashruth,* quite by accident. Some years ago I contributed a series of Chinese cooking classes to a fund-raising auction at my children's school. A friend bought and gave the series to her friend Helen Nash, an accomplished cook and noted author who specializes in kosher cookbooks. Helen was eager to learn Chinese cooking, and as I taught her, she taught me about Jewish dietary laws.

The more I learned about Jewish dietary laws, the more I realized that Chinese cooking and those laws, as well as Jewish culinary tastes, go hand in hand. This eventually led to my teaching Chinese kosher-cooking classes for the 92nd Street YMHA in New York City. The classes, which I started in 1981, are held at the Spanish-Portuguese Synagogue on Manhattan's West Side and have become very popular. Rabbi Marc Angel, the rabbi of the synagogue, together with his wife, Gilda, have guided me in the laws of kashruth.

It is because my Chinese kosher classes are so popular that I decided to write this book. I would like to share the variety of Chinese cooking techniques, methods and ingredients with those who follow Jewish dietary laws and open up a whole new culinary world.

## CHINESE COOKING

Jewish dietary laws have religious and spiritual foundations based on a reverence for life. These beliefs are similar to those shared by the Chinese early in the development of their cuisine. Buddhists forbade consuming the flesh of all animals and the Taoists had similar restrictions. The foundation of Chinese cooking, however, is not religious but ethical and pragmatic, and these two influences developed together.

Confucius has been the ethical and spiritual voice of China for 2,500 years. He taught ritual and ceremony in the service of order. He extolled simple dishes. A follower of the Confucian ethic shunned luxury and sought out moderation and natural foods. One special offering for guests, a Grand Stew, was prepared without seasoning to emphasize its humbleness. The ideas of Confucius ritualized daily life, from how to set the table to elaborate ceremonies and menus for betrothals, weddings, funerals and even national disasters. Yet practical concerns also shaped Chinese cuisine. The scarcity of fuel meant shorter cooking times, so stir-frying rather than roasting or boiling became the preferred method of cooking. In time, simplicity gave way to elaboration and elaboration to sumptuousness, particularly in the Imperial Court. Chinese still follow the Confucian ideas of ritual; the link between food and ceremony has endured. The range of dishes, however, is now very broad, from the vegetarian dishes of the Buddhists to highly seasoned banquet fare.

Today, Chinese, who live all over the world, care passionately about food. We spend time looking for the freshest ingredients. We invite family and friends to try a new dish, and even as we eat, we talk enthusiastically about food. To many of us, food is the joy of life—and most Chinese willingly pay well for a good meal. Expensive edible delicacies such as bird's nest, shark's fin or black mushrooms are considered prized gifts. Although we seldom give parties, we celebrate birthdays, weddings and anniversaries with feasts.

Chinese love variety in their cooking. Even a simple meal has more than one dish, and within each dish there are always several ingredients. Meat, fowl, fish, vegetables and bean curd are often all served at the same meal. Variety means more than just different dishes; it also means a wide range of tastes, textures, shapes and colors. The human palate can distinguish among five different flavors: salty, sweet, sour, acrid and bitter. Often a good Chinese cook will try to include all these tastes in several dishes. Sweet-and-sour sauce is well known. Orange Beef (page 108) is sweet, spicy and tangy all at once. For different textures, we contrast crunchy with slick, crispy with soft, chewy with gelatinous. For instance, Peking Duck (page 82) combines crispy skin with soft wheat pancakes. Because we eat with chopsticks, ingredients are cut bite size, some cubed, others in balls, shreds or slices, allowing for variety in shapes. For color contrast, green vegetables are mixed with white ones and dark mushrooms. By using these special touches, even a modest meal becomes a sensual treat.

The Chinese eat much less meat than Westerners. With its huge population and limited suitable land, the Chinese long ago discovered that cultivation of vegetables ultimately produces more protein and other nutrients than does raising animals. To the Chinese, grazing animals is an inefficient use of scarce land. Because there are few pastures with cows, dairy products never became a part of Chinese cuisine. Instead, a wide range of vegetables were developed and grown. The soybean, a complete vegetable protein, is used in many forms, such as soybean sprouts (different from the more common mung bean sprouts), soybean milk, bean curd, bean-curd skins and pressed bean curd. A large variety of cabbages, from bok choy to mustard greens, which are high in calcium, are raised. Of course, rice and wheat are the staples.

Chinese food is considered healthy for many reasons. First, the Chinese diet contains a higher proportion of grains and plants than meat. Second,

Chinese use fresh ingredients. Although many prepared ingredients are also used, they are a small part of the diet. Third, stir-frying preserves many of the nutrients in the fresh ingredients. Fourth, we use a wide variety of dried plants rich in vitamins and minerals. Finally, although we stir-fry many dishes, we use polyunsaturated oil. For these reasons, Chinese food is low in cholesterol and high in fiber, with many vitamins and other essential nutrients.

# CHINESE FOOD AND JEWISH DIETARY LAWS

Jewish dietary laws are based on Biblical scriptures: Leviticus, chapter 11, and Deuteronomy, chapter 14. The laws of kashruth are sacred and define a way of life for the observant Jew who strives for holiness and compassion. For the observant, the home is a sanctuary, the dining table an altar and eating a hallowed act. Thus it follows that what is served at the table must be kosher, following Jewish dietary laws. Now, let's look at how Chinese cuisine adapts to these laws.

First, the laws of kashruth permit only certain foods.

1. All vegetables are permitted, which allows the vast majority of Chinese dishes to be served. With a varied climate, China developed many vegetables, and these form the basis of Chinese cooking. This is one of the reasons for the compatibility between Jewish dietary laws and Chinese food. Grains, nuts, spices, fruits and most oils, like vegetables, are *pareve* (neither meat nor dairy products), which means they can be used. Chinese cooking uses these ingredients abundantly.

2. Domestic fowl such as chicken, turkey, duck and goose and their eggs are permitted and are mentioned in the Torah. Chinese chefs use all of these in their recipes. One dish, Peking Duck (page 82), has become almost legendary.

3. Meat (which includes fowl) is treated with greater complexity in Jewish dietary laws. These laws prescribe not only the kind of meat permitted but also how it is slaughtered and prepared. Only cloven-hoofed animals who chew their cud may be eaten. Beef is scarce in China and used sparingly. Pork, however, is the most common meat used in Chinese cooking. Although the pig has cloven hooves, it does not chew its cud, so pork is not kosher. I have had great success using properly seasoned turkey and veal as a substitute for pork.

4. Fish is permitted if it has both fins and scales, which means shellfish is not permitted. Fish is pareve, which means it can be served when

 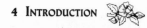

eating meat or dairy. Fish such as sea bass and pike are frequently used in both Chinese and Jewish cuisines. Catfish, monkfish, mackerel and swordfish are not permitted because they do not have scales.

The second key to the appropriateness of food is how it is prepared. Jewish life is rich with observance. Proper preparation, from the butcher shop to the table, is very important. First, animals and fowl must be ritually slaughtered and *koshered* (made kosher). Hindquarters of beef are not sold in kosher butcher shops in this country because it is financially impractical to remove the sinews, veins and fat embedded in them. You can either kosher your own meat or purchase it from a kosher butcher who works under approved rabbinical supervision. Throughout this book I have used only kosher cuts of meat.

Third, the laws of kashruth require that there be a complete separation between meat and milk products. Not only must the products themselves be separated, but the utensils used in their preparation and consumption must be kept separate. There is even a prescribed time period between consuming the two. Chinese cuisine does not use milk products, making this rule relatively easy to observe. Because dairy products never developed as a part of the Chinese diet, most Chinese cannot digest the lactose in milk. This is also true of about 50 percent of all Sephardic Jews, who share this lactose intolerance.

Finally, the most important reason for the adaptability of Chinese cuisine to the Jewish dietary laws is that Chinese cooking is based on techniques more than ingredients; a major advantage to the kosher cook is its flexibility and the ease with which ingredients can be substituted. For instance, pork—the principal meat in China—is forbidden in the kosher kitchen, but turkey, veal, chicken and beef are excellent substitutes. Cantonese Roast Veal or Turkey (page 97) replaces Cantonese roast pork; barbecued spareribs turn into Barbecued Chicken Wings (page 49). Although shellfish is important in Chinese cuisine and not permitted in the kosher kitchen, you can still delight in the taste and color contrast of salmon in place of shrimp, stir-fried with a green vegetable. In fact, you can take almost any Chinese recipe and change the ingredients to fit kosher requirements. I believe you will find, as I have, that Chinese cooking adapts beautifully to Jewish dietary laws. The reason I wrote this book is to provide you with authentic Chinese recipes adapted to Jewish dietary laws; to instruct you in the concept, method and techniques of Chinese cooking; and to help you add variety to your kosher meals. You will find you can create delicious Chinese meals using kosher ingredients.

# CHINESE FOOD AND JEWISH TASTE

The popularity of my Chinese kosher-cooking classes reveals the interest and affinity Jewish people have for Chinese food. A Jewish friend told me this joke: Jewish civilization is two thousand years older than Chinese civilization, but how did the Jews survive all those years without Chinese food?

There are several thriving Chinese kosher restaurants in New York City that attest to the popularity of Chinese food among those who adhere to Jewish dietary laws. The well-known kosher restaurant Bernstein-on-Essex Street on the Lower East Side in Manhattan has served kosher food with a Chinese flair for more than twenty years. A Jewish friend and I recently dined on a number of traditional Jewish dishes: tongue Polonaise, stuffed cabbage, stuffed derma and meat kreplach. As we ate, I noticed that the sweet-and-sour taste of the traditional Jewish sauces was similar to a Chinese sweet-and-sour sauce. Like wontons, the kreplach were folded and served in chicken broth. My friend noted that the sauces were thinner than she remembered, and it became clear why when the chef was introduced: he was Chinese. M. K. Bill Lee has been the chef at Bernstein's for nineteen years. The lighter sauces, a result of Mr. Lee's Chinese touch, were thickened with cornstarch rather than flour.

The two cultures have mingled in the past. Jews who settled in the Chinese city of K'ai-feng in Hunan Province were known as the Sect Which Plucks Out the Sinews and also as the Blue-Cap Moslems. The mingling continues today through the cuisine of both cultures. On occasion my Chinese friends have substituted gefilte fish for Chinese fishballs. Chicken soup is commonly used in both cuisines. Many Chinese dishes are flavored with chicken broth, and nearly all Chinese soups use chicken stock as a base.

Chinese dishes can fit into daily kosher meals as easily as they can in traditional Jewish feasts. Smoked fish, a classic delicatessen special, is unique when made with five-spice powder. Serve wonton soup rather than the traditional matzah ball soup. Vary the main dish of your holiday meal with White-Cut Chicken (page 60), Braised Beef with Garlic (page 103) or an exotic Shanghai Braised Duck with Onions (page 80). Do the reverse of my Chinese friends and serve Chinese fishballs in place of gefilte fish. For those who observe the Sabbath, many Chinese dishes can be cooked a day ahead. Try Soy-Sauce Chicken (page 79), Star-Anise Beef (page 109), Curried Beef (page 102) or Cantonese Roast Veal (page 97) instead of the usual pot roast or brisket. (See comments on page 27 for more do-ahead tips.) Look at the chart at the beginning of each chapter for recipes that can be prepared ahead.

The light and healthful quick-cooking methods of Chinese cuisine offer alternatives to some of the heavily sauced and longer-cooked traditional

Jewish dishes. Stir-frying is so quick that I often hear this comment in my classes: "It's cooked already?"

It's not necessary to prepare as many dishes for one meal as the Chinese do. Many of my recipes will fit into the routine meal. One Chinese dish in a meal is plenty except for special occasions, and one Chinese dish will be enough to make that meal memorable, whether it's an appetizer, soup or main course.

## HOME COOKING VS. RESTAURANT COOKING

Why does Chinese food prepared at home taste so subtle while food served in a restaurant is more pungent? The reason is simple: in order to produce many dishes quickly, restaurant chefs shorten cooking times by using larger woks, more oil and, most important, higher temperatures. The high temperatures produced by a commercial stove cannot be achieved at home and because of this, restaurant woks impart a different flavor than does a home wok.

# INGREDIENTS, EQUIPMENT AND COOKING TECHNIQUES

*T*he various methods of Chinese cooking allow for the easy substitution of ingredients, so keep this in mind when planning your menu. Buy the freshest ingredients and best-quality products you can find, but remember that you can also improvise with whatever you might have on hand. For the occasional dish that requires a special ingredient not readily available, choose a substitute that will retain the character of the dish as much as possible. For example, the crunchy, slightly sweet white flesh of jicama, a tuber from Mexico that is becoming more popular here, is an excellent substitute for fresh or canned water chestnuts. Use kohlrabi in place of bamboo shoots and chicken for veal or turkey, or interchange beef and lamb. Once you understand the cooking methods and the general character of the recipes, feel free to experiment.

I have divided the ingredients used in Chinese cooking into the following categories: Chinese flavorings, vegetables and vegetable products, dried products, and fresh noodles and wrappers. All these ingredients are found in supermarkets, Asian groceries and health-food stores. If you can't find kosher brands, many of these ingredients can be made from recipes in this book.

# INGREDIENTS

## Chinese Flavorings

Chinese flavorings are created from a variety of sauces and seasonings, which are listed below.

**Chicken Broth**   Kosher chickens make excellent broth. Many stir-fry recipes in this book require a few tablespoons of chicken broth. Since homemade chicken broth is superior to any of the canned kosher varieties, make your own (page 155) and freeze it in ice-cube trays. Keep the broth cubes in a plastic bag in the freezer and use them as needed.

**Cinnamon Stick**   The Chinese use the cinnamon-flavored brown bark of the cassia tree. It is found in Asian groceries and is thinner than the cinnamon stick usually found in supermarkets, but either one may be used.

**Coriander**   This fresh herb from the parsley family is also called Chinese parsley or cilantro. It has a distinctive, almost medicinal flavor and is used in fillings and as a garnish for soups and fish dishes. Do not substitute ground coriander.

**Cornstarch**   This fine, powdery starch made from corn is the most common thickening agent used in Chinese cooking. Cornstarch is added to a marinade to give the ingredients a smooth texture and allows the seasonings to adhere to the ingredients. When used for thickening, cornstarch is first dissolved in cold liquid and then added to hot food during the last stages of cooking. It must be cooked and stirred until the sauce thickens or forms a glaze.

**Dried Hot Chili Peppers**   Many varieties of dried hot chili peppers can be found in Asian groceries and supermarkets, and their size and degree of spiciness differ. You may have to experiment with the kind and amount to find what suits your taste. They are used mainly in Sichuan dishes. I prefer the larger ones because they can be easily picked out of a prepared dish and not eaten.

**Dried Tangerine Peel**   Available in Asian groceries, these sun-dried peels are used to flavor master sauces and in the well-known Orange Beef (page 108) dish. To dry your own, place tangerine peels on a flat baking pan in a slow oven (200° F.) until dry.

**Duck Sauce**   A sweet-and-pungent sauce made from assorted fruits, vinegar and sugar, duck sauce is served as a condiment with duck and meats. The recipe is on page 33.

**Fermented Black Beans** (Salted Black Beans)  These imported small black beans have been fermented and preserved in salt. I could not find any brand of fermented black beans with rabbinical approval, so I have not used them in any of the recipes in this book. They are an important spice in Chinese cooking and are a pure vegetable product sold packaged in Asian groceries. These beans are soft and chewy with a pungent aroma, and they add a delightful flavor to dishes cooked with minced garlic and fresh ginger and are especially good with stir-fried beef or steamed fish. They can be stored indefinitely in the refrigerator in an airtight container.

**Five-Spice Powder**  This is a blend of ground star anise, cloves, cinnamon, fennel seeds and Sichuan peppercorns. Like curry powder, the combination of spices can vary according to the manufacturer, however star anise is usually the flavor that stands out. Store in an airtight container. It is easy to make your own (page 35).

**Ginger**  Ginger is a plant that grows a chain of rhizomes, or underground stems. Used extensively in Chinese cooking for its sharp, peppery, spicy flavor, fresh ginger "root" is especially good with fish. Choose an unblemished, firm piece with a smooth, shiny skin. The color of the skin can vary from light tan to beige, while the color of the interior varies from pale yellow to a yellowish green and its texture can be smooth and firm or woody. Usually, the lighter the skin color, the younger the ginger piece; a woody texture indicates a very mature piece. Fresh ginger is peeled before using. The younger, less pungent ginger is best used in stir-fried or steamed dishes while the harsher peppery mature ginger is good for braised dishes. It keeps best in the refrigerator vegetable compartment wrapped in a paper towel placed inside a plastic bag. Cut away any dried or moldy parts to expose the fresh interior. Ground dried ginger cannot be substituted.

**Hoisin Sauce**  A thick, smooth, dark reddish brown bean sauce made with sugar, garlic and other spices, this has a spicy-sweet taste that complements meat dishes and dumplings. Best known as the sauce served with Peking Duck, it is available in cans or jars, or you can make your own (page 31). It also makes a terrific barbecue sauce for chicken or beef.

**Hot Bean Sauce**  This sauce is a combination of hot chili sauce and brown bean sauce. It is used in spicy Sichuan and Hunan dishes. Although I could not find a brand with rabbinical approval, it is a pure vegetable product sold in small cans in Asian groceries. After opening, transfer to a clean airtight jar and refrigerate.

**Hot Chili Oil**  This is vegetable oil in which dried hot chili peppers and other spices have been fried. When the oil becomes very spicy, the spices

 INGREDIENTS  11

are removed and the oil transferred to an airtight jar. The hot oil is served as a condiment at the table or stirred into a dish during the final stages of cooking. A recipe is on page 36.

**Hot Chili Sauce**   This fiery sauce is made from crushed dried hot chilies, sweet red peppers and soy sauce. If you like Sichuan or Hunan food, this sauce is essential. It is available in jars or you can make your own (page 32).

**Hot Mustard Powder**   Hot mustard powder is ground mustard seeds. It makes a very spicy condiment when combined with equal amounts of water and stirred until smooth. Serve it with egg rolls or dumplings or add it to salad dressing.

**Kosher Salt**   A course-grain salt used for koshering meat and cooking. I prefer to use kosher salt when cooking because less salt is needed to make a dish tasty. I used kosher salt in testing the recipes in this book, so if you are using a fine-grain salt, use less than the recipe indicates and, of course, whichever salt you use, do so to suit your own taste.

**Madras Curry Powder**   This curry powder is kosher and readily available from Durkee.

**Master Sauce**   This spicy concentrated sauce or marinade is known as *lu* in Chinese. There are two types of master sauce: one is made with spices, rice wine, sugar and soy sauce and is called Brown Master Sauce; the other is made with the same ingredients except for the soy sauce, for which salt is substituted, and is called White Master Sauce. Different kinds of meats or fowl can be cooked simply by immersing in either a Brown or White Master Sauce and simmering until done. Food prepared this way is always cooked whole or in large chunks and is served cut up and at room temperature. This method of cooking is perfect for meals that must be cooked in advance, such as for Shabbat. Food cooked in a Brown Master Sauce is lighter in flavor than that which is red-cooked (stewed in soy sauce). Soy-Sauce Chicken (page 79) is cooked in a Brown Master Sauce.

**Monosodium Glutamate** (MSG)   A chemical food enhancer in the form of white granules that look like coarse salt. The Chinese have used it for centuries to deepen and bring out the natural flavors of foods. Used in a very small amount, it can add a sparkle to the taste of a dish. However, if used in large amounts, MSG can cause severe allergic reactions when ingested. If top quality, fresh ingredients are used, MSG is not necessary, so I do not include it in any of the recipes in this book.

**Oil**   Corn, safflower, soy or peanut oil are all excellent for Chinese cooking, since these oils do not have a strong flavor. Olive oil is too strong and is never used. Peanut oil is often used in Chinese recipes, but I prefer the lighter flavor of corn oil and have used it to test the recipes in this book. In China, soybean oil is more widely used because it is most available. Used oil can be saved, but strain it through several layers of cheesecloth and store it in the refrigerator. Discard frying oils that have darkened in color, that flow more slowly than they did originally, or that foam to the top of the pot when you put the food in. Store unused oils in a cool place.

**Rice Wine**　Because rice wine is a grain product, it can be used in the kosher kitchen. The best substitute is dry, kosher white wine.

**Rock Sugar**　Rock sugar is crystallized raw sugar. Its flavor is more mellow and not as sweet as refined sugar. It is used in braised dishes and in the master sauce. It is available in Asian groceries.

**Scallions**　A scallion is a young onion with long green stems and a small white bulb at the root end. Because of its crisp, sharp fresh taste and its bright green and white color, it is used extensively in Chinese cooking. The recipes in this book use both the green stem and white bulb unless specified.

**Sesame Oil**　Oriental sesame oil made from roasted sesame seeds has a dark orange hue and a strong, nutty, slightly smoky flavor. Use it sparingly as a flavoring, but never use it for cooking, since it burns easily. Store in a cool place or in the refrigerator.

**Sesame Paste**　Roasted sesame seeds are ground into a paste. Peanut butter can be used as a substitute. Do not use tahini, which is made from unroasted sesame seeds, because the taste is different.

**Sichuan Peppercorns**　These dried, reddish, aromatic berries are slightly peppery and give a numbing sensation to the tongue. They have a strong, distinct aroma when roasted and are used whole or crushed into a powder (page 35).

**Soy Sauce**　Brewed from fermented soybeans, wheat, salt, sugar and yeast, soy sauce is the most important flavoring in Chinese cuisine. It is salty and tangy in flavor and is dark brown—almost black—in color. There are two main kinds of imported soy sauces available—light (thin) or dark (black). Both kinds are used for cooking; however, the light soy sauce is saltier than the black and is preferred for dipping. Imported soy sauces are better than approved domestic brands because the flavor is deeper, richer and more consistent. Some of the kosher brands are not even made from soybeans.

Of the kosher brands, I find La Choy and Kikkoman the best and have used them in testing the recipes for this book.

**Star Anise**   Its name is derived from the eight seed pods that come together in the shape of a star. Its licorice flavor is not unlike aniseed, and it is used to flavor braised dishes and the master sauce. Remove the star anise from the dish before serving, since it is not to be eaten. Store in an airtight jar.

**Sweet Red Bean Paste**   Made from a purée of azuki red beans cooked with sugar and corn oil, it is used as a sweet filling for desserts. A recipe is found on page 217.

**Vinegar**   Most of the recipes in this book call for distilled white vinegar or apple cider vinegar, available in any supermarket. The Chinese make a black rice vinegar called Chinkiang vinegar, which is mild with a distinct flavor. It is used mostly for dipping and is originally from the city of Chinkiang in the province of Kiangsu.

**White Pepper**   Chinese prefer ground white pepper because of its penetrating, potent flavor.

## Vegetables and Vegetable Products

Many of the green leafy vegetables such as bok choy and Chinese mustard greens used in Chinese cooking are from the cabbage family. They are usually stir-fried or cooked in soups for a short time so that they retain their bright color, crispness and vitamins. Chinese cabbages are a good source of calcium.

**Bamboo Shoots**   Bamboo shoots are cream-colored and shaped like small pine cones. There are several kinds of bamboo shoots. I recommend the winter variety for its firm texture and flavor. They are cut in large pieces and canned in water.

**Bean Curd** (Tofu)   This is a pure vegetable product made from ground dried soybeans and water, to which a coagulant, gypsum powder, is added to curdle the mixture. Bean curd, which the Chinese have eaten for centuries, is a high-quality, complete vegetable protein; it is totally free of cholesterol. Now readily available in supermarkets and Asian groceries, its texture can be soft and custardlike, medium firm, very firm or even grainy, depending on how it is processed and how much water is retained. Many supermarket brands have rabbinical approval; some are marked as pareve and are packaged in a one-pound cake, while the brands found in Asian groceries are sold both in large cakes and as four squares in a package. Packaged brands are marked soft or firm. All bean curd should be covered in cold water, whether sold packaged or loose. Asian markets sometimes sell it loose by the pad. Fresh bean curd has almost no smell and a rather bland, slightly beany flavor. This bland flavor and soft texture make it a good foil for spicy, strong flavors. See the Braised Bean Curd recipe on page 138. Bean curd tends to spoil quickly, especially if it is not refrigerated; when it does, a strong sour odor and taste are apparent. To store loose bean curd, place it in a container, cover with cold water, top with an airtight lid and refrigerate. If you are keeping the bean curd more than a day or two, change the water daily.

**Bean Sprouts**   Bean sprouts are the tender shoots of the mung bean. They are long, pearly white sprouts with tiny yellow bean heads. When fresh they are crunchy and have a sweet taste. Prepare them promptly—within a day or two—because they lose flavor quickly.

**Bok Choy**   Bok choy has a bright green leaf and a chalky white stalk with small yellow flowers. Some have short, thick stalks while others have long, narrow stalks, but they all have more or less the same shape. They are available throughout the year in Asian groceries and supermarkets.

**Chinese Cabbage** (Napa Cabbage or Celery Cabbage)   This pale green cabbage is available all year. There are two kinds: one long and narrow, and the other shorter and rounder. The Chinese prefer the shorter, rounder cabbage because it is sweeter and more tender, but the long, narrow one is more common in supermarkets.

**Chinese Mustard Greens**   Sold only in Asian groceries, these greens have thick smooth stems with crisp swirling leaves and a strong, pungent, slightly bitter mustard flavor. They are delicious in soups or stir-fried with meat.

**Daikon** (Chinese Radish)   A large, long, tapered, sweet and juicy radish that can be eaten raw or cooked and is available in most markets.

**Fresh Hot Chili Peppers**   I used fresh Anaheim hot green peppers in testing my recipes. They are long and narrow, about the size of a small parsnip, and slightly twisted; they can be mild or very hot. If it is not indicated, you can ask the grocer about their spiciness or you might taste one yourself.

**Oriental Eggplant** (Banana Eggplant)   Long and narrow, these eggplants are sweeter and have fewer seeds than the common thicker variety.

**Seasoned Pressed Bean Curd**   Fresh bean curd is pressed to remove much of the water, then simmered in soy sauce and spices. A recipe is on page 144.

**Snow Peas**   Unlike peas that are shelled, these peas have thin, edible pods.

They are delicious blanched or stir-fried. Although thought to be Chinese in origin, there is some evidence that snow peas were first cultivated in Europe. The Cantonese name for them is *ho lan dow,* or "Holland bean."

**Taro Root**   A starchy tuber, taro is often deep-fried or cooked with duck because it absorbs the fat and flavor without becoming greasy. Shredded, it can be deep-fried into the shape of a basket. It is dark brown, nappy, and barrel shaped with a faint chestnutlike flavor. Peel before using.

**Water Chestnuts**   Water chestnuts, available mostly in Asian markets, are not part of the chestnut family. They look like muddy little tulip bulbs, with black skin and crisp white sweet flesh, and taste almost like a crisp apple. They must be peeled before using. The canned are flavorless by comparison, so it is worth the expense and effort to use the fresh whenever possible. If you can't find the fresh, use the canned or substitute jicama, a tuber that also has a crisp white flesh and can be found in Asian and Latin markets and some supermarkets. Fresh water chestnuts bruise and spoil easily, so choose the very hard ones with no soft spots. Free of any blemishes, fresh water chestnuts will keep for weeks in the refrigerator vegetable compartment. Peeled, they can be frozen raw for a month or so.

**Winter Melon**   A member of the squash family, this large melon has a hard outer light-green skin that is coated with a chalky white powder. It is usually cooked in soup. The flesh becomes transparent and soft when cooked and has a subtle taste that is enriched with the flavor of chicken broth. It is found in Asian markets and sold by the pound in wedges. Store loosely wrapped in the refrigerator to prevent spoiling.

## Dried Products

Most Chinese packaged dried products, such as plants or noodles, have been sun-dried. You may want to consult your rabbi for approval.

**Agar-agar**   This gelatinous substance is derived from seaweed. It is a pure plant product and comes as a powder, in long rectangular blocks, or in thin sticks. Some of the powdered brands have rabbinical approval. The thin strips are soaked in cold water to soften and are used in salads. Agar-agar dissolves in hot or boiling water and is used to make gelatin. Stored in a dry place, it will keep for months.

**Black Mushrooms**   Dried black mushrooms come in varying price depending on the quality. They have a distinctive, slightly earthy flavor and a chewy texture. The more expensive ones are thicker and have a richer, more intense flavor. You can store dried mushrooms indefinitely in a clean, dry, covered jar. Soak them in warm water until soft (about 30 minutes)

before using. The thicker mushrooms require longer soaking than do the thin ones, so soak them the night before and refrigerate.

**Cellophane Noodles** (Bean Threads)   These dried thin noodles are made from mung-bean flour. They become transparent when braised, hence the name cellophane. They become very crisp when deep-fried.

**Glutinous Rice** (Sweet Rice)   This round, short-grain rice becomes sticky and somewhat gummy when cooked. It is used mostly for stuffings or fried rice. You can find it in Asian markets.

**Rice**   Chinese prefer long-grain rice cooked plain—either boiled or steamed (page 167)—and it is served with every meal. It is the staple of the southern Chinese diet, while in the north, because of the cold climate and shorter growing season, wheat is used more than rice. Rice is also used to make congee (page 168), a rice gruel eaten for breakfast. Fried Rice is made with leftover rice (page 169).

**Rice Noodles**   Thin, dried rice noodles are made from rice flour and can be found in Asian groceries. These noodles come in two thicknesses: one is the size of cellophane noodles and the other even thinner. You need only to soak them in water before stir-frying with other foods. The noodles are sold in one-pound packages separated into four bundles.

**Tiger Lily Buds** (Golden Needles)   These dried, pale-golden lily buds are delicate in flavor, used mostly for texture, and are often combined with tree ears. They must be soaked in boiling water before being added to a dish. They are good in steamed or stir-fried dishes and in soups.

**Tree Ears**   They are also called black fungus, wood ears or cloud ears, depending on their size. When soaked in warm water, they triple in bulk. Tree ears should be washed thoroughly after soaking and any foreign matter removed. Like tiger lily buds, they are used mostly for texture.

## Fresh Noodles and Wrappers

**Egg Noodles**   Fresh or dried noodles are made from wheat flour, eggs and water. If fresh, they are kept in the refrigerated section of Chinese grocery stores or the produce section of supermarkets. They can be refrigerated for two days or frozen up to three weeks.

**Egg-Roll Wrappers**   These are large square sheets of fresh egg-noodle dough, found in the refrigerated section of Chinese grocery stores. They can be refrigerated for two days or frozen for three weeks. A recipe is on page 193.

 INGREDIENTS  **17**

**Rice Noodle Sheets**   Fresh or dried rice noodles are made from ground rice and water spread on a flat surface and steamed into sheets. Rice noodle sheets are found in Chinese grocery stores; they must be kept refrigerated. A recipe is on page 180.

**Spring-Roll Wrappers**   Fresh spring-roll wrappers are thin wheat crêpes found in the refrigerated section of Chinese grocery stores. They are much thinner than egg-roll wrappers and can be refrigerated (for two days) or frozen (for three weeks).

**Wonton Wrappers**   These are small squares of fresh egg-noodle dough found in the refrigerated section of Chinese grocery stores or in supermarkets. They must be refrigerated or frozen. A recipe is on page 193.

# BUYING KOSHER PRODUCTS

Many of the products and ingredients I have used in my recipes have the registered kosher symbol, or *hecksher*, and are available in oriental shops, supermarkets and health-food stores. More and more kosher oriental and oriental-style products appear on the market all the time. A few of the companies such as La Choy have nationwide distribution while others distribute only locally. I have given brand names with their symbols whenever possible, but it is important to keep checking for the symbol of approval on these products because it is not uncommon for products to lose their rabbinical approval without warning to the consumer. Some symbols to look for are:

Ⓤ —the Union of Orthodox Jewish Congregations, New York, New York. This symbol is the best known and most widely used because it is under the aegis of a large communal organization.

Ⓚ —O.K. (Organized Kashruth) Laboratories, Brooklyn, New York

Ⓜ —(K.V.H.) Kashruth Commission of the Vaad Horabanim (Rabbinical Council) of New England, Boston, Massachusetts

⒦ —Rabbi J. H. Ralbag, New York, New York

⒝ —Kosher Supervision Service, Hackensack, New Jersey

𝕂 —Kosher Overseers Association of America, Beverly Hills, California

Ⓥ —Vaad Hoeir of St. Louis, St. Louis, Missouri

♛ —Board of Rabbis, Jersey City, New Jersey

✰ —Vaad Hakashrus of Baltimore, Baltimore, Maryland

The following is a list of companies, their hecksher, some of their addresses and the labels to look for. These companies produce all or some of the following products: soy sauce, hoisin sauce, sweet-and-sour sauce, duck sauce, hot mustard sauce, sesame oil, hot pepper oil, bamboo shoots, water chestnuts, even kosher "oyster" sauce (which I do not recommend) and various other oriental-style kosher products.

Allied Old English Co. Ⓤ, Port Reading, New Jersey 07064. Soy sauce, hoisin sauce, hot mustard sauce, duck sauce, sweet-and-sour sauce and kosher oyster sauce, under the following labels: Meetu Ⓤ, Polynesian Ⓤ and China Pride Ⓤ.

Arrowhead Mills Inc. Ⓤ, Box 2059, Hereford, Texas 79045. Rice flour.

Durkee and Shop Rite Ⓤ. Seasonings. Durkee Famous Foods, SCM Corporation, Westlake, Ohio 44145.

Eden Ⓚ, Clinton, Michigan 49236. Soy sauce, sesame oil, agar-agar and rice noodles.

Erewhon Inc. Ⓚ, Wilmington, Massachusetts 01887. Soy sauce and agar-agar.

Fantastic Foods Inc. Ⓚ (pareve), Novato, California 94947. A variety of Chinese-style products.

Gomasio Ⓚ, Lima USA, Inc., P.O. Box 566096, Atlanta, Georgia 30356. Soy sauce.

Hain Pure Foods Inc. Ⓤ, Los Angeles, California 90061. Barbeque sauce.

Kikkoman International Inc., Box 784, San Francisco, California 94133. Although the Kikkoman brand soy sauce does not have a hecksher, it is often sold in approved kosher markets.

La Choy Ⓚ (pareve), Beatrice/Hunt Wesson Inc., P.O. Box 4800, Fullerton, California 92634. Soy sauce, bamboo shoots, water chestnuts.

Mitoku Co. Ltd. Ⓤ, Tokyo. Soy sauce.

Rokeach Ⓤ, Rokeach & Sons, 25 E. Spring Valley Avenue, Maywood, New Jersey 07607. Clear chicken broth.

San-J Ⓚ, imported by San-J International, Colonial Heights, Virginia 23834. Soy sauce.

The following companies make tofu, fresh egg noodles and egg-roll and wonton wrappers. These ingredients are found in the refrigerated section of oriental stores or in the produce section of supermarkets.

Azumaya Ⓚ (pareve), 1575 Burke Avenue, San Francisco, California 94133
Canton Noodle Co. Ⓤ, 101 Mott Street, New York, New York 10013
Nasoya Foods Ⓚ (pareve), 23 Jytek Drive, Leominster, Massachusetts 01453
Tomsum Ⓚ (pareve), Greenfield, Massachusetts 01301
West Lake Noodle Co. Ⓤ, 183 E. Broadway, New York, New York 10013

The following nationally known companies produce kosher vegetable oils.

Ⓤ Krasdale Corn Oil
Ⓤ Mazola Corn Oil
Ⓚ Planters Peanut Oil
Ⓤ Rokeach Peanut Oil    (available during Passover only)
Ⓤ Shop-Rite Vegetable Oil    (pure soybean oil)
Ⓚ Wesson Vegetable Oil    (pure soybean or corn oil)

# EQUIPMENT

All of the recipes in this book can be prepared without any of the Chinese utensils described below. For instance, a chef's knife can be used instead of a cleaver, or you can stir-fry in a skillet rather than a wok, but using a Chinese cleaver for cutting and a wok for cooking ensures preparation will be faster and cooking easier—with better results. Once you become adept at using these utensils you will find you can't cook without them!

**Chopping Board**    The chopping board is an important tool because Chinese cooking requires so much cutting. I recommend a large wooden one 16 × 10 × 1½ inches. Also, the thickness of the wood as well as the material itself cushions the cutting, making you less tired. I keep mine clean by scrubbing it with detergent after each use.

**Chinese Cleaver**    Since most ingredients are cut into bite-size pieces, more time is spent cutting than cooking. It's important to cut the ingredients of each dish into approximately the same size and shape so they will absorb seasonings and cook evenly. Obtaining a good cleaver, and learning how to use it properly, makes chopping much easier.

Good-quality cleavers are made of stainless steel or a combination of carbon and stainless steel. I prefer the combination because it holds an edge well and always looks sleek and clean. They cost a bit more but are well worth it. The most useful size is a cleaver with a rectangular blade about 3½ inches wide and 8 inches long. Cleavers come in three different weights: light (½ pound, 3/32 inch thick at the top) with a thin blade for slicing vegetables and fancy cutting; medium (¾ pound, ⅛ inch thick at the top) for general cutting and chopping through bone; and heavy (more than 1 pound) for bone chopping alone. I suggest buying two sizes—the light and the medium.

Once you learn to handle a cleaver it will become indispensable. In addition to chopping meat and vegetables, you will use it on its side to crush garlic, to transport food from chopping board to platter to wok and occasionally as a pastry scraper. The blunt back edge can be used for tenderizing meat. It is important to keep a sharp edge on the cleaver. Use a sharpening stone or rod periodically.

**Wok** The wok, a concave, multipurpose Chinese cooking pan, is centuries old. Its shape is perfect for stir-frying, deep-frying, braising and, with a rack and lid, even steaming. Though its shape is not ideal for an ordinary stove, it adapts well when a metal ring is placed around the burner with the wok on top of the ring. For this reason, the wok, a ring and a lid are usually sold as a set. Woks are available in stainless steel, aluminum, anodized aluminum and carbon steel. The best woks are made of carbon steel because this metal heats and cools quickly. This property is important for stir-frying, during which quick temperature changes affect taste and texture. Carbon steel can also be properly cured. Stainless steel burns easily and can't be cured. Aluminum retains heat too long for quick cooling. The wok comes in different sizes, with either two metal handles or a long wooden one. I use a 14-inch, two-handled wok.

If you have an electric stove, use a flat-bottomed wok because the flat bottom makes good contact with the heating element. To adjust heat rapidly while stir-frying, use two electric burners—one on high and the other on medium. Transfer the wok quickly between the two or take the wok off the burners altogether for quick temperature changes.

An electric wok will do in a pinch, and it is handy to use as a hot pot for cooking at the table, but because it cannot be cured like a carbon steel wok, it will never develop the wok flavor that the Chinese prize.

A new wok must first be cured so that food will not stick. This curing and subsequent use over hot heat replaces an objectionable metallic taste with a characteristic "wok flavor." First, wash the wok thoroughly with soap or detergent. Place it on the stove over medium heat and, when it is completely dry, add 1 teaspoon of vegetable oil. With a paper towel, wipe the entire inside surface of the wok with the oil. Continue heating and, as the oil dries, add more oil and wipe again, repeating this for about 10 minutes until a clean paper towel is not stained gray from the new metal. The wok is now cured and ready to use. Each time you finish cooking with the wok, wash it with water, a trace of detergent and a brush while it is still warm. Do *not* use a metal scouring pad. Remove all traces of food, but leave as much oil on the wok as possible, for this is what keeps the wok cured. Over time and with use the wok will take on a dull black patina.

**Wok Spatula** This is a light, stainless-steel, shovel-shaped spatula that helps lift and turn ingredients while you are stir-frying. I suggest buying a 15-inch spatula; a shorter one brings your hand too close for comfort and a longer one is awkward to use.

**Ladle**   A long-handled ladle is ideal for dishing out food from the wok and for serving soup.

**Perforated Strainer**   For deep-frying, an 8-inch stainless-steel perforated strainer with a long wooden handle is useful for removing food from the hot oil and draining it.

**Steamers**   The Chinese have steamed food for centuries and have developed various utensils for this purpose. There are two types of round steamers: bamboo and metal. Both come with three tiers, which can be used singly or stacked in layers. The bamboo steamer is placed in a wok with boiling water, while the metal steamer has its own metal pot to hold the boiling water. Any large pot with a close-fitting lid will do as a makeshift steamer, as long as the dish being steamed can be elevated at least 1½ inches above the boiling water with enough room for the hot steam to circulate.

Dim sum buns or dumplings can be placed directly on the oiled bamboo rack to steam. Chicken, fish or ingredients with a marinade or sauce, however, are placed on a ceramic platter or baking dish before they are put into the steamer.

A large 16½ × 12-inch oblong turkey roaster with a lid is indispensable as a steamer for large items such as duck, chicken or fish. A round metal rack 1½ inches high and about 8 inches round is handy to hold the platter for steaming in a roaster.

**Food Processor**   The food processor is ideal for mincing and chopping meats coarsely. I have included recipes for yeast doughs, fishballs and other dishes using a food processor, with alternative instructions if you do not have one.

# PREPARATION TECHNIQUES

**Cutting**   There is a definite relationship between cutting and cooking ingredients in Chinese cooking. When ingredients are cut up properly they can be cooked quickly, enhancing natural flavors without losing texture, as well as adding visual appeal to a dish.

Cutting vegetables into small, uniform pieces ensures they can be cooked quickly and evenly yet still retain their crunchiness. They can also absorb the flavors of the seasonings and oil in a short cooking time.

Beef or chicken are cut into thin slices, shreds or cubes, then marinated according to the recipe. When meat is cut into the appropriate size, the seasonings penetrate it more thoroughly.

Place your cutting board close to the edge of the counter so you can look directly down on the top of the cleaver as you cut. Hold the handle of the cleaver firmly, but without tension, in your cutting hand. Place your slightly curved index finger and your thumb on opposite sides of the blade. With your knuckles slightly curved and relaxed over your fingertips, place your other hand on top of and holding the food to be cut. Angle the cleaver so that the side of the blade touches the protruding knuckles of your other hand. Start slicing by moving the cleaver away from you in a forward gliding motion as you cut downward. The weight of your arm and the sharp edge of the cleaver will do much of the work of cutting. The cleaver and your other hand should be moving in the same direction as you make successive cuts, with the other hand continuously exposing more of the food to be cut. Never lift the cleaver higher than the piece of food. The protruding knuckles on your other hand will keep your fingers safe.

**Slicing**  By changing the angle of the cleaver you can slice straight across or on the diagonal. This is important when you want to adjust the length of the slice. The thickness of the slice is controlled by the hand holding the food. The more of the ingredient you expose, the thicker the slice; the less you expose, the thinner the slice. Generally, slices should be about ⅛ to ¼ inch thick and about 1½ inches wide by 2 inches long.

**Parallel or Horizontal Cutting**  This method of slicing is for cutting thin, flat slices of chicken breast and the like. If the ingredient is meat or fowl, freeze thoroughly and then allow it to thaw for 15 minutes, or until just soft enough to slice but still firm. Hold the cleaver so that the flat side is parallel to the cutting board. Begin to cut a thin slice and, as the edge of the cleaver cuts its way into the food, put the fingertips of the hand holding the meat over the part of the slice that has been cut. Be careful to keep your fingertips away from the sharp edge of the cleaver. Continue in this manner until you complete the cut.

**Shredding or Julienning**  Start with flat, thin slices of the ingredient. Place them flat so they overlap in a small mound. Press the mound to flatten it slightly and then cut the slices into thin strips about 2 inches long.

**Mincing and Fine Chopping**  First, shred the ingredient thin, then cut across the shreds until they are minced fine. Ginger is minced fine in many Chinese recipes. Meat can also be chopped fine.

**Dicing**  First cut ¼-inch strips, then cut across the strips, making small cubes. The size of the dice can vary according to the recipe.

**Roll-Cutting**  Roll-cut long, cylindrical vegetables to be stewed or braised, such as carrots or oriental turnips. Hold the vegetable with one hand. With your cutting hand, place the cleaver perpendicular to the cutting board diagonally over the vegetable, then cut. Roll the vegetable a quarter turn toward you and make another diagonal cut. The resulting piece should be an asymmetrical wedge shape that exposes a fair amount of inner surface to cook quickly. Continue making quarter turns and cutting on the diagonal until the entire vegetable is cut up. Adjust the diagonal slant as you cut to make thicker or thinner pieces in order to keep the size and shape as uniform as possible.

**Chopping**  To chop through bone, hold the handle of the cleaver firmly, lift it straight up and bring it straight down, striking the item with the sharp edge of the cleaver at a point close to the handle. Be careful not to twist or turn the edge of the cleaver if the cut is not complete; the edge can be damaged. Keep your free hand clear! If you find this method too difficult, place the cleaver where you want to make the cut and hammer the top of the cleaver with a rubber mallet until it cuts through.

To cut the bone of a whole cooked chicken or duck to make bite-size pieces, chop through the joints of the wings, thighs and legs and remove them from the body. Then chop the body in half lengthwise through the backbone and breastbone. Chop each half lengthwise again. Chop all the sections in the following sequence: wings, thighs, legs, backbone and breast—all into ¾ × 2-inch-wide pieces. As you finish chopping each section, use the flat side of the cleaver to transfer the pieces by section. Place them on a large, oblong serving platter, with the wings at the top and the legs at the bottom, leaving the breast pieces for the top of the center of the platter. When arranging on the platter, try to reconstruct the shape of the bird.

# COOKING TECHNIQUES

**Braising**  Braising is cooking by searing the food first in hot oil, then simmering it in a covered pot with seasonings and a little liquid until tender. Red-cooking is a form of braising with soy sauce, which gives the food a reddish color.

**Deep-Frying**  The goal of deep-frying is to cook the ingredients in hot oil until they are crispy on the outside—never greasy—and tender on the inside.

When deep-frying, use a flat-bottom wok, or place the wok over a ring to be sure it will not tip. Use at least 2 cups or more of oil, since the food should float freely and not be crowded. The oil must be between 325° to 350° F. Use a candy thermometer to determine the temperature. If the oil is too hot the food will brown before it is cooked, and if the oil is not hot enough the food will be soggy and oily.

Use tongs gently and carefully to lower the ingredients into the oil, being careful not to splash. Turn the food frequently to fry evenly. Never crowd too many ingredients at one time.

After frying, allow the oil to cool. Using a funnel, strain the oil through a paper towel into a glass jar. Cover and store in the refrigerator to use again.

**Poaching**   Poaching is cooking in a simmering liquid; therefore water, broth or oil can be used to poach food. When poaching in water or broth, use enough liquid to cover the ingredients and bring the liquid to a boil before adding the ingredients. Then lower the temperature, add the food and cook at a low simmer until done.

When poaching in oil, use 1 to 2 cups of oil. Have the temperature of the oil at about 280° F. to cook quickly without browning. In the recipes in this book, the ingredients will have been marinated so they will not absorb much oil while cooking.

**Roasting**   In China, almost no roasting is done at home because few homes have ovens. Instead, roasting is done in restaurants and markets, which have very large ovens. In these ovens, the meat or fowl is hung from rods to roast. Peking Duck and Cantonese roast pork are roasted this way; the key to this method is that they are self-basting.

I have adapted this self-basting technique for the American kitchen. For example, in Cantonese Roast Veal (page 97), the meat is hung from the oven rack to roast.

**Steaming**   Steaming is a quick-cooking method that brings out the natural flavor of the food. The ingredients are usually cut up, marinated and steamed in a heatproof serving dish that can be taken right to the table.

When steaming, make sure the boiling water is at least 1½ inches deep, and the dish or food is elevated 1½ inches above the boiling water. If the recipe requires a long steaming time, check the water level occasionally and add more *boiling* water if necessary. Remove the lid slowly, so the steam rises away from your face and hands.

**Stir-Frying**   The most well-known and most common cooking method in Chinese cooking is stir-frying. Stir-frying is best done in a wok, because its round bowl shape makes it easy to toss and flip the ingredients. Heat the wok, then add and heat a small amount of oil, add the ingredients and, with a spatula, quickly flip and toss them until they reach the desired doneness. Adjusting the heat quickly is important because this affects taste and texture. Pay close attention to the ingredients as you stir-fry them; they should sizzle as they cook. If they start to turn brown after a few seconds in the wok, turn the heat down. If they become watery, turn the heat up.

Have all the ingredients cut up and placed on a platter or tray in separate mounds near the stove. This makes it easy to slide them into the wok at the appropriate time. Meat or fowl should be cut up and marinated according to the recipe directions before cooking. Sauces, salt and sugar should also be near the stove before you begin stir-frying.

Always heat the wok over medium heat until hot. (The wok should be hot but not smoking.) Then add the oil and heat a few seconds before adding the ingredients so that they will not stick to the wok.

Keep the spatula continuously in motion, lifting and turning the ingredients and blending the mixture and its sauces. Separate pieces of meat by pressing them with the tip of the spatula against the side of the wok. If you have a delicate ingredient like soft bean curd, lift it gently with the spatula and return it without turning it over.

Stir-fry leafy vegetables such as spinach and watercress over very high heat. When stir-frying thicker vegetables such as broccoli, use medium-high heat, add liquid, and cover the wok according to the recipe. Vegetables can also be parboiled or steamed until partially done, tender yet crisp, then stir-fried as the final step. Vegetables are done when they wilt or become translucent.

You'll notice in the recipes that meat and vegetables are stir-fried separately, then returned to the wok to stir-fry together. Don't try to skip the first step. When an ingredient is stir-fried alone, its flavor and texture have a chance to develop. When each ingredient is stir-fried separately and then mingled, the results are deeper, richer, more complex flavors.

To ensure the best results, do not cook a larger quantity of food than required for one recipe at a time.

## MIXING CHINESE AND WESTERN FOOD

If you are planning only one Chinese dish to supplement a Western menu, a vegetable dish is the best choice, with many to choose from. For instance, Stir-Fried Snow Peas with Ginger (page 150) or Braised Chinese Cabbage with Chestnuts (page 146) go very well with traditional braised beef. Stir-Fried Broccoli (page 149) complements roast chicken, in both taste and color. A soup is also a good choice. Egg Drop Soup (page 160) is an excellent beginning for a Western meal. Finally, the Chinese have few desserts compared to Westerners, but those that I've included are the favorites; try one.

## IMPROVISATION

Much of Chinese cooking is based on improvisation. While these recipes are very specific, an experienced cook will substitute what might be fresh in the market or what is in the refrigerator. Use the freshest ingredients available and, in stir-frying, cut them into equal, bite-size pieces. Consider the water content of a vegetable before making a substitution. Spinach and watercress, for instance, have a high water content and become limp when stir-fried. Stir-fry them separately from other ingredients; do not mix, but place the other ingredients on top of the vegetable.

# TEAM COOKING

If you like company in the kitchen, cook Chinese food with a group. A wonton or dim sum party can be great fun. Prepare the fillings before guests arrive, then have them make their own dumplings.

# DO-AHEAD CHINESE COOKING

Cooking a few hours or days in advance can make a big difference; many Chinese dishes can be prepared ahead. See the chart at the beginning of each chapter for a list of do-ahead recipes. Most of the braised dishes, such as Braised Beef with Garlic (page 103) and Curried Beef (page 102), actually taste better if cooked a day in advance, and many of the poached dishes, such as Soy-Sauce Chicken (page 79), do not lose flavor if cooked a day ahead.

If you are pressed for time in stir-frying, there are a few steps that can be done earlier. You can cut and refrigerate meat and vegetables a day earlier, but if you do this, be sure not to marinate the meat until 20 or 30 minutes before cooking unless the directions instruct otherwise. Wrap the vegetables well so they stay crisp and do not lose moisture.

On rare occasions, you may wish to stir-fry the day before. A few dishes, such as Stir-Fried Lamb with Scallions (page 111), Lamb Hunan Style (page 112) and Vegetarian Lo Mein (page 178), can tolerate this. They reheat well in a microwave oven or in a skillet on top of the stove.

Doing steps ahead of time is important for some of the more difficult recipes that require many steps. Roast Boneless Chicken Stuffed with Glutinous Rice (page 66) is an example. As I mention in the recipe, bone the chicken a week in advance and freeze it. Then, the day before the chicken is to be cooked, make the filling and refrigerate it. On the day you want to serve it, all you need to do is stuff and roast the chicken.

Although dim sum recipes can be complicated, most of them can be made ahead and frozen. Break up a recipe by doing part of it one day and finishing it the next day. For instance, make the filling one day and the dough and dumplings the next day. This works well with steamed buns, which also freeze well.

# BEVERAGES

There are no set rules about what to drink with Chinese food. Traditionally, a simple soup is served at family meals, while a warm rice wine is served throughout a banquet, with many toasts during the meal. Today, you will find many beverages from tea to soft drinks, beer to cognac. Nevertheless, there are a few beverages that go particularly well with Chinese food. Beer is appropriate with spicy dishes, and a slightly fruity white or rosé wine is good with most Chinese food. If you prefer tea, there are many from which to choose.

# TEA

It's customary for Chinese to wait until after the meal to drink tea. Chinese teas are divided into three groups according to their curing or fermentation process. Green tea has not been allowed to ferment and remains green. Oolong, also known as red, is semifermented and often scented with flowers such as jasmine, lychee, rose or laurel. Black tea is fully fermented and became popular in the West because it goes well with milk and sugar. Chinese, as well as many of my students, favor the scented lychee, oolong or jasmine teas for their fragrant bouquet and mild flavor.

# SAUCES AND CONDIMENTS

Chinese sauces are made from various vegetable products, fruits and spices. Used as dips or for flavoring a dish, these sauces give even the simplest dish a more interesting, exotic flavor. Keep them on hand so you can prepare the recipes in this book when the spirit moves you. Be creative and serve them with traditional Jewish fare. You'll be delighted when you pep up a roast chicken with hoisin sauce or add zest to pickled tongue or pot roast with a touch of hot mustard sauce.

| Recipes | | Prepare Ahead | Serving Temperature |
|---|---|---|---|
| Hoisin Sauce | Mildly spicy | Yes | Room temp. |
| Hot Mustard Sauce | Spicy hot | Yes | Room temp. |
| Hot Chili Sauce | Spicy hot | Yes | Room temp. |
| Duck Sauce | Mildly sweet | Yes | Room temp. |
| Roasted Salt and Sichuan Peppercorns | Salty-spicy | Yes | Room temp. |
| Sweet-and-Sour Sauce | Sweet-sour | Yes | Hot |
| Five-Spice Powder | Spicy | Yes | Room temp. |
| Roasted Sichuan Peppercorns | Spicy | Yes | Room temp. |
| Soy Sauce Dip | Salty | Yes | Room temp. |
| Hot Chili Oil | Spicy hot | Yes | Room temp. |

# HOISIN SAUCE

*B*ecause it can be difficult to find kosher hoisin sauce, I have developed a homemade version. The recipe is in two parts. The azuki beans must first be cooked and puréed into a paste, then the sauce made. Properly stored in a well-sealed jar in the refrigerator, this sauce will keep for months.

## Unsweetened Red Bean Paste

*1 cup dried azuki red beans (found in health-food stores)*
*4 cups water*

*1.* Sort the beans and discard those that are broken and discolored. Rinse the beans and place them in a saucepan. Add the water and bring to a boil. Turn down the heat and simmer for 1½ hours, or until the beans are very soft and the liquid has been absorbed.

*2.* Put the metal blade into the bowl of a food processor and pour in the cooked beans. Process into a fine paste. The beans can also be mashed by hand. This purée is now ready to use in sauces or sweetened for desserts. Transfer to a clean jar with a lid and store in the refrigerator up to a week or freeze for a month.

## Sauce

*2 tablespoons corn oil*
*2 garlic cloves, minced*
*4 dried hot chili peppers*
*½ cup Unsweetened Red Bean Paste*
*1 teaspoon kosher salt*
*½ cup sugar*
*2 tablespoons soy sauce*
*3 tablespoons distilled white vinegar*
*3 tablespoons water*

*1.* In a small saucepan, heat the oil and add the garlic and peppers. Stir and cook over medium heat for 2 minutes, or until the flavors are released and the garlic browns slightly. Be careful not to burn the garlic.

*2.* Remove and discard the peppers. Add the bean paste. Stir until blended, then add the remaining ingredients, continuing to stir until blended. Simmer over very low heat for 20 to 30 minutes, or until the sauce thickens slightly.

*3.* Pour the sauce into a food processor and blend until smooth, or mash by hand into a smooth paste. Pour into a clean jar with an airtight lid. Cover and store in the refrigerator to use as needed.

# HOT MUSTARD SAUCE

Serve as a spicy dip for any of the dumpling recipes, Cantonese Egg Rolls (page 192) or Shanghai Spring Rolls (page 205). Be cautious: First you will feel it in your nose, then your eyes and finally it will go straight to the top of your head.

6 tablespoons hot
   mustard powder
6 tablespoons water
1 teaspoon distilled
   white vinegar
1 teaspoon oriental
   sesame oil

*1.* Combine the mustard powder and water in a small bowl and mix until smooth. Let the mixture stand for 1 minute.

*2.* Stir in the vinegar and sesame oil. Pour the mixture into a clean jar and cover. Store in the refrigerator for up to 3 or 4 weeks.

# HOT CHILI SAUCE

This is a delicious hot sauce that you can substitute for commercial Chinese chili paste. Add it to a cooking sauce or use it as a condiment for dishes such as lo mein or wonton. A note of warning about working with fresh or dried hot chili peppers: Be careful not to touch your eyes with your fingers after handling hot peppers. Coat your fingers with corn oil before touching the peppers.

30 dried hot chili
   peppers, each about
   1½ inches long
½ cup warm water
6 tablespoons corn oil
3 garlic cloves, minced
1¼ pounds red bell
   peppers, seeded and
   chopped coarse
6 tablespoons soy
   sauce

*1.* Soak the peppers in warm water until very soft. Drain and chop fine.

*2.* In a heavy saucepan over low heat, heat the oil. Add the peppers and garlic; cook, stirring constantly, for 1 minute until the garlic browns slightly. Take care not to burn the garlic.

*3.* Add the bell peppers and soy sauce. Stir several times and bring to a boil. Simmer for about 30 minutes, until most of the liquid has evaporated and the peppers are very soft.

**4.** Remove from the heat and allow the sauce to cool completely. Pour into a clean jar, cover with plastic wrap and screw on the lid. Turn the jar upside down and store in the refrigerator. The oil will rise to the surface and inhibit mold from forming. Discard the sauce at the first sign of mold.

# DUCK SAUCE

*Makes 1 quart*

*T*his chutney-style sauce, made from plums and other fruit, combines the sweet taste of fruits with a sour touch of vinegar. Serve it with Cantonese Roast Duck (page 86), Cantonese Egg Rolls (page 192), Cantonese Roast Turkey (page 97) and other roasted meats.

*3 large peaches, or 1 1-pound, 13-ounce can peaches, drained*

*9 large plums, or 1 1-pound, 14-ounce can plums, drained*

*1 cup diced red bell peppers*

*1 cup coarsely chopped dried apricots*

*½ cup dark brown sugar (omit if using canned fruit)*

*¾ cup granulated sugar (omit if using canned fruit)*

*⅔ cup distilled white vinegar*

*2 teaspoons minced Candied Ginger (page 212), or to taste (optional)*

**1.** If using fresh fruit, skin the peaches and plums by plunging them into boiling water for a few seconds. Rinse and peel under cool water. Quarter the plums and divide the peaches into eighths, and discard the pits. There should be about 5 cups of peaches and plums.

**2.** Combine all the ingredients in a large, non-corrosive pot and bring to a boil, stirring several times. Reduce the heat to low. Simmer, uncovered, for 1½ hours, stirring occasionally.

**3.** Press the mixture through a coarse food mill or strainer. Cool and store in an airtight jar in the refrigerator.

# Roasted Salt and Sichuan Peppercorns

*Makes ¼ cup*

Served as a dry dip with Puffed Fish Fillets in Mock Seaweed Batter (page 116), Sichuan Crispy Duck (page 84) or Chinese "Southern" Fried Chicken (page 77), this salty, peppery and numbing condiment also goes well with deep-fried dishes. It is salty so use it sparingly.

¼ cup kosher salt
2 tablespoons Sichuan
   peppercorns

**1.** Put the salt and peppercorns in a small, dry skillet. Over medium heat shake the skillet and toss the ingredients until the salt browns slightly and the peppercorns become fragrant, about 4 minutes.

**2.** Cool, then grind the mixture in a blender or spice mill. Strain through a sieve. Store in a covered jar.

# Sweet-and-Sour Sauce

*Makes 1 cup*

Serve this all-purpose sauce with fried wontons (page 194) or chicken, turkey or fish.

4 tablespoons distilled
   white vinegar
4 tablespoons sugar
1 tablespoon catsup
2 tablespoons soy
   sauce
½ cup Chicken Broth
   (page 155)
1 tablespoon
   cornstarch mixed
   with 3 tablespoons
   water

**1.** Combine all the ingredients except the cornstarch mixture in a small saucepan. Place the saucepan over medium heat and bring to a boil. Turn down the heat to low.

**2.** Stir the cornstarch mixture and slowly pour it into the simmering liquid while stirring constantly for about 2 minutes, or until the sauce thickens and becomes clear. Serve as a dip for fried foods.

# FIVE-SPICE POWDER

*Makes approximately 4 tablespoons*

*T*his powder is a combination of five ground spices and can be found in most supermarkets. Kosher brands of five-spice powder are difficult to find, but it is easy to prepare your own. Use ground spices when available and grind the Sichuan peppercorns and star anise, which are not usually available ground.

*2 teaspoons Sichuan peppercorns*
*8 star anise, or 4 teaspoons ground anise*
*½ teaspoon ground cloves*
*1 tablespoon ground cinnamon*
*1 tablespoon ground fennel seeds*

**1.** In a dry skillet, roast the peppercorns by shaking the pan over low to medium heat until the aroma of the peppercorns is released, about 3 minutes.

**2.** Grind the roasted peppercorns and star anise separately in a blender or a spice mill. Strain. Mix in other spices and grind again until very fine. Store in an airtight container.

# ROASTED SICHUAN PEPPERCORNS

*S*ichuan peppercorns have a distinctive aroma that is released when they are roasted.

*2 tablespoons Sichuan peppercorns*

**1.** Place the peppercorns in a small, dry skillet. Shake the skillet over medium heat until the peppercorns become fragrant, about 3 to 4 minutes. Cool.

**2.** Crush the peppercorns with a rolling pin or grind in a blender. Strain through a fine sieve and store in an airtight jar.

# SOY SAUCE DIP

**U**se this basic, simple dip for Shanghai Spring Rolls (page 205), fried or steamed dumplings (pages 196–198), Wontons (page 194) and Cantonese Egg Rolls (page 192).

*⅓ cup soy sauce*
*2 tablespoons distilled white vinegar*
*2 teaspoons sugar*
*2 tablespoons finely minced fresh ginger*
*1 tablespoon finely minced garlic*
*2 teaspoons Hot Chili Oil (page 36) or Hot Chili Sauce (page 32)*

In a bowl, combine the soy sauce, vinegar and sugar, stirring to dissolve the sugar. Stir in the ginger, garlic, and chili oil or sauce just before serving. Add additional chili oil to taste.

# HOT CHILI OIL

**H**ot Chili Oil is easy to make and will keep well for several months in the refrigerator.

*½ cup corn oil*
*20 dried hot chili peppers*
*½ teaspoon Sichuan peppercorns*
*1 teaspoon paprika*

**1.** Line a small, fine strainer with a paper towel and set it aside.

**2.** In a small, heavy saucepan heat the oil. When the oil is very hot, turn down the heat to very low and add the peppers. Cook, stirring, until peppers turn dark brown. Add the peppercorns and paprika, and continue to cook just until mixed.

**3.** Pour the oil through the strainer into a bowl. Discard the solids. Pour the oil into a small jar and cover with a lid. Store in the refrigerator.

# APPETIZERS AND COLD DISHES

With the exception of the Northern-Style Chicken Nuggets, every one of these unusual dishes can be made ahead to spice up any meal. Try serving them with cocktails, too.

| Recipes | | Prepare Ahead | Serving Temperature |
|---|---|---|---|
| Duck Salad | | Yes | Room temp. |
| Broccoli Salad | | Yes | Cold |
| Chinese Chicken Salad | | Yes | Room temp. |
| Shredded Chicken and Cucumber Salad | | Yes | Cold |
| Cucumber Salad | | Yes | Cold |
| Hot and Spicy Cucumbers | Spicy hot | Yes | Cold |
| Green Bean Salad | | Yes | Cold |
| Marinated Chinese Cabbage | Spicy hot | Yes | Cold |
| Sautéed Eggplant with Spicy Sauce | Spicy hot | Yes | Hot or cold |
| Fish Toast | | Yes | Hot |
| Barbecued Chicken Wings | Spicy | Yes | Hot |
| Tea Eggs | | Yes | Warm or cold |
| Northern-Style Chicken Nuggets | | No | Hot |
| Smoked Fish | Smoky | Yes | Hot or cold |
| Candied Pecans | Sweet | Yes | Room temp. |
| Steamed Egg-Crêpe Roll | | Yes | Warm |
| Steamed Eggplant | Spicy hot | Yes | Cold |

# DUCK SALAD

*T*his elegant salad is well worth the effort. The contrasting textures and flavors with a mustard dressing make this a tantalizing treat. This salad can be made in advance and is great for picnics.

*2 ounces rice sticks (to make 3 cups fried rice sticks)*
*2 cups corn oil, for frying*
*½ Cantonese Roast Duck (page 81), or simple roast duck*

### Mustard Sauce

*3 tablespoons soy sauce*
*2 teaspoons Hot Mustard Sauce (page 32), or to taste*
*1 tablespoon water*
*1 teaspoon sugar*
*2 teaspoons cider vinegar*
*1 tablespoon oriental sesame oil*
*1 tablespoon corn oil*

*2 cups shredded romaine lettuce*
*1 scallion, shredded fine*
*1 tablespoon chopped fresh coriander*

**1.** Put rice sticks into a large paper bag (this prevents pieces from scattering). Break the bundle in half lengthwise and pull the pieces apart slightly to separate the sticks into 2 or 3 loose batches.

**2.** Heat a wok and add the 2 cups of oil. When the oil is very hot, 375° F., drop one batch of rice sticks into the hot oil. Quickly, as soon as they puff and expand in volume, turn them over. Remove immediately and place on paper towels to cool and drain. Repeat the procedure with the remaining batches of rice sticks to make the necessary 3 cups.

**3.** When cool enough to handle, with your hands crush the rice sticks into small pieces about 3 inches long.

**4.** Bone and shred the duck into small pieces.

**5.** Combine the sauce ingredients in a small bowl and stir until well blended. Set aside.

**6.** Arrange the crushed rice sticks on a large serving platter. Place the shredded lettuce over the rice sticks and the shredded duck on top of the lettuce. Garnish the top of the duck with the scallion and coriander. Drizzle on the sauce just before serving. Toss and serve.

# BROCCOLI SALAD

*B*roccoli attractively arranged and topped with a sesame oil–soy sauce dressing makes a beautiful, simple salad you'll want to serve often.

*1 bunch broccoli*
*1 teaspoon kosher salt*

### Dressing

*3 tablespoons soy*
  *sauce*
*1 tablespoon cider*
  *vinegar*
*1 teaspoon sugar*
*2 teaspoons oriental*
  *sesame oil*

*1.* Using a sharp paring knife, start from the bottom of each broccoli stem and peel back the tough outer skin until you reach the flowerets. Cut the skin away at the base of the flowerets and discard it. Separate the flowerets and their stems from the large stem. Cut the flowerets into bite-size pieces. Cut the stems into 1½ × ½ × ½-inch pieces.

*2.* Bring 2 quarts of water to a boil. Add the salt and broccoli. Return to a boil and remove the pot from the heat as soon as the broccoli turns bright green, about 1 minute. Pour the contents of the pot into a large strainer and immediately rinse with cold water to cool the broccoli. Drain and dry thoroughly.

*3.* Arrange the broccoli stems on a serving platter and garnish attractively with the flowerets. In a small bowl, mix the dressing ingredients. Drizzle the dressing over the broccoli just before serving. Serve cold.

# CHINESE CHICKEN SALAD

$T$ry various kinds of lettuce in this colorful salad. The dressing has the characteristic taste of Chinese cuisine.

½ *skinned and boned chicken breast*

2 *large, ripe plum tomatoes*

3 *cups shredded romaine or red leaf lettuce*

2 *tablespoons coarsely chopped fresh coriander*

2 *tablespoons chopped scallions*

### Sauce

2 *tablespoons soy sauce*

1 *teaspoon sugar*

1 *tablespoon oriental sesame oil*

**1.** Put the chicken breast in a saucepan and cover with water. Bring to a boil. Turn down the heat, cover the pan and simmer for 10 minutes. Turn off the heat and let chicken cool in the saucepan. Remove the chicken breast and shred it with your fingers into thin strips. Set aside.

**2.** Bring 2 cups of water to a boil. Drop in the tomatoes for 10 seconds, then remove and plunge into cold water. Remove the skins, which will come off easily. Cut the tomatoes in half and remove the seeds. Cut the halves into ⅛-inch-wide slices. Set aside.

**3.** Arrange the shredded lettuce on a serving platter in a wide mound. Spread the tomato slices on top, leaving a ½-inch border around the edge. Scatter the chicken shreds over the tomatoes, leaving a narrow border of tomato. Garnish the top with coriander and scallions.

**4.** Combine the sauce ingredients in a small bowl. Drizzle the sauce over the salad at the table just before serving. Toss and serve.

# Shredded Chicken and Cucumber Salad

*A*gar-agar adds an unusual texture to this delicious salad. Use this salad as the main course for a light summer lunch.

*½ pound boned and skinned chicken breast*

### Marinade

*¼ teaspoon kosher salt*
*½ extra-large egg white*
*2 teaspoons rice wine*
*1 teaspoon cornstarch*
*2 teaspoons corn oil*

*½ ounce agar-agar sticks*
*2 cucumbers*

### Dressing

*4 tablespoons soy sauce*
*1 teaspoon sugar*
*2 teaspoons oriental sesame oil*

*1.* Freeze the chicken. Thaw until semifrozen, then shred fine.

*2.* In a medium bowl, combine the marinade with the chicken and mix to coat well. Refrigerate for at least 1 hour or overnight.

*3.* In a 2-quart saucepan, bring 1 quart of water to a boil. Turn off the heat and add the chicken shreds, stirring quickly to separate them. Turn on the heat and simmer until the chicken just turns white. Pour the chicken into a colander to drain. Spread on a platter to cool.

*4.* With a pair of scissors cut the agar-agar into 2-inch lengths. Cover with cold water and soak for 15 minutes or until soft. Drain and shake dry. Chill the agar-agar in the refrigerator.

*5.* Peel the cucumbers. Cut crosswise into 2-inch sections. Place each section flat on a cutting board and cut down to make thin slices from one edge until you reach the seeds (which will be discarded). Rotate the section one-quarter turn and continue to cut thin slices until you reach the seeds. Rotate and slice the two remaining sides until the seeds are left in a solid core. Discard the seeds. Stack the slices of cucumber and cut into lengthwise shreds. Continue this procedure until all the cucumber is shredded. Chill.

**6.** In a large mixing bowl, combine and toss the salad ingredients. Combine the ingredients for the salad dressing in a jar with a tight-fitting lid.

**7.** Just before serving, shake the salad dressing well, add to the salad and toss lightly. Serve the salad on a decorative platter.

# CUCUMBER SALAD

*Serves 4*

*T*he Chinese do not usually eat raw vegetables, but cucumbers are an exception. Removing the seeds prevents the salad from becoming watery.

*2 medium cucumbers*

**Sauce**
*½ teaspoon kosher salt*
*1½ teaspoons sugar*
*2 tablespoons soy sauce*
*1 tablespoon cider vinegar*
*2 teaspoons oriental sesame oil*

**1.** Peel the cucumbers and cut in half lengthwise. Remove and discard the seeds. Cut the cucumbers crosswise into ¼-inch slices.

**2.** In a jar with a tight-fitting lid combine the sauce ingredients and shake until thoroughly blended. Pour over the slices of cucumber and toss just before serving. Serve cold.

# HOT AND SPICY CUCUMBERS

2 medium cucumbers
1 tablespoon soy sauce
½ teaspoon salt
2 tablespoons sugar
2 tablespoons corn oil
1 large garlic clove,
   lightly crushed with
   a cleaver
4 dried hot chili
   peppers
⅛ teaspoon ground
   Sichuan
   peppercorns
1 tablespoon distilled
   white vinegar

**1.** Wash and dry the cucumbers, but do not peel them. Trim off the ends and cut in half lengthwise. Remove the seeds and cut each half lengthwise into 4 long strips and then cut each strip into 3-inch lengths. Have the soy sauce, salt and sugar measured and ready near the stove.

**2.** Heat a wok until it is hot and add the oil. Turn the heat to low. Add the garlic and chili peppers, stirring and pressing the spices against the wok to release their flavors. Stir-fry until the garlic is lightly brown and the peppers turn dark brown. Add the Sichuan peppercorns.

**3.** Turn off the heat and add the cucumbers. Stir-fry for about 30 seconds, or until the cucumber skin turns bright green. Sprinkle the soy sauce, salt and sugar over the cucumbers. Continue stirring until the sugar is dissolved, then pour the contents of the wok into a bowl. Refrigerate until thoroughly chilled. Stir the cucumber slices a few times while chilling.

**4.** Remove the cucumber slices from the sauce and transfer to a serving dish. Add the vinegar. Toss well and serve.

# Green Bean Salad

A cool addition to a summer buffet.

*½ pound chicken livers*
*Kosher salt*
*1 pound fresh green beans (youngest, most tender you can find)*
*2 teaspoons finely shredded fresh ginger*

**Mustard Dressing**

*3 tablespoons soy sauce*
*2 teaspoons Hot Mustard Sauce (page 32), or to taste*
*1 teaspoon sugar*
*2 teaspoons cider vinegar*
*1 tablespoon oriental sesame oil*
*1 tablespoon corn oil*

**1.** Kosher the chicken livers by sprinkling with kosher salt and broiling 2 minutes on each side. Cut the livers lengthwise into ¼-inch slices and set aside.

**2.** Snap off and discard the ends of the green beans. Break beans in half; you should have about 4 cups. Bring 2 quarts of water to a boil. Add the beans and return the water to a boil. Cook for about 5 minutes, or until the beans are tender yet crisp. Remove with a slotted spoon, rinse with cold water and drain. Dry the beans with paper towels and set aside.

**3.** Bring the same water back to a boil. Add the chicken livers and simmer for 3 minutes or until they are just firm. Drain and cool them in cold water. Drain again and dry with paper towels.

**4.** Put chicken livers, beans and ginger in a salad bowl.

**5.** Combine the mustard dressing ingredients in a small bowl and blend with a wire whisk. Pour the dressing over the beans and chicken livers and toss well. Chill in the refrigerator for 30 minutes and serve.

# MARINATED CHINESE CABBAGE

### Serves 6 to 8

*S*weet, sour, spicy and slightly crunchy, this salad is delightful served with cold meat dishes. It's great for large parties because it can be made several days in advance.

*1½ pounds Chinese cabbage (white part only and preferably the tender stems from the heart)*
*2 teaspoons kosher salt*
*⅓ cup distilled white vinegar*
*7 tablespoons sugar*
*1 fresh red chili pepper, shredded fine*

**1.** Separate the leaves of the cabbage. Trim away the leafy part from the stems. (Reserve the leafy parts for use in salads, soups or stir-fry dishes.) Cut stems crosswise into 2-inch sections. Cut these sections lengthwise with the grain into narrow matchstick strips. You should have about 8 cups of cabbage strips.

**2.** Put cabbage strips into a large mixing bowl. Sprinkle the salt over the cabbage and toss to mix. Set aside for 1 hour.

**3.** Wrap the cabbage in a dish towel and wring to remove much of the liquid. Return cabbage to the mixing bowl.

**4.** Put the vinegar and sugar in a small saucepan and bring to a boil. Pour over the cabbage. Cover and let stand for 30 minutes.

**5.** Strain the liquid from the cabbage and pour it back into the saucepan. Bring to a boil. Once again, pour the liquid over the cabbage. Cover and refrigerate the cabbage for 2 to 3 days. For a more intense flavor, refrigerate for as long as a week.

**6.** When ready to serve, take out the cabbage and pour off the excess liquid. Add the chili pepper. Toss to mix. Serve chilled.

# Sautéed Eggplant with Spicy Sauce

### Serves 4 to 6

*L*ook for oriental eggplants, which are sweeter and have fewer seeds than the common variety. Their long, narrow, banana shape is easily distinguished from the larger round eggplant. Try these chunks of soft, sweet eggplant bathed in a spicy sauce flecked with ginger and garlic. This is another do-ahead dish that tastes better the next day.

1 small eggplant
   (about ¾ pound)
6 tablespoons corn oil

### Sauce
1 tablespoon corn oil
1 tablespoon finely
   minced fresh ginger
1 garlic clove, minced
   fine
2 tablespoons Hot
   Chili Sauce (page
   32), or to taste
2 tablespoons water
1 tablespoon soy sauce
½ teaspoon sugar
½ teaspoon kosher
   salt

*1.* Cut off and discard stem of eggplant; without removing skin, cut eggplant into 2-inch cubes. Soak in cold water for 10 minutes to keep eggplant from absorbing too much oil when fried.

*2.* Drain the eggplant and shake to remove most of the water. Heat a large skillet to medium hot and add the 6 tablespoons oil. Sauté the eggplant cubes about 5 minutes. Remove with a slotted spoon and drain on paper towels. Transfer to a serving platter.

*3.* To prepare the sauce, heat 1 tablespoon oil in a small saucepan over medium-low heat and add the ginger and garlic. Stir-fry for a few seconds until the flavors are released. Add the remaining sauce ingredients, stir and bring to a boil, then pour the sauce over the eggplant. Serve hot or cold.

# FISH TOAST

*L*ightly seasoned fish adds a delicate taste to this toast. This excellent appetizer can be made in advance and frozen without losing flavor.

**¾ pound fish fillets, such as sea bass or yellow pike (walleye)**
**1 tablespoon minced scallions**
**2 tablespoons finely minced water chestnuts**

### Seasoning

**1 teaspoon salt**
**1 tablespoon rice wine**
**2 teaspoons cornstarch**
**1 small egg white**
**3 tablespoons water**

**6 thin slices white bread**
**24 whole fresh coriander leaves, rinsed and dried with paper towels**
**2 cups corn oil, for frying**

*1.* Cut the fish into small cubes. Using the metal blade in a food processor, add the fish, scallion, water chestnuts, and seasoning ingredients to the bowl. Process only until mixture holds together. Do not overprocess! (If you do not have a food processor, chop the fish cubes with a cleaver until they form a coarse paste. Add minced scallion, water chestnuts and seasoning ingredients. Stir in one direction until the mixture becomes light and sticky.)

*2.* Remove the crusts from the bread and cut each slice into quarters. Spread each quarter with the fish paste, mounding it slightly in the center. Place a coriander leaf on the top of each fish toast and press it down lightly.

*3.* Heat a wok and add the oil. When the oil reaches 325° F., place the fish toast in the hot oil *fish side down.* Deep-fry the toast until golden brown, turning once or twice during the frying. Remove and drain. Arrange on a serving platter and serve hot as an appetizer.

**Note:** To freeze, wrap the fried fish toast in foil and put into a plastic bag. To serve, preheat oven to 350° F. and place the fish toast on a rack in a single layer over a shallow baking pan. Heat for 10 minutes.

# BARBECUED CHICKEN WINGS

*H*oisin sauce makes a terrific barbecue sauce. East meets West.

*18 chicken wings*
*1½ tablespoons soy*
*sauce*
*¾ cup Hoisin Sauce*
*(page 31)*

**1.** Preheat the broiler and line the broiler pan with foil. Rinse and dry the chicken wings. Cut away the wing tip at the joint; save the tips for stock. Arrange the wings in the pan so that they do not touch and brush with the soy sauce.

**2.** Broil the wings, not too close to the heat, for 5 minutes. Brush on the sauce. Broil, being careful the sauce does not burn, for another 5 or 7 minutes.

**3.** Turn the wings over. Broil them for 5 minutes, then brush with more sauce and broil another 5 to 7 minutes, or until done. Serve as an appetizer.

*Note:* Try this sauce on other chicken parts. If larger chicken parts are used, broil 10 minutes on each side before brushing on the sauce and then watch closely so the sauce doesn't burn.

# TEA EGGS

*T*ea Eggs are terrific for picnics or buffets. They are popular street food in China because they are easy to make and can be cooked in advance. This traditional method cooks the eggs for several hours so they will absorb the flavor of the tea.

*12 extra-large eggs*
*2 tablespoons kosher salt*
*3 tablespoons black tea*
*3 tablespoons soy sauce*
*½ teaspoon sugar*
*2 star anise*

**1.** Place the eggs in a large pot and cover with cold water. Bring the water to a boil and cover the pot. Turn the heat to low and cook for 5 minutes. Turn off the heat and let stand for 20 minutes.

**2.** Pour out the hot water, remove the eggs and, using a spoon, gently crack the shells all around the eggs but do not remove the shell.

**3.** Return the eggs to the pot and add just enough cold water to cover. Add the remaining ingredients and stir once or twice. Bring to a boil, then turn the heat as low as possible. Cover the pot and cook for 2 or 3 hours. Turn off the heat and let the eggs remain overnight in the cooking liquid.

**4.** To serve, peel the eggs and cut into halves or quarters. Arrange the eggs on a platter to show the whites with their finely cracked lines from the shells. Serve warm or cold. The eggs may be stored in a covered container in the refrigerator for up to 2 weeks.

# NORTHERN-STYLE CHICKEN NUGGETS

*T*his deep-fried chicken recipe uses coarse bread crumbs as a batter to add a tasty crispiness.

**2 whole chicken breasts, skinned, boned and cut in half**

**Marinade**

**1 large egg white**
**3 tablespoons cornstarch**
**1½ teaspoons kosher salt**
**1 tablespoon rice wine**
**⅛ teaspoon white pepper**

**¾ cup all-purpose flour**
**1 extra-large egg, slightly beaten**
**2 cups coarse bread crumbs**
**2 cups corn oil, for deep-frying**

*1.* Cut the chicken breasts into 2½ × 1½ × ¼-inch slices. In a mixing bowl, combine the chicken with the marinade ingredients. Blend thoroughly.

*2.* Dredge the slices of chicken in the flour, dip them in the beaten egg and coat them on both sides with the coarse bread crumbs. Set aside.

*3.* Pour the oil into a wok and heat to about 350° F. Deep-fry as many chicken pieces as will float freely in the hot oil until golden and crisp. Turn once or twice while frying. Drain and serve hot.

# SMOKED FISH

*T*he smoky flavor in this recipe comes from the five-spice powder. This goes well with cold dishes, such as Cucumber Salad (page 43), for a summer meal.

## Marinade

3 tablespoons soy
    sauce
1 tablespoon chopped
    scallions
1 teaspoon finely
    minced fresh ginger
1/8 teaspoon white
    pepper
1/4 teaspoon kosher
    salt

3/4-pound flounder
    fillet, cut into
    2 × 2-inch pieces

## Sauce

1/4 cup rice wine
2 teaspoons sugar
1/4 teaspoon
    Five-Spice Powder
    (page 35)

2 cups corn oil, for
    frying

*1.* In a small bowl combine the marinade ingredients. Pour over the fish and marinate for 15 minutes. Drain the fillets, reserving the marinade.

*2.* Heat a small skillet over very low heat. Add the reserved marinade and the sauce ingredients. Keep sauce warm while frying the fish.

*3.* Heat a wok and add the oil. When the oil reaches 356° F., fry the drained fish 5 or 6 pieces at a time. Be careful not to crowd the pieces. Fry 2 minutes on each side, or until golden brown. Take out the fish pieces when they are done and immediately put them in the small skillet with the marinade sauce, so that the fried fish is coated on all sides with the sauce. Continue with this procedure until all the pieces are cooked. Serve hot or cold.

# CANDIED PECANS

Candied nuts are often served at the beginning of a Chinese banquet to add a sweet taste and a crunchy texture to the variety of small dishes offered to perk up the appetite. For Westerners, they're more appropriate as an after-dinner sweet. They are hard to resist at any time.

**8 ounces (about 2¼ cups) shelled large pecans**
**4 cups water**
**½ cup sugar**
**2 cups corn oil, for frying**

**1.** Put the nuts in a saucepan and add water. Bring to a boil and simmer for 5 minutes. Drain and immediately put the nuts back into the pan and add the sugar. Toss and mix the nuts well to coat them evenly. Pour the nuts onto wax paper and spread out to dry for about 10 minutes.

**2.** Heat a wok over moderate heat and add the oil. When the oil reaches 320° F. (use a candy thermometer), fry half the nuts for 6 to 8 minutes, or until the sugar has caramelized around each nut. Stir constantly so the nuts fry evenly and use a slotted spoon to transfer them to a shallow baking pan. Spread them apart in a single layer to cool, then put them on paper towels to absorb excess oil. Continue with the balance of the nuts. After cooling, store the nuts in an airtight container. They will remain crisp and crunchy for months.

*Note:* Walnuts can be substituted but it is difficult to remove the bitter skin.)

# STEAMED EGG-CRÊPE ROLL

*T*he Chinese appreciate the color of eggs as much as the taste. The yellow of these rolls is striking when contrasted with the meat filling. Serve as an attractive appetizer, sliced on top of a stir-fried vegetable dish, or with Hot Pot (page 158).

*3 extra-large eggs*
*⅛ teaspoon kosher salt*

### Filling

*½ pound ground beef*
*½ teaspoon kosher salt*
*⅛ teaspoon pepper*
*½ teaspoon sugar*
*1 teaspoon rice wine*
*1 teaspoon oriental sesame oil*
*1 tablespoon soy sauce*
*1½ teaspoons cornstarch*
*¼ cup Chicken Broth (page 155)*

**1.** Beat the eggs well with the salt. Pour through a fine strainer and discard the solids. Measure 3 tablespoons of the beaten egg into a small cup and set aside.

**2.** Combine the filling ingredients and stir in one direction until light and sticky. (Stirring the filling in one direction makes the mixture stick together.)

**3.** Heat a 9- or 10-inch nonstick or well-cured skillet. Turn the heat to low and allow pan to cool slightly. Brush the skillet with oil, then pour in enough egg to coat the skillet. Tilt the skillet and swirl the egg to make a thin, even layer. When the egg sets and the edges begin to curl, carefully lift the egg-crêpe out of the skillet and transfer to a plate. Repeat this process with the rest of the egg to make a second crêpe.

**4.** Divide the filling mixture into 2 equal portions. Using a spatula, spread one portion of the meat mixture evenly in a thin layer over the entire surface of each crêpe.

**5.** Starting at the edge, tightly roll the crêpe like a jelly roll. Brush a little of the reserved raw egg on the exposed edge of the crêpe and press to seal. Place on a flat plate. Do the same with the second crêpe.

**6.** Place the plate in a steamer over boiling water and steam for 10 minutes. Turn off the heat and allow the rolls to cool in the covered steamer for 5 minutes. Carefully transfer the rolls to a cutting board and cut them diagonally into ¼-inch-thick slices. Arrange the slices in an overlapping circle and serve.

# STEAMED EGGPLANT

*Serves 4*

Steamed vegetables are healthful. They sometimes are bland but not if prepared this way. This is a tasty, cold dish that contrasts the sweetness of eggplant with the spiciness of the sauce. Best of all, it is simple to prepare.

**1 medium eggplant (about 1 pound)**

**Sauce**

**2 tablespoons soy sauce**
**2 teaspoons sugar**
**2 teaspoons cider vinegar**
**1 tablespoon oriental sesame oil**
**1 to 2 teaspoons Hot Chili Sauce (page 32), or to taste**

**1.** Wash the eggplant and remove the stem. Cut into quarters lengthwise. Arrange the eggplant in one layer in a deep heatproof dish, such as a glass pie plate. Place in a bamboo or metal steamer over boiling water and steam for 15 to 20 minutes or until soft.

**2.** Remove the eggplant from the steamer and discard the accumulated liquid. With a fork in each hand, carefully pull each section of eggplant apart into thin, lengthwise strips. Remove any seeds and tough parts. Chill the eggplant in the refrigerator.

**3.** When you are ready to serve, mix the sauce ingredients and pour over the eggplant.

# CHICKEN AND DUCK

**K**osher chickens are excellent and some people attribute this to the method of slaughtering, which is to drain the blood immediately after killing the fowl.

Large chickens, or pullets, are the best for making stock or for any of the recipes requiring whole chicken. However, a small chicken or a pound or so of bones can also make a small quantity of excellent stock.

Chicken "cutlet," a label often seen in kosher butcher shops, is chicken breast with the skin and bone removed.

Chinese love duck, especially the skin, which they will go to great lengths to make crispy. You will be delighted to learn the different ways to eliminate the fat from duck and bring out its delectable flavor.

I prefer fresh kosher ducks when I can get them, but they are difficult to find and have to be ordered. Frozen ducks will do nicely so don't despair, but be aware they can be very salty. Soak the duck for an hour or so to remove the salt before proceeding with the recipe. Also, because hot water cannot be used to remove the feathers from kosher fowl, many of the pin feathers remain. The feathers of the duck are particularly difficult to extract, so the skin of the duck is often torn. Using a pair of tweezers to remove the feathers is effective but time-consuming. Pass the bird lightly over a low flame to singe any feathers, moving the bird quickly so it does not become heated.

| Recipes | | Prepare Ahead | Serving Temperature |
|---|---|---|---|
| White-Cut Chicken | | Yes | Room temp. |
| Chinese Roast Chicken | | Yes | Room temp. |
| Chicken Velvet | | No | Hot |
| Silver-and-Gold Shredded Chicken | | No | Hot |
| Mu Shu Chicken with Peking Pancakes | | No | Hot |
| Braised Chicken with Ginger | | Yes | Hot |
| Roast Boneless Chicken Stuffed with Glutinous Rice | | Yes | Hot |
| Sweet-and-Sour Chicken | | No | Hot |
| Steamed Chicken | Mild | No | Hot |
| Lemon Chicken | | No | Hot |
| Kung Pao Chicken | Spicy hot | No | Hot |

| Recipes | | Prepare Ahead | Serving Temperature |
|---|---|---|---|
| Stir-Fried Chicken with Broccoli | | No | Hot |
| Steamed Whole Chicken | | Yes | Room temp. |
| Chicken with Cashew Nuts | Spicy hot | No | Hot |
| Smoked Chicken | | Yes | Room temp. |
| Chinese "Southern" Fried Chicken | | Yes | Hot or room temp. |
| Spicy Chicken | Spicy hot | No | Hot |
| Soy-Sauce Chicken | | Yes | Room temp. |
| Shanghai Braised Duck with Onions | | Yes | Hot |
| Roast Duck | | Yes | Room temp. |
| Peking Duck | | No | Hot |
| Sichuan Crispy Duck | | Yes | Hot |
| Cantonese Roast Duck | | Yes | Room temp. |
| Stir-Fried Duck with Ginger | Spicy | No | Hot |

# WHITE-CUT CHICKEN

*Serves 4 to 5 as a main course, or 6 to 8 if served with other dishes*

This is the basic Chinese method of poaching chicken, a task at which the Cantonese excel. The chicken is poached until just cooked, then chilled quickly for a firm yet tender texture and to enhance its natural flavor. If served with soy sauce it becomes Shanghai style; when served with garlic, it's Northern. Here, the pure chicken flavor is contrasted with a piquant ginger-scallion sauce.

*1 large chicken, about 4 to 5 pounds*
*1 tablespoon kosher salt*
*8 cups Chicken Broth (page 155)*

**Ginger-Scallion Sauce**
*½ tablespoon finely minced fresh ginger*
*4 scallions, white part only, minced fine*
*½ teaspoon sugar*
*1 teaspoon hot mustard powder mixed with 2 teaspoons water*
*¼ cup corn oil*
*1 teaspoon kosher salt*

*Few sprigs fresh watercress, for garnish*

**1.** Rinse and dry the chicken. Rub the inside and outside with the salt. Refrigerate for a minimum of 4 hours or overnight.

**2.** Pour the broth into a pot large enough to submerge the chicken. Bring the broth to a boil.

**3.** Insert a metal spoon into the cavity of the chicken. (This helps to conduct heat to the inside of the chicken while cooking.) Carefully lower the chicken, breast side down, into the broth. Add boiling water if necessary to cover the chicken.

**4.** Bring the broth back to a boil. Cover and turn the heat down to low. Simmer gently for 30 minutes. Turn off the heat and allow the chicken to cool slightly, still covered in the broth, for 1 hour.

**5.** Remove the chicken from the broth. (Save the broth for other recipes.) Take out the metal spoon. Plunge the chicken into 8 cups of ice water. When the chicken has chilled, remove and place it on a platter. Refrigerate until the chicken is thoroughly cold, about 2 hours.

**6.** With a sharp cleaver or knife, disjoint the chicken. Carefully remove the bone from each section and cut the chicken into bite-size pieces. Arrange the pieces on a serving platter and garnish with sprigs of fresh watercress.

**7.** To make the sauce, put the ginger, scallions, sugar and mustard mixture into a heatproof dish. Heat the oil and salt in a small skillet until very hot but not smoking. Pour the hot oil over the ginger-scallion mixture and stir.

**8.** Pour the sauce over the chicken and serve at room temperature.

# CHINESE ROAST CHICKEN

*Serves 4 to 5*

**H**ere is a simple Chinese-flavored roast chicken with a crispy skin.

*1 roasting chicken, 4 to 5 pounds*
*1 teaspoon kosher salt*

### Glaze

*1 tablespoon light corn syrup mixed with 1 tablespoon boiling water*
*1 tablespoon soy sauce*
*1 tablespoon distilled white vinegar*
*½ teaspoon Five-Spice Powder (page 35)*

*Few sprigs fresh coriander, for garnish*

**1.** Preheat the oven to 350° F. Rinse the chicken with cold water and pat dry with paper towels. Rub both the inside and the outside of the chicken with the salt.

**2.** Combine the ingredients for the glaze and mix thoroughly. Using a pastry brush, cover the outside of the chicken with the glaze. Place the chicken on a rack over a shallow baking pan and allow to dry in a cool, breezy place for 1 to 2 hours or until dry. Alternatively, dry in front of a room fan for 1 hour.

**3.** Put the chicken breast side down on the rack and place in baking pan. Bake for 20 minutes, then turn it breast side up, being careful not to break the skin. Roast for another 50 minutes or until done. Let the chicken cool.

**4.** Transfer chicken to a chopping board. Using a cleaver, disjoint and chop through the bone to make bite-size pieces, or carve Western-style at the table. Arrange pieces on a serving platter and garnish with coriander. Serve at room temperature.

# CHICKEN VELVET

**P**rized for its velvety texture and its subtle flavor, this dish is served at northern Chinese banquets. A food processor or blender is needed to turn the chicken into a smooth paste.

1 whole chicken breast
1½ cups Chicken
  Broth (page 155)
1 teaspoon kosher salt
1 teaspoon sugar
1 tablespoon rice wine
1 tablespoon
  cornstarch
6 extra-large egg
  whites
4 dried black
  mushrooms
2 cups corn oil, for
  poaching
½ cup frozen peas,
  thawed; or 20 fresh
  snow peas, blanched
¼ cup sliced bamboo
  shoots
2 teaspoons cornstarch
  mixed with 2
  tablespoons water
¼ cup finely minced
  kosher smoked
  turkey (optional)

*1.* Bone and skin the chicken breast, remove tendons and cut meat into small cubes. Put the cubed chicken into a blender or food processor. Blend or process by turning the machine on and off while gradually adding 1 cup of the broth and the salt, sugar and rice wine. Scrape the mixture down with a spatula to be sure the chicken is thoroughly blended into a smooth paste. Add the cornstarch and mix well, then add the egg whites and process briefly until the mixture is light and creamy. (The dish can be prepared up to this point and refrigerated overnight.)

*2.* Soak the mushrooms in warm water for 30 minutes. Remove the stems and cut caps into quarters. Set aside.

*3.* Place a strainer over a pot near the stove. Heat a wok until hot and add the oil, heating to 280° F. over medium heat. Add the chicken mixture and gently stir, breaking up the mixture. As soon as the chicken turns white, pour the contents of the wok into the strainer and allow the oil to drain into the pot.

*4.* Reheat the wok and add 2 tablespoons of the drained oil. Add the peas or snow peas, mushrooms and bamboo shoots. Stir-fry for 1 or 2 minutes, then add the chicken and the remaining ½ cup broth. As the broth begins to boil, add the cornstarch mixture. Cook and stir gently until the sauce thickens. Dish out onto a serving plate and garnish with the minced smoked turkey. Serve at once.

# SILVER-AND-GOLD SHREDDED CHICKEN

*Serves 4 to 5*

An attractive dish, this recipe is typically Chinese in its presentation and subtle flavor. Shredded raw chicken is divided into two portions. One portion is marinated in soy sauce and turns golden when cooked; the other is cooked without soy sauce and remains white, or silver. Stir-fried spinach is placed between the gold and silver mounds on the serving platter.

**1½ pounds boned and skinned chicken breasts**

**Marinade**
½ large egg white
½ teaspoon salt
1 tablespoon dry sherry
1 teaspoon oriental sesame oil
2 teaspoons cornstarch

1 tablespoon soy sauce
3 tablespoons corn oil
1 large garlic clove, crushed slightly with the cleaver
1 pound fresh spinach, washed, drained and tough stems removed
1 teaspoon kosher salt
½ teaspoon sugar
½ cup corn oil, for poaching

**1.** Freeze the chicken in separate pieces. Thaw until semifrozen, then shred fine. Mix the chicken with the marinade ingredients and marinate for at least 1 hour, or as long as overnight. Divide the chicken shreds into two equal portions and mix the soy sauce into one portion.

**2.** Heat a wok over high heat until very hot and add the 3 tablespoons of corn oil. Add the garlic and stir-fry for a few seconds, being careful not to let it burn. Add the spinach and stir-fry until the ingredients are thoroughly mixed with the oil. Add the salt and sugar. As soon as the spinach wilts, use a pair of tongs or chopsticks to transfer the spinach to the center of an oblong serving platter. Discard the garlic and any accumulated liquid. Wipe the wok clean with a paper towel.

**3.** Reheat the wok. Place the strainer over a pot near the stove. Add the ½ cup of corn oil to the wok, heat to about 280° F. and add the chicken portion without the soy sauce. Stir quickly to separate the pieces of chicken. As soon as the chicken turns white, pour the contents of the wok into the strainer and allow the oil to drain away. Transfer the chicken to one side of the spinach. Cook the chicken portion with the soy sauce in the same manner and arrange on the opposite side of the spinach. Serve hot.

# MU SHU CHICKEN WITH PEKING PANCAKES

**Serves 4 to 6**

*T*his northern Chinese dish is traditionally served as a filling with Peking Pancakes, but it is also delicious plain. Veal, turkey or beef can be substituted for chicken.

*¾ pound boned and
  skinned chicken
  breast
20 tiger lily buds
3 tablespoons tree ears*

### Marinade

*1 teaspoon cornstarch
1 tablespoon water
½ teaspoon sugar
1 tablespoon soy sauce*

*6 tablespoons corn oil
4 extra-large eggs,
  well beaten
3 scallions, shredded
1 cup shredded green
  cabbage
1 teaspoon salt
1 tablespoon oriental
  sesame oil
20 Peking Pancakes
  (page 200), warmed*

**1.** Freeze the chicken in separate pieces. Thaw until semifrozen, then shred fine.

**2.** Soak the tiger lily buds and tree ears separately in warm water in bowls for 30 minutes. Cut off and discard the hard ends of the lily buds, then cut the buds in half. Clean and wash the tree ears and cut them into small pieces. Discard soaking liquid. Place the shredded ingredients in separate mounds on a large platter near the stove.

**3.** In a medium bowl mix the marinade ingredients and add the chicken. Mix well and also place near the stove.

**4.** Heat a wok over medium heat until hot, then add 3 tablespoons of corn oil and the eggs. With a spatula, slowly push the eggs back and forth in the wok; as the eggs cook and coagulate, break them up into large pieces—they should be dry. Transfer the cooked eggs to a bowl.

**5.** Reheat the wok and add the remaining corn oil. Add the chicken and stir-fry until it changes color. As you stir, use the spatula to separate the shredded chicken. Add the shredded tree ears, lily buds, scallions and cabbage, blend well, then add the salt. Continue to stir-fry until the cabbage wilts, about 2 to 3 minutes.

**6.** Return the eggs to the wok and stir until well blended, breaking up the eggs into smaller pieces. Mix in the sesame oil, turn off the heat and transfer the mixture to a serving platter. Serve hot with pancakes.

---

*Note:* To serve, offer each guest a pancake. The guest puts 1 tablespoon of the chicken mixture in the center of the pancake and rolls the pancake around the filling. The pancake is then eaten with the fingers.

# BRAISED CHICKEN WITH GINGER

*Serves 4*

---

*B*raising the chicken with these flavorings creates a savory sauce.

---

*1 frying chicken, about 3 pounds (have your butcher disjoint the chicken and cut through the bone of each piece to make 16 pieces)*

### Marinade
*1 teaspoon kosher salt*
*1½ teaspoons sugar*
*1½ tablespoons cornstarch*
*5 tablespoons soy sauce*
*1 teaspoon oriental sesame oil*

*6 dried black mushrooms*
*3 tablespoons corn oil*
*3 garlic cloves*
*3 slices fresh ginger, each about the size of a quarter*
*2 scallions, cut into 1-inch pieces*
*1 tablespoon rice wine*

**1.** Rinse the chicken in cold water and pat dry with paper towels. Put the pieces in a large mixing bowl, add the marinade ingredients and mix thoroughly.

**2.** Soak the mushrooms in warm water for 30 minutes. Remove stems and cut caps in half.

**3.** Heat a heavy pot or casserole over medium heat until hot. Add the oil, then the garlic, ginger and scallions and stir-fry for 1 minute. Add the chicken and mushrooms, and stir-fry for 2 minutes. Add the rice wine, stir, cover and turn down the heat to low. Cook for about 30 minutes, or until the chicken is tender. Stir several times during cooking. Serve hot with Boiled Rice (page 167).

# Roast Boneless Chicken Stuffed with Glutinous Rice

This classic Cantonese banquet dish only looks complicated. Everything can be done ahead, and your guests will be astonished at your accomplishment. You might want to practice once or twice.

1½ cups glutinous rice
5 dried black
 mushrooms
1 roasting chicken,
 about 4 to 5 pounds
1 chicken liver
4 tablespoons corn oil
1 tablespoon soy sauce
1 tablespoon rice wine
¼ cup diced bamboo
 shoots
3 water chestnuts
1 tablespoon chopped
 scallions
1 tablespoon chopped
 fresh coriander
2 teaspoons kosher salt
⅛ teaspoon white
 pepper
½ teaspoon sugar
¼ cup Chicken Broth
 (page 155)

## Glaze

1 quart boiling water
1 tablespoon light corn
 syrup

Few sprigs fresh
 coriander, for
 garnish

*1.* Rinse the rice and soak it in water for 4 hours. Drain and transfer to a heatproof mixing bowl. Pour 3 or 4 inches of water in a steamer and bring the water to a boil. Place the rice in the steamer and steam for 30 minutes. Using a fork, fluff up the rice and allow to cool.

*2.* Soak the mushrooms in warm water for 30 minutes. Discard the stems and dice the caps.

*3.* Bone the chicken, leaving the skin intact. Start at the neck opening and, using a kitchen shears and a sharp paring knife, begin by making small cuts close to and around the bone of the neck, freeing the meat with the skin and pulling it away from the carcass. (Watch that the sharp tip of the knife does not pierce the skin as you cut. However, if you make a hole don't worry; just sew it up with a dark thread, so the thread can be easily found and removed after cooking.) Work downward, pulling and cutting the meat and skin away from the bone as carefully as possible down around the main body. Keep as close to the carcass as possible. Turn the chicken around as you cut so that you are cutting at the same level all around. Cut the meat away from around the thigh bone and sever the joint between the thigh bone and the drumstick. Continue cutting and pulling until you reach the joint where the backbone and tailbone meet. Cut through that joint, leaving the tail attached to the skin and meat. Carefully remove the breast and thigh meat from the skin. Dice the meat and set aside.

**4.** Salt the chicken liver, broil 2 minutes on each side and dice.

**5.** Heat a wok and add the oil. Add the diced chicken and chicken liver. Stir-fry for about 2 minutes, or until they both change color. Add the soy sauce and wine. Stir in the mushrooms, bamboo shoots, water chestnuts, scallions and coriander. Then stir in the rice, salt, pepper, sugar and broth. Stir to blend thoroughly. Transfer the mixture to a platter and let cool.

**6.** Close the chicken skin at the top with a skewer. Using the rice mixture, stuff the chicken skin from the cavity opening, trying to recreate the shape of the chicken. Close the bottom end with another skewer. Place the stuffed chicken breast side down on a rack in the sink.

**7.** For the glaze, bring water to a boil, add the corn syrup and mix. Slowly ladle half the boiling liquid over the chicken. Turn the chicken over, breast side up, and ladle the remaining boiling liquid over it. This coating tightens the skin so that as the chicken is roasted, the skin becomes golden brown and crispy. Allow the chicken to drip-dry for 30 minutes.

**8.** Preheat the oven to 375° F. Place the chicken breast side up on a rack in a shallow roasting pan. Roast for 1 hour. Transfer to a warm serving platter, remove the skewers and garnish with coriander sprigs. Cut and serve the chicken at the dinner table.

---

*Note:* You can bone the chicken several days or even a week in advance and freeze the skin and meat until ready to use. The filling can also be made a day in advance and refrigerated until ready to use.

# SWEET-AND-SOUR CHICKEN

### Serves 4

**A**s with much in Chinese food, contrast is the key: sweet with sour, a crispy golden crust with moist, tender meat. Try this recipe with chunks of turkey breast or veal.

*12 large chicken wings, the thickest segment only (save other segments for stock)*

### Marinade

*1 tablespoon light soy sauce*
*½ teaspoon kosher salt*
*1 teaspoon oriental sesame oil*

*1 tablespoon corn oil*
*1 garlic clove*
*1 cup assorted vegetables, such as sliced peppers, carrots, snow peas cut in half, sliced water chestnuts*

### Sauce

*4 tablespoons sugar*
*4 tablespoons distilled white vinegar*
*2 tablespoons catsup*
*2 tablespoons soy sauce*
*½ cup Chicken Broth (page 155)*
*1 tablespoon cornstarch*

**1.** Using a sharp knife, loosen the skin, meat and cartilage from the narrow end of each chicken wing. Pull the meat back over the meatier end, turning the skin inside out and exposing the meat on the inside so wing looks like a lollipop. In a bowl combine the marinade ingredients, add the chicken and let stand for 20 minutes.

**2.** Heat the tablespoon of corn oil in a medium saucepan and toss in the garlic and vegetables. Stir-fry with a wooden spoon for 2 minutes, then turn off the heat. Discard the garlic. Combine the sauce ingredients and stir into the saucepan mixture. Place the saucepan near the stove, to be cooked later. In a bowl mix the batter ingredients until smooth.

**3.** Heat the 2 cups of oil in a wok to about 325° F. While the oil is heating, remove 1 tablespoon of warm oil from the wok and stir it into the batter. Dip each wing into the batter and deep-fry as many pieces as will float freely until golden brown, crisp and cooked, about 5 or 6 minutes. Turn once or twice while frying so the pieces fry evenly. Remove and drain. The chicken can be kept warm on a rack over a shallow baking pan in a 180° F. oven. Continue the procedure until all the chicken is fried.

**4.** When the chicken is almost finished frying, restir the sauce to dissolve the cornstarch. Place

## Batter

½ cup all-purpose
  flour
¼ cup cornstarch
½ teaspoon salt
2 teaspoons baking
  powder
⅔ cup cold water,
  approximately

2 cups corn oil, for
  frying
½ cup pineapple
  chunks or lychees

saucepan over medium heat and, while stirring, boil until the sauce thickens and becomes clear. Stir in the fruit and turn off the heat.

**5.** Place the chicken on a large serving dish. Pour the sauce with the vegetables and fruit over it, and serve immediately.

# STEAMED CHICKEN

*Serves 6*

This is a simple, low-calorie, delicious way to cook chicken.

2 pounds boneless
  chicken

### Seasoning

1½ teaspoons sugar
2 tablespoons rice
  wine
2 tablespoons soy
  sauce
1½ teaspoons kosher
  salt
1 tablespoon
  cornstarch

6 dried black
  mushrooms
3 thin slices fresh
  ginger, each about
  the size of a quarter
2 tablespoons corn oil
2 fresh hot green chili
  peppers, shredded

**1.** Remove the excess skin from the chicken and cut chicken into ½-inch chunks. Put in a mixing bowl, add the seasoning ingredients and mix until pieces are coated.

**2.** Soak the mushrooms in warm water for 30 minutes. Remove the stems and discard.

**3.** Place the chicken in a heatproof serving dish with a 2-inch rim. Arrange the ginger slices over the chicken and then the mushrooms over all. Place the dish in a steamer on a rack set over 1½ inches or more of boiling water. Cover and steam for 40 minutes. Stir the chicken once or twice during the cooking.

**4.** Meanwhile, heat a saucepan and add 1 tablespoon oil. Add the peppers and stir-fry for a few seconds.

**5.** Remove the chicken from the steamer, arrange the peppers on top of the steamed chicken and serve at once.

# LEMON CHICKEN

*L*emon chicken is a big hit with my students, perhaps because they rediscover the familiar lemon taste in a new and delectable way. The recipe looks complicated at first glance, but when done step by step it all falls into place and the effort brings raves!

**2 whole chicken breasts**

### Marinade
**½ teaspoon salt**
**1 tablespoon light soy sauce**
**1 teaspoon oriental sesame oil**

### Batter
**½ cup all-purpose flour**
**¼ cup cornstarch**
**2 teaspoons baking powder**
**¼ teaspoon kosher salt**
**⅔ cup cold water**

### Lemon Sauce
**4 tablespoons fresh lemon juice, strained**
**4 tablespoons sugar**
**4 tablespoons mild Japanese rice vinegar**
**¾ cup Chicken Broth (page 155)**
**4 teaspoons cornstarch**

**1.** Skin and bone the chicken and cut each breast in half. Combine the marinade ingredients with the chicken. Mix to coat the chicken pieces thoroughly, then set aside for 20 minutes.

**2.** Combine the batter ingredients in a bowl. Stir until smooth.

**3.** Combine the sauce ingredients in a small bowl, stirring until the cornstarch dissolves. Place near the stove.

**4.** Heat a wok until hot and add the 2 cups of oil. As the oil is heating, remove 1 tablespoon of warm oil and add it to the batter. Stir to blend. When the oil reaches about 325° F., or when a drop of batter sizzles instantly when dropped into the wok, quickly dip the pieces of chicken into the batter and then gently place them in the hot oil. Deep-fry the chicken until golden brown and crispy, turning the pieces several times. Remove chicken pieces as they are done, in about 5 or 6 minutes, and drain on a rack placed over a pan. Keep warm in oven.

**5.** Heat 1 tablespoon of oil in a small saucepan until warm. Briefly stir the sauce, then add to the oil. Turn up the heat and, while stirring constantly, bring the sauce to a boil. Immediately reduce the heat to a simmer. Cook and stir until the sauce thickens and becomes clear.

2 cups corn oil, for
frying, plus 1
tablespoon for
sauce
1 cup shredded iceberg
lettuce
½ lemon, sliced thin,
for garnish

**6.** Cut the chicken into bite-size pieces with a cleaver. Arrange on a serving platter over the shredded lettuce and garnish the platter with the lemon slices. Pour the sauce over the chicken just before serving or, for a crispier chicken, serve sauce as a dip.

---

*Note:* Marukan brand vinegar adds a pale yellow color to the sauce. If you substitute distilled white vinegar, the sauce will be slightly more acidic and less colored.

# KUNG PAO CHICKEN

*Serves 4*

---

A classic, spicy Sichuan dish, this is said to have been created during the Qing dynasty for a banquet in honor of a new governor of Sichuan, Ting Pao-Ts'en. He was called Kung Pao, hence the name of this dish.

---

¾ pound boned and
skinned chicken
breast

### Marinade
½ small egg white
2 teaspoons cornstarch
¼ teaspoon kosher
salt

6 to 8 large dried hot
chili peppers
2 garlic cloves, sliced
thin
2 thin slices fresh
ginger
2 scallions, cut into
¼-inch pieces

**1.** Cut the chicken into ¼-inch cubes. In a bowl, combine the marinade ingredients and add the cubed chicken. Mix thoroughly to be sure the chicken is well coated. Refrigerate for at least 1 hour or overnight.

**2.** Put the chili peppers, garlic, ginger and scallions separately on a plate. Combine the sauce ingredients in a small bowl. Place both near the stove. Put a large strainer over a bowl and place it near the stove.

**3.** Heat a wok and add the corn oil. When the oil is warm, about 280° F., add the chicken and stir gently until the meat turns white and separates. Pour the contents of the wok into the strainer and allow the oil to drain. (continued)

## Sauce

½ teaspoon sugar
1 teaspoon distilled
   white vinegar
1 tablespoon rice wine
2 tablespoons dark soy
   sauce
1 teaspoon oriental
   sesame oil
3 tablespoons Chicken
   Broth (page 155)
Dash of white pepper

1 cup corn oil, for
   poaching
1 teaspoon cornstarch
   mixed with 2
   tablespoons water
½ cup unsalted roasted
   peanuts

**4.** Reheat the wok and add 2 tablespoons of the drained oil. Add the chili peppers and stir-fry over medium-low heat until the peppers turn dark brown. Add the scallions, garlic and ginger, then stir-fry for a few seconds to release the flavors. Add the sauce and the cooked chicken. Stir the cornstarch mixture and add to the wok while stirring constantly. Cook and stir until the sauce thickens and coats the chicken. Add the peanuts, stir and transfer to a serving platter. Serve hot.

# STIR-FRIED CHICKEN WITH BROCCOLI

### Serves 4

*T*his is a basic stir-fry chicken dish in which you can vary the vegetables. For instance, try it with zucchini, cauliflower, carrots or asparagus.

½ pound boned and
   skinned chicken
   breast

### Marinade

½ egg white
1½ teaspoons
   cornstarch
1 tablespoon soy sauce
½ teaspoon kosher
   salt

**1.** Cut the chicken into 1½ × 2 × ⅛-inch slices and combine with the marinade ingredients. Set chicken aside for 30 minutes.

**2.** Soak the mushrooms in warm water for 30 minutes. Remove the stems and cut caps into quarters.

**3.** Using a sharp paring knife, start from the bottom of the broccoli stem and peel back the tough outer skin until you reach the flowerets.

¼ teaspoon sugar
1 tablespoon water
1 tablespoon corn oil

4 dried black
   mushrooms
   (optional)
1 stalk broccoli (or
   more if not using
   mushrooms and
   bamboo shoots)
½ teaspoon kosher
   salt
¼ cup sliced bamboo
   shoots (optional)
¼ teaspoon sugar
2 teaspoons cornstarch
   mixed with ¾ cup
   Chicken Broth
   (page 155)
4 tablespoons corn oil

Cut the peel away at the base of the flowerets and discard. Separate the flowerets and their branches from the large stem. Cut the flowerets into bite-size pieces, and then cut the stems into 1½ × ½ × ½-inch pieces.

**4.** Bring 2 quarts of water to a boil. Add the salt and broccoli. Return to a boil and remove the pot from the heat as soon as the broccoli turns bright green, about 1 minute. Pour the contents of the pot into a large strainer, then rinse with cold water until the broccoli is cooled. Drain and shake dry.

**5.** Place the mushrooms, bamboo shoots and broccoli separately on a platter. Have the platter, sugar and cornstarch mixture near the stove.

**6.** Heat a wok over medium heat until hot. Add 3 tablespoons of oil and then the chicken. Use the edge of a spatula to separate the pieces of chicken, then stir-fry until chicken turns white, about 2 minutes. Remove to a bowl.

**7.** Reheat the wok over low heat and add the remaining 1 tablespoon oil. Turn the heat to medium and add the mushrooms. Stir and add the bamboo shoots and broccoli. Stir-fry for a few seconds, then sprinkle on the sugar. Stir and return the cooked chicken to the wok. Give the cornstarch mixture a stir and add to the wok. Stir-fry until the sauce thickens and forms a glaze over the ingredients, then transfer to a serving platter and serve immediately.

# STEAMED WHOLE CHICKEN

Steaming is a quick and easy alternative to poaching a chicken. You won't end up with a large quantity of rich chicken broth, as you do when you poach a chicken, but you will have 1 or 2 cups of pure chicken juice, which can be used for flavoring stir-fried vegetables. Like poached chicken, steamed chicken can be used in many other dishes, Chinese or Western, such as chicken salad.

*1 large chicken, 4 to 5 pounds*
*1 tablespoon kosher salt*
*2 tablespoons finely shredded scallions*
*Soy sauce or Hot Mustard Sauce (page 32)*

**1.** Rinse the chicken with cold water. Dry with paper towels. Rub the salt on both the inside and the outside of the chicken. Place the chicken in a heatproof dish with a 2-inch rim. Cover with plastic wrap and refrigerate for 1 hour.

**2.** To steam the chicken, use a large oblong roasting pan with a lid. Put a 1½-inch-high rack in the pan. Pour 1½ inches of water in the pan and bring to a boil. Place the dish with the chicken on the rack, cover the roasting pan, and steam for 50 minutes or until done. Save the accumulated juice for flavoring stir-fried dishes or soups. Set chicken aside to cool.

**3.** Disjoint the chicken and cut each section into bite-size pieces. Arrange on a platter and sprinkle the scallions over the top. Serve at room temperature, with soy sauce or Hot Mustard Sauce.

*Note:* Chicken parts can be steamed as well. Steam for 20 to 30 minutes or until done.

# CHICKEN WITH CASHEW NUTS

*¾ pound boned and
 skinned chicken
 breast*

### Marinade

*1 tablespoon
 cornstarch*
*1 tablespoon soy sauce*
*1 tablespoon water*

*3 dried black
 mushrooms*
*3 tablespoons corn oil*
*½ cup diced red bell
 pepper*
*1 scallion, cut into
 ⅛-inch pieces*
*½ cup diced fresh
 water chestnuts or
 bamboo shoots*
*½ teaspoon kosher
 salt*
*1 tablespoon rice wine*
*3 tablespoons Hoisin
 Sauce (page 31), or
 to taste*
*1 to 2 teaspoons Hot
 Chili Sauce (page
 32), or to taste*
*½ cup roasted unsalted
 cashew nuts*

**1.** Cut the chicken into ¼-inch cubes and mix with the marinade.

**2.** Soak the mushrooms in warm water for 30 minutes. Remove the stems and dice the caps.

**3.** Heat a wok and add 1 tablespoon of oil. Add the red pepper, scallions, water chestnuts, mushrooms and salt. Stir-fry for 2 minutes, then transfer to a serving platter.

**4.** Reheat the wok and add the remaining oil. Stir the chicken and marinade, add to the wok and stir-fry quickly until the chicken separates and turns white.

**5.** Splash on the rice wine. Mix in the Hoisin Sauce and Hot Chili Sauce, then return the cooked vegetables to the wok and stir-fry until well blended. Transfer to the serving platter and sprinkle the nuts on top. Serve hot.

# SMOKED CHICKEN

*S*moke a chicken in your own wok. Prepare it a day or two in advance, then slice the chicken very thin for a delicious treat. It is wonderful served cold as an appetizer, at room temperature for a first or main course, or in a cold buffet.

*1 large chicken, 4 to 5 pounds*
*3 tablespoons kosher salt*
*1 tablespoon Sichuan peppercorns*
*4 slices fresh ginger, each about the size of a quarter*
*2 scallions, cut into 2-inch lengths*
*3 tablespoons rice wine*
*¼ cup hickory chips*
*3 tablespoons black tea*
*Few sprigs fresh coriander or parsley, for garnish*

**1.** Rinse and dry the chicken well. Combine the salt and Sichuan peppercorns in a small, dry skillet. Shake the skillet over medium heat until the salt turns light brown and the aroma is released from the peppercorns. Rub the chicken inside and out with the salt mixture. Place in a deep heatproof dish and put the ginger slices and scallions in the cavity. Cover with plastic wrap and refrigerate overnight.

**2.** Remove the chicken from the refrigerator and sprinkle with the rice wine. Put at least 2 inches of water in a large oblong enamel roaster with a lid and place a rack inside. Bring the water to a boil. Place the dish with the chicken on the rack, cover the roaster and steam for 45 minutes. Check the water level in the steamer every 20 minutes and add more boiling water if necessary. When chicken is done, remove and allow to dry. Brush off the peppercorns and remove the ginger and scallions from the cavity.

**3.** To smoke the chicken, line a wok and its cover with large sheets of heavy-duty aluminum foil. Sprinkle the hickory chips and tea on the aluminum foil at the bottom of the wok, and over them place the chicken on an oiled rack. Cover the wok and press it down to be sure it is tightly closed. Put the wok on the burner and turn the heat to high. Smoke for 8 minutes. Turn off the heat, but do not uncover for at least 5 minutes to allow the smoke to dissipate.

**4.** Transfer the chicken to a chopping board and, using a sharp cleaver, disjoint it and carefully remove the thigh and leg bones, trying to leave the thigh and leg meat in one piece. Cut the thigh and leg meat into thin slices and arrange on a serving platter. Remove the breast meat from the bone and slice thin. Arrange these slices attractively over the other chicken slices. Garnish with coriander or parsley and serve.

*Note:* Open the windows and turn on the exhaust fan while the chicken is smoking. (Smoke alarms may be triggered). Discard the aluminum foil linings as quickly as possible to reduce the lingering smell.

# CHINESE "SOUTHERN" FRIED CHICKEN

*Serves 4*

*I* developed this method for giving fried chicken a Chinese flavor. Browning the chicken in oil, then baking it on a rack allows the oil to drain away. The crust becomes light and crispy, and the inside is moist and delicious. It can be prepared ahead, frozen and reheated in the oven.

### Marinade
*1 garlic clove, minced*
*1½ teaspoons minced fresh ginger*
*½ teaspoon kosher salt*
*2 teaspoons sugar*
*3 tablespoons soy sauce*
*1 tablespoon rice wine*

*1 frying chicken, about 3 pounds, cut into 8 pieces*
*Flour, for dredging*
*1 cup corn oil, for frying*

**1.** Combine the marinade ingredients with the chicken and set aside for 1 hour.

**2.** Preheat the oven to 350° F. Dredge the pieces of chicken in the flour. Place a rack in a shallow baking pan and put pan near the stove.

**3.** Heat a large skillet and add the oil. When the oil is hot, fry the pieces of chicken on both sides until lightly browned, about 4 or 5 minutes. Arrange the chicken on the rack so they don't touch and bake for 45 minutes or until done. Serve hot or at room temperature.

Serve Spicy Chicken plain or as a spectacular banquet dish when presented in a deep-fried basket of taro root.

*¾ pound boned and skinned chicken breast*

### Marinade
*½ small egg white*
*½ teaspoon cornstarch*
*1 tablespoon soy sauce*
*¼ teaspoon kosher salt*
*1 tablespoon cold water*

### Sauce
*1 teaspoon sugar*
*½ teaspoon cornstarch*
*¼ teaspoon kosher salt*
*1 tablespoon soy sauce*
*½ teaspoon distilled white vinegar*
*1 teaspoon oriental sesame oil*
*2 tablespoons Chicken Broth (page 155)*

*½ cup corn oil, for poaching*
*1 garlic clove, lightly crushed*
*½ cup cubed fresh medium-hot chili peppers*
*¼ cup sliced fresh mushrooms*
*2 Taro-Root Baskets (page 136), heated (optional)*

**1.** Cut the chicken into ¼-inch cubes. Combine with the marinade, mix thoroughly and refrigerate for at least 1 hour or overnight.

**2.** Combine the sauce ingredients in a small bowl. Mix until the cornstarch is dissolved, then set the bowl aside. Place a strainer over a pot and place it near the stove.

**3.** Heat a wok over moderate heat until hot. Add the oil and then the chicken. Stir-fry until the chicken turns white, then pour the contents of the wok into the strainer and allow the oil to drain away.

**4.** Reheat the wok and add 2 tablespoons of the drained oil. Add the garlic and stir-fry for a few seconds until it browns slightly. Add the chili peppers, stir, then add the mushrooms. Stir-fry for a few more seconds. Slide the strainer of cooked chicken into the wok. Stir and pour in the sauce. Continue to cook and stir until the sauce thickens and forms a glaze over the chicken.

**5.** If you are serving the chicken in taro baskets, put half the chicken mixture in each basket. Or serve the chicken plain on a large serving platter. Serve hot.

# SOY-SAUCE CHICKEN

## *Serves 4 to 5 as a main dish, or 8 to 10 if served with other dishes*

*T*he Cantonese way of poaching a chicken in a Brown Master Sauce gives it a slightly sweet soy-sauce flavor, with a hint of herbs and a glistening, reddish brown glaze. Racks of these chickens, ready to eat, are seen hanging in the windows of Chinese grocers.

*1 large chicken, 4 to 5 pounds*
*2 teaspoons kosher salt*
*1 cinnamon stick*
*2 star anise (16 pods)*
*1 large piece dried tangerine peel*

### Brown Master Sauce

*2½ cups soy sauce*
*⅓ cup granulated sugar or crushed rock sugar*
*1 cup rice wine*
*5 cups water*

*Few sprigs fresh coriander or parsley, for garnish*

*1.* Rinse and dry the chicken. Rub the inside and outside with the salt, then refrigerate for 4 hours.

*2.* Place the cinnamon, star anise and tangerine peel on a double layer of 4-inch-square cheese-cloth and tie in a bundle. Combine the sauce ingredients in a large, heavy pot and bring to a boil. Add the spice bundle. Cover and simmer for 15 minutes.

*3.* Uncover the pot and slowly lower the chicken into the sauce, breast side down. The sauce should cover at least three-quarters of the chicken. Simmer gently for 35 minutes, and baste the exposed part of the chicken with the sauce frequently while it cooks.

*4.* Carefully turn the chicken over and continue to simmer for 35 more minutes, repeating the basting procedure. Pierce the thick part of the thigh; if the juices run clear, the chicken is done. Remove from the sauce and cool. Save the sauce.

*5.* Transfer the chicken to a chopping board and, with a sharp cleaver, disjoint it. Carve the chicken or chop each section through the bone into 3 or 4 bite-size pieces. Arrange the pieces on a serving platter. Garnish with coriander or parsley and serve at room temperature.

*Note:* The Brown Master Sauce can be refrigerated for weeks or frozen for months. Renew with one-quarter of each sauce ingredient every other time the sauce is used to retain its strength. Duck, squab or game hen can be cooked in the sauce, with the cooking time depending on the size of the bird.

# SHANGHAI BRAISED DUCK WITH ONIONS

*Serves 4*

*R*oasting the duck removes much of the fat before it is braised in soy sauce until it is so tender chopsticks can pull the meat off the bones. The onions are then cooked in the sauce to absorb the rich flavor of the duck.

*1 duck, about 5 pounds, fresh or frozen*
*5 tablespoons soy sauce*
*2 cups water*
*¼ cup rice wine*
*2 tablespoons crushed rock sugar or granulated sugar*
*1½ pounds onions, cut into ¼-inch wedges*
*1 teaspoon cornstarch mixed with 2 tablespoons water*
*Coriander sprigs, for garnish*

**1.** Thaw the duck if frozen. Remove and discard any excess fat around the cavity and neck area. Rinse, then dry with paper towels. Preheat oven to 400° F.

**2.** Rub the duck with 1 tablespoon soy sauce. Place on a rack 2 inches high, set into a shallow roasting pan. Roast the duck for 45 minutes, breast side up. Turn the duck over and roast for 30 minutes more. Remove from the oven.

**3.** Place the duck in a heavy casserole. Add the water, remaining 4 tablespoons soy sauce, rice wine and sugar. Bring to a boil, reduce the heat, cover and simmer very gently for about 1¾ hours. Carefully turn the duck every 30 minutes during cooking. Check the level of liquid from time to time and add more water, ½ cup at a time, if necessary. The duck is done when it is tender enough to be pulled apart with a fork. There should be about 1½ cups of liquid remaining. Carefully transfer the duck to a large serving platter and cover it to keep warm.

**4.** Skim fat from the braising sauce in the casserole. Add the onions and cook over medium heat, stirring frequently, until they are translucent, about 5 minutes. Reduce the heat to a simmer. Stir the cornstarch mixture and add to the simmering liquid. Cook and stir until sauce thickens. Spoon the sauce and onions over the duck. Garnish with coriander and serve.

# ROAST DUCK

*T*his is a simplified version of the Cantonese Roast Duck, using the steaming method to first remove the fat. Serve this duck as given here, or use it in Stir-Fried Duck with Ginger (page 87) or Duck Salad (page 39).

*1 duck, about 5 pounds, fresh or frozen*
*1 tablespoon kosher salt*
*1 scallion*
*3 slices fresh ginger*

### Glaze

*1 tablespoon light corn syrup*
*2 tablespoons water*
*1 tablespoon soy sauce*

*Few sprigs fresh coriander, for garnish*

*1.* Thaw the duck, if frozen. Remove any excess fat, and rinse and pat dry with paper towels. Rub the entire surface of the duck, inside and out, with the salt. Cover and refrigerate for several hours or, even better, overnight.

*2.* Put the scallion in the cavity and lay the slices of ginger on top of the duck. Add at least 2 inches of water to a large flameproof roasting pan with a lid and put the pan on the stove. Place a large rack in the roasting pan and bring the water to a boil. Choose an oval casserole large enough to hold the duck and small enough to fit into the roasting pan. Place the duck in the casserole and then put the casserole on the rack. Cover and steam for 1 hour, checking the water level from time to time and adding more boiling water if necessary. Save the duck broth to use in soups or stir-fry dishes. When done, remove the duck from the casserole and place it on a rack to dry.

*3.* Combine the ingredients for the glaze in a small saucepan and bring to a boil. With a pastry brush, paint the hot glaze over the surface of the duck. Allow duck to dry for 1 hour.

*4.* Preheat the oven to 375° F. Roast the duck, breast side down, for 20 minutes. Turn over and continue to roast for 40 more minutes.

*5.* Transfer duck to a chopping board and allow to cool slightly. Using a cleaver, disjoint and cut the duck through the bone into bite-size pieces. Arrange the pieces on a serving platter, garnish with coriander and serve.

# PEKING DUCK

*Serves 4*

*P*eking duck is the high point of banquets in northern China. The dish is a study in contrasts: the crispness of the skin with the softness of the pancake wrapper; the red-brown glaze against the pearly white and light green of the scallion brushes, served on a white wrapper; and finally, the mingling of the sweetness and spiciness of all the ingredients. The duck skin is the main feature of this dish—the Chinese prize this delicacy. To produce it, you hang the duck to dry for several hours, giving your kitchen the temporary appearance of a Chinese shop. This dish takes patience, but you'll be enormously satisfied with the results.

*1 duck, about 5 pounds, fresh or frozen*
*6 cups water*
*2 tablespoons honey*
*1 slice fresh ginger*
*1 scallion*
*2 tablespoons rice wine*
*1 tablespoon distilled white vinegar*
*3 tablespoons cornstarch mixed with ½ cup water*
*10 small scallions, for scallion brushes*
*20 Peking Pancakes (page 200)*
*½ cup Hoisin Sauce (page 31)*

*1.* Cut off two lower wing joints of duck and save them for making stock. Remove and discard excess skin and fat at the neck and cavity. Rinse, then dry the duck with paper towels. Prepare for hanging by pushing a chopstick into the neck and through the flesh out the joint of one wing, keeping close to the bone as you push chopstick through. Push the other end of the same chopstick through to the other wing joint. The wings should extend straight out from the body. Tie a 10-inch length of string around the exposed part of the chopstick at the neck opening, then make a loop at the free end for hanging.

*2.* Put the water in a wok and bring to a boil. Mix in the honey. Add the ginger, scallion, sherry and vinegar, and simmer for 1 minute. Stir the cornstarch mixture and slowly add it to the simmering wok, stirring constantly until the liquid thickens. Keep at a simmer.

*3.* Take the duck by the string, hold it just above the simmering wok and ladle the hot liquid over, making sure you coat the entire surface of the duck. The duck will be heavy and the liquid hot, so have someone assist you. Repeat the ladling process twice. This coating will make the skin crispy and give it a glistening reddish brown color.

**4.** Hang the dripping duck, with a pan under it, in a cool, airy place near an open window for at least 4 hours, or until the skin feels very dry to the touch. (Or use an electric fan to dry the hanging duck.) This extended drying period is why most restaurants require a one-day notice for this dish.

**5.** Make the scallion brushes. Using only the white part of the scallions, cut each into 3-inch-long pieces. Use the tip of a sharp knife to cut several lengthwise slits at both ends of each section. Place the scallions in a bowl of cold water and refrigerate until the ends curl. Drain.

**6.** Oil the center of the top rack of your oven. Place a roasting pan on the lowest level of the oven and pour 2 to 3 inches of water in the pan. The water reduces the splattering from the fat as it drips from the duck.

**7.** Preheat the oven to 350° F. Untie the duck and remove the chopstick. Place the duck breast side up on the oiled rack. Put duck in the oven and roast for 30 minutes. Turn duck breast side down and roast for 45 minutes more. Turn the duck breast side up again and roast for another 30 minutes or until reddish brown.

**8.** About 30 minutes before the duck is done, wrap the Peking Pancakes in a damp cloth and steam them for 10 minutes; keep hot in the steamer over low heat until ready to serve.

**9.** Use a cleaver to cut off duck wing stubs and drumsticks. Make a cut down the skin on both sides of the duck. With your finger, carefully pull off the hot, crisp skin from the breast and back. Scrape off and discard the fat, if any, then cut the skin into 2 × 2-inch pieces. Arrange the skin on a large, warm serving platter. Remove the meat

(continued)

from the carcass and slice into 2 × ½-inch pieces and arrange with the drumsticks and wings on another warm serving platter. Place Hoisin Sauce on a small plate and arrange scallion brushes around it. Serve the duck, pancakes, and sauce together.

*10.* Each guest takes a pancake and a scallion brush, then dips the scallion brush into the Hoisin Sauce and brushes some of it on the pancake. The guest then places the scallion, a piece of duck skin and a piece of duck meat in the center of the pancake, folds up one end of the pancake and rolls it into a cylinder, to be eaten by hand.

# SICHUAN CRISPY DUCK

*Serves 4*

*T*he weather in the western region of China is so hot and humid that chefs devised an alternative method of steaming and then roasting to make this Sichuan-style Peking duck. This version, easily made in advance, is served with steamed buns.

*1 duck, about 5 pounds, fresh or frozen*
*5 slices fresh ginger, crushed lightly with a cleaver*
*1 scallion, white part crushed with a cleaver*
*1 tablespoon Sichuan peppercorns*
*1 teaspoon Five-Spice Powder (page 35)*
*1 tablespoon dark soy sauce*
*20 steamed Lotus Leaf Buns (page 186)*

*1.* Thaw the duck, if frozen. Remove excess fat from the neck and cavity. Rinse and dry well.

*2.* Place the duck on a hard surface and press down hard on the breastbone to break the ribs and backbone. (The broken bones release their flavors when steamed, or when deep-fried in the traditional recipe.) With a small paring knife, cut deep slashes into the thickest part of the thigh and leg. Rub the crushed ginger and scallion on the entire surface of the duck, inside and out.

*3.* Roast the Sichuan peppercorns in a dry skillet over medium heat until their aroma is released. Add the Five-Spice Powder, shaking the skillet gently, and then remove from the heat. When cool, rub the entire surface of the duck, inside and out, with the peppercorn mixture. Cover and refrigerate overnight.

**4.** Hold the duck over the sink and brush off the peppercorns. Discard the peppercorns and place the duck in a heatproof dish with a 1½-inch rim.

**5.** Put a 3-inch-high rack into an oblong roaster, then pour in 3 inches of boiling water. Place the dish with the duck on the rack, cover and steam over medium heat for 1½ hours. Check the water level every 20 minutes to be sure the water does not dry out; add more boiling water if necessary.

**6.** Carefully remove the duck to a rack over a shallow pan. Allow to cool completely, then rub the outside of the duck with the soy sauce and let dry thoroughly.

**7.** Preheat the oven to 375° F. Place the pan with the duck in the middle of the oven and roast for 1 hour.

**8.** Just before serving, put the buns in a single layer in a bamboo steamer, cover and steam for 10 minutes.

**9.** Cut the duck into bite-size pieces, removing the large bones. Arrange on a serving platter and serve hot between split steamed buns, like sandwiches.

# Cantonese Roast Duck

*L*ike Soy-Sauce Chicken (page 79), this duck hangs glistening and ready to eat in Chinatown shops.

*1 duck, about 5 pounds, fresh or frozen*

### Sauce

*2 teaspoons minced fresh ginger*
*2 garlic cloves, minced*
*3 tablespoons soy sauce*
*2 teaspoons honey*
*2 tablespoons light brown sugar*
*1 tablespoon Hoisin Sauce (page 31)*
*½ teaspoon Five-Spice Powder (page 35)*
*1 cinnamon stick*
*1 large piece dried orange peel*

### Glaze

*1 quart boiling water*
*1 tablespoon light corn syrup*

*Few sprigs fresh coriander, for garnish*

**1.** Thaw the duck, if frozen. Remove any excess fat around the neck and cavity. Wash, then dry it thoroughly with paper towels. Close the opening at the neck of the duck as tightly as possible by overlapping one side of the skin over the other and threading a metal skewer through. Mix the sauce ingredients in a small bowl. Pour the sauce into the cavity of the duck and rub to coat the entire inside surface. Close the cavity with metal skewers.

**2.** To glaze the duck, in a saucepan mix boiling water and corn syrup, stirring until it is thoroughly mixed. Continue boiling. Meanwhile, place the duck, breast side down, on a rack about 2 inches high over a large, deep roasting pan. Ladle half the boiling liquid over the entire back of the duck. Turn the duck over and ladle the remaining boiling liquid over the front. Pour the liquid collected in the roasting pan back into the saucepan and boil again. Repeat the process, taking care to cover the duck evenly, then discard the liquid. Coating the duck with the sweet syrup tightens the skin, which will turn crispy and a beautiful reddish brown when roasted.

**3.** Dry the duck by placing it on a rack near a cool, breezy window or in front of a fan for several hours until the skin feels dry to the touch.

**4.** Preheat the oven to 425° F.

**5.** Roast the duck breast side down for 30 minutes. Reduce the temperature to 350° F., turn the duck over and roast for 1 hour more. Allow the duck to cool for 15 minutes.

**6.** Remove the skewers and cut duck into bite-size pieces, Chinese style, then arrange pieces on a large serving platter. Garnish with coriander sprigs and serve plain or with Duck Sauce (page 33).

# STIR-FRIED DUCK WITH GINGER

*Serves 6*

$\mathcal{M}$ake this dish using leftover roast duck.

½ boned, roasted duck
1 red bell pepper
1 green bell pepper
1 cup bamboo shoots
2 scallions
1 garlic clove
3 very thin slices fresh
  ginger

### Sauce
½ tablespoon Hot
  Chili Sauce (page
  32)
2 tablespoons Hoisin
  Sauce (page 31)
1 tablespoon rice wine
1 teaspoon sugar
⅓ cup Chicken Broth
  (page 155)
2 teaspoons cornstarch
  mixed with 2
  tablespoons water
4 tablespoons corn oil
1 teaspoon oriental
  sesame oil

**1.** Cut the duck with the skin into shreds about ⅛ inch thick and 1½ inches long. Cut the peppers in half lengthwise, remove the seeds and trim away the ribs and curved ends. Cut the peppers, bamboo shoots and scallions into shreds 1½ inches long and ⅛ inch thick. Slice the garlic. Shred the ginger fine. Place the garlic and the shredded ingredients separately on a platter.

**2.** Combine the sauce ingredients in a small bowl. Have the cornstarch mixture, sauce and platter of shredded ingredients near the stove.

**3.** Heat a wok until hot and add 2 tablespoons corn oil. When the oil is hot, add the peppers and bamboo shoots. Stir-fry the ingredients for 2 minutes, then transfer to a serving platter. Wipe out the wok.

**4.** Reheat the wok and add the remaining corn oil. When the oil is hot, add the ginger, garlic and scallions. Stir-fry for a few seconds to release the flavors, then add the sauce ingredients and stir quickly. Add the shredded duck and cooked vegetables. Stir to blend the sauce with the ingredients. Stir the cornstarch mixture and add it to the wok. Continue to stir and cook until the sauce thickens and forms a glaze. Stir in the sesame oil and transfer to a serving platter. Serve hot.

# TURKEY AND VEAL

*T*hough turkey and veal are seldom used in Chinese cooking, I have found that they make a credible substitute for a meat we often use: pork. Although not as sweet as pork, these two meats are somewhat neutral in flavor and will accept Chinese seasonings without changing the essential character of the dish. I have even been told by some of my students who have recently begun keeping kosher that Cantonese Roast Turkey (page 97) tastes just like pork.

These eight translations of traditional and essential pork recipes offer a whole new opportunity for kosher diners, and through these versions you can participate much more fully in Chinese cuisine than ever before.

| Recipes | | Prepare Ahead | Serving Temperature |
|---|---|---|---|
| Lettuce Packages | | Yes | Hot |
| Stir-Fried Veal or Turkey with Bok Choy | | No | Hot |
| Turkey or Veal in a Spicy Sauce | Spicy hot | No | Hot |
| Egg Fu Yung | | No | Hot |
| Scallops of Veal or Turkey in Scallion Sauce | | No | Hot |
| Sweet-and-Sour Turkey Balls | | Yes | Hot |
| Cantonese Roast Veal or Turkey | | Yes | Hot or warm |
| Spicy Bean Curd | Spicy hot | No | Hot |

# LETTUCE PACKAGES

*T*he crisp, cold lettuce-leaf wrapper is a surprising contrast to the finely minced warm filling. Find the best iceberg lettuce in the market.

## Marinade

½ teaspoon kosher salt
2 teaspoons cornstarch
1 tablespoon soy sauce
1 tablespoon water
1 tablespoon corn oil

½ pound ground turkey or veal
1 head iceberg lettuce
6 dried black mushrooms
4 tablespoons corn or peanut oil
½ cup finely minced bamboo shoots
12 fresh water chestnuts, peeled and minced fine
2 tablespoons rice wine
1 cup finely minced celery
1 teaspoon kosher salt
1 teaspoon sugar
½ cup pine nuts, raw or fried (optional)

**1.** In a bowl combine the marinade ingredients and add the ground turkey or veal. Mix well and set aside. Soak the lettuce in lukewarm water for 5 minutes and separate the leaves. (The warm water makes the leaves more flexible and easier to take apart.) Using a pair of scissors, cut the lettuce leaves in the shape of cups 6 inches in diameter. Dry the leaves thoroughly and place them in a plastic bag; refrigerate until ready to serve.

**2.** Soak mushrooms in warm water for 30 minutes. Remove stems and mince caps fine.

**3.** Heat a wok over moderate heat and add 2 tablespoons of oil. When the oil is hot, add the meat and stir-fry to separate the pieces until the meat changes color. Transfer to a bowl and keep warm. Wipe out the wok.

**4.** Reheat the wok and add the remaining oil, mushrooms, bamboo shoots and water chestnuts. Stir-fry for 1 minute. Splash the wine around the edge of the wok, then add the celery, salt and sugar. Return the cooked meat to the wok and stir-fry a few seconds more, until the ingredients are blended. Transfer to a large serving platter. Place the nuts on top of the mixture, arrange the lettuce leaves around the edge of the platter and serve.

**5.** To make a lettuce package, each person takes a lettuce cup and spoons 2 tablespoons of filling onto the center, then rolls up the leaf into a cylinder around the filling and eats with the fingers.

# STIR-FRIED VEAL OR TURKEY WITH BOK CHOY

### Serves 4

Ṃore and more Chinese vegetables are available in supermarkets. They are delicious when stir-fried, tender yet crisp. This recipe calls for bok choy, but you can use broccoli or zucchini. Also, beef or chicken can be substituted for the veal or turkey. In fact, this recipe illustrates what Chinese cooks typically do: use what is fresh or on hand.

*½ pound lean boneless veal shoulder or turkey breast*

**Marinade**

*1 teaspoon cornstarch*
*2 tablespoons soy sauce*
*¼ teaspoon sugar*
*1 teaspoon oriental sesame oil*

**Sauce**

*½ teaspoon cornstarch*
*1 tablespoon soy sauce*
*½ teaspoon sugar*
*1 teaspoon oriental sesame oil*
*3 tablespoons Chicken Broth (page 155)*

*1 pound bok choy*
*5 tablespoons corn oil*
*1 teaspoon kosher salt*
*½ teaspoon sugar*
*2 tablespoons water*

**1.** Cut the veal or turkey into 1 × 2-inch thin slices. Mix the marinade ingredients and combine with the meat to coat evenly; set aside for 30 minutes. Combine the sauce ingredients and set near the stove.

**2.** Separate the bok choy stalks and wash in warm water to remove any sand. Cut into ½ × 2-inch pieces, separating the stalks and leaves into individual mounds.

**3.** Heat a wok or large skillet over medium heat until hot. Add 2 tablespoons corn oil. Add the bok choy stalks, stir briskly and sprinkle on the salt and sugar. Stir, then add the bok choy leaves. Continue stirring a few seconds, then add water. Cover and cook for 2 minutes, stirring once or twice, until the vegetable is tender yet crisp. Turn off the heat, transfer to a large serving platter and keep warm. Wipe the wok clean.

**4.** Reheat the wok and add the remaining 3 tablespoons oil. Add the meat and stir-fry until it just changes color. Give the sauce ingredients a stir and add them to the wok. Stir several times to blend the sauce with the meat and continue stirring until the sauce thickens slightly. Turn off the heat and ladle the meat and sauce on top of the vegetables. Serve hot.

# TURKEY OR VEAL IN A SPICY SAUCE

## Marinade

1 tablespoon soy sauce
1 tablespoon rice wine
2 teaspoons cornstarch
1 tablespoon corn oil

¾ pound boneless
   turkey breast or
   lean boneless veal
   shoulder, diced into
   ¼-inch cubes
1 garlic clove, minced
1 tablespoon minced
   fresh ginger
1 large scallion, cut
   into ⅛-inch pieces
1 cup diced green bell
   pepper
½ cup diced bamboo
   shoots

## Sauce

2 tablespoons Hoisin
   Sauce (page 31)
2 teaspoons Hot Chili
   Sauce (page 32), or
   to taste
2 teaspoons sugar
1 tablespoon rice wine
3 tablespoons soy
   sauce
1 tablespoon oriental
   sesame oil
½ teaspoon cornstarch

4 tablespoons corn oil

**1.** Combine the marinade ingredients with the meat in a mixing bowl. Mix to coat evenly. Set aside for 30 minutes. Place the other cut-up ingredients separately on a work platter. Combine the sauce ingredients in a small bowl and place near the stove.

**2.** Heat a wok over medium heat until hot. Add 2 tablespoons corn oil. When the oil is hot, swirl it and add the meat. Stir-fry until the meat changes color, about 2 minutes. Transfer to a mixing bowl. Wash out the wok.

**3.** Reheat the wok until hot and add the remaining 2 tablespoons oil. Add the garlic, ginger and scallion, and stir-fry until the flavors are released. Add the diced pepper and bamboo shoots, and stir-fry about 1 minute. Stir and add the sauce ingredients; stir briskly.

**4.** Turn the heat to high and return the cooked meat to the wok. Continue stirring to blend all the ingredients with the sauce. Remove the wok from the heat, transfer the contents to a serving bowl and serve hot with Boiled Rice (page 167).

# EGG FU YUNG

*E*gg Fu Yung, a deep-fried omelet served with a sauce, is a well-known Chinese-American restaurant dish, but in China omelets are not deep-fried and are never served with a sauce. Here are both versions using the same ingredients, although the listing is arranged for the first version.

## Sauce

*1 cup Chicken Broth (page 155)*
*2 tablespoons soy sauce*
*1 tablespoon rice wine*
*Dash of white pepper*
*1 tablespoon cornstarch dissolved in 3 tablespoons water*
*1 teaspoon oriental sesame oil*

*¾ cup finely shredded cooked turkey, veal or chicken*
*½ cup finely shredded onions*
*½ cup bean sprouts*
*¼ cup shredded celery*
*¼ cup thinly sliced fresh mushrooms*
*5 extra-large eggs, well beaten*
*1 teaspoon kosher salt*
*⅛ teaspoon white pepper*
*2 cups corn oil for deep-frying, or 5 tablespoons for stir-frying*

## Deep-Fried Version

**1.** Bring the broth to a boil in a saucepan. Add the soy sauce, wine and pepper. Turn down the heat. Give the cornstarch mixture a stir and gradually pour it into the broth while stirring constantly until the sauce thickens. Add the sesame oil and stir once more. Keep the sauce warm.

**2.** Combine the meat, vegetables, eggs, salt and pepper and mix well.

**3.** Heat a wok and add the 2 cups corn oil. When the oil is very hot, about 350° F., ladle in one-fourth of the egg mixture. The egg will float; as it sets, ladle in another fourth of the mixture. Continue until you have 4 omelets frying. Deep-fry the omelets until the bottoms are lightly browned, then turn them over and brown the other side. Use 2 spatulas to remove each omelet from the wok, pressing lightly to squeeze out some of the excess oil. Place on a serving platter. Reheat the sauce until hot, stirring once or twice. Pour the sauce over the omelets and serve.

## Stir-Fried Version

**1.** Heat a wok over medium heat until hot. Add 2 tablespoons corn oil. Add the meat and vegetables. Stir-fry a few seconds and add the salt and pepper. Continue to stir-fry for 2 minutes. Turn off the heat and spread the cooked mixture on a platter to cool slightly. Clean out the wok.

**2.** In a large mixing bowl, combine the beaten eggs with the meat-and-vegetable mixture.

**3.** Reheat the wok. Add 3 tablespoons oil. When the oil is very hot, pour in the egg mixture. Use a spatula to push the mixture back and forth as the eggs set. Flip portions of the egg mixture over so that it browns slightly on the outside, and turn off the heat while the egg mixture is still soft on the inside. Serve hot.

# SCALLOPS OF VEAL OR TURKEY IN SCALLION SAUCE

*Serves 4*

*T*his is another variation of sweet-and-sour, prepared with veal scallops or sliced breast of turkey. Serve it with rice and a stir-fried vegetable for a simple meal.

*6 large slices turkey breast or veal scallops, cut ¼ inch thick and pounded thin*

### Marinade

*½ teaspoon kosher salt*
*1 teaspoon sugar*
*1 teaspoon oriental sesame oil*
*½ tablespoon soy sauce*

### Sauce

*½ teaspoon kosher salt*
*3 tablespoons sugar*
*3 tablespoons distilled white vinegar*
*2 tablespoons soy sauce*

*½ cup corn oil*
*1 scallion, chopped fine*

**1.** Cut each slice of meat into 3 pieces, about 1 × 2 inches each.

**2.** In a mixing bowl combine the meat with the marinade ingredients and mix well. Marinate for 30 minutes.

**3.** In a small saucepan combine the sauce ingredients. Place near the stove to be heated later.

**4.** Heat a skillet over medium heat until hot and add the corn oil. When the oil is hot, pan-fry about half the meat pieces on both sides until lightly browned. Transfer to a serving platter and fry the remaining pieces of meat.

**5.** Heat the sauce until hot, then add the minced scallion. Pour the hot scallion sauce over the meat and serve.

# SWEET-AND-SOUR TURKEY BALLS

## Marinade

½ cup minced
  scallions
½ teaspoon finely
  minced fresh ginger
2 tablespoons soy
  sauce
1 tablespoon corn oil
1½ teaspoons kosher
  salt
1 teaspoon rice wine
1 extra-large egg
3 tablespoons water

1 pound ground veal
  or turkey
3 tablespoons corn oil
1 pound Chinese
  cabbage, shredded
½ teaspoon kosher
  salt
½ teaspoon sugar
2 cups corn oil

## Sauce

4 tablespoons sugar
3 tablespoons distilled
  white vinegar
2 tablespoons soy
  sauce
½ teaspoon kosher
  salt
1 tablespoon
  cornstarch mixed
  with ⅔ cup water
1 teaspoon oriental
  sesame oil

**1.** Combine the marinade ingredients with the ground meat. Stir in one direction until the mixture feels light and sticky.

**2.** Heat a wok and add the 3 tablespoons corn oil. When the oil is hot, stir-fry the Chinese cabbage until it is coated with oil. Sprinkle on the salt and sugar, stir and cover for a few minutes until soft. Transfer to a serving platter and keep warm. Wipe the wok clean.

**3.** Reheat the wok and add the 2 cups of corn oil. While the oil is heating, wet your hands and form the meat mixture into balls each about the size of a large walnut. When the oil reaches 325° F., deep-fry the meatballs for 3 minutes, turning frequently until done. Remove and drain on paper towels. Place them on top of the cooked cabbage and keep both warm.

**4.** Add 2 tablespoons of the frying oil to a saucepan. Heat and add the sauce ingredients, stirring constantly until the sauce simmers and thickens. Pour the sauce over the turkey balls and cabbage and serve hot.

# CANTONESE ROAST VEAL OR TURKEY

*T*his is a versatile recipe. You can prepare it in advance; you can slice and serve the meat as is; you can stir-fry it with vegetables, bean curd or noodles. You can also dice it and use as a filling for steamed or roasted buns, and, finally, you can use it for great sandwiches.

*2 pounds boneless veal shoulder or white and dark meat turkey*

### Marinade

*5 tablespoons soy sauce*
*2 tablespoons cold water*
*3 tablespoons brown sugar*
*1 tablespoon honey*
*1 teaspoon Five-Spice Powder (page 35)*
*2 garlic cloves, minced fine*

*Few sprigs fresh coriander, for garnish*

*1.* Cut the meat into 6 strips 1½ inches wide, 5 inches long and 2 inches thick.

*2.* Combine the marinade ingredients, blending thoroughly. Add the meat strips, and turn them several times in the marinade to be sure they are well coated. Marinate for 1½ hours.

*3.* Heat the oven to 350° F. Fill a large roasting pan with 2 inches of water and place it on the bottom of the oven. The pan of water will catch the drippings and reduce smoking in the oven. Place a rack at the top of the oven.

*4.* Insert the pointed end of an **S** hook into one strip of meat. Use the other end of the hook to hang the meat from the top rack of the oven, placing the meat directly over the pan of water. Do the same with the remaining strips of meat. Roast for 25 minutes, or until done but not dry.

*5.* Cut the meat into diagonal slices and arrange on a serving platter. Garnish with coriander and serve hot or warm.

*Note:* Metal curtain hooks are available in hardware stores.

# SPICY BEAN CURD

*B*ean curd with a real punch! Make it as spicy as you like, since tradition-ally it is very hot. Serve rice with this dish.

## Marinade

½ teaspoon sugar
1 teaspoon cornstarch
1½ tablespoons soy
    sauce
1 tablespoon water
1 tablespoon corn oil

4 ounces ground veal
    or turkey
4 squares fresh bean
    curd, or 1-pound
    package soft bean
    curd
¼ teaspoon kosher
    salt
3 tablespoons corn oil
1 garlic clove, minced
2 teaspoons minced
    fresh ginger
3 tablespoons finely
    chopped scallions
2 teaspoons Hot Chili
    Sauce (page 32)
½ cup Chicken Broth
    (page 155)
2 tablespoons soy
    sauce
2 teaspoons cornstarch
    mixed with 2
    tablespoons water
¼ teaspoon Roasted
    Sichuan Pepper-
    corns (page 35)
1 teaspoon oriental
    sesame oil

**1.** Combine the marinade ingredients, add the meat and mix well. Cut the bean curd into ¼-inch cubes. Sprinkle with salt. Set aside.

**2.** Heat a wok over moderate heat until hot and add corn oil. Add the garlic, ginger and scallions, and stir-fry a few seconds until the flavors are re-leased. Add the meat and stir-fry to separate the pieces. When the meat changes color, add the chili sauce. Stir well.

**3.** Place the bean curd atop the meat. Add the broth and soy sauce and slowly bring to a boil. Turn the heat to a simmer and cover. Cook for 3 or 4 minutes, stirring gently once or twice dur-ing the cooking.

**4.** Stir the cornstarch mixture well and add to the wok, gently stirring until the sauce thickens. Sprinkle mixture with ground peppercorns and sesame oil, and serve piping hot.

# BEEF AND LAMB

**B**raised Beef with Garlic (page 103), Star-Anise Beef (page 109) or Curried Beef (page 102) instead of the usual pot roast or brisket will add variety to your traditional meal. These dishes taste better cooked a day or two ahead, and they need only the simplest accompaniments.

The cuts of kosher meat vary from region to region and sometimes from shop to shop, so labels can be misleading. For instance, I have tried cuts labeled "minute steak" or "London broil" for stir-frying, and at times they have been very tender and at others not. Meat for stir-frying must be very tender, so I have specified steak for all the stir-fried recipes. Consult your butcher for less expensive cuts you might use and about appropriate cuts for different methods of cooking. I recommend kosher cuts of boneless beef such as brisket, foreshank, chuck, flanken or shoulder for any of the braised dishes.

| Recipes | | Prepare Ahead | Serving Temperature |
|---|---|---|---|
| Spicy Sichuan Beef | Spicy | No | Hot |
| Curried Beef | | Yes | Hot |
| Braised Beef with Garlic | | Yes | Hot |
| Stir-Fried Beef with Bean Sprouts | Spicy | No | Hot |
| Tomato Beef | | No | Hot |
| Stir-Fried Beef with Broccoli | | No | Hot |
| Stir-Fried Beef with Onions | | No | Hot |
| Orange Beef | Spicy | No | Hot or room temp. |
| Star-Anise Beef | Spicy | Yes | Hot or cold |
| Jellied Lamb | | Yes | Cold |
| Stir-Fried Lamb with Scallions | | No | Hot |
| Lamb Hunan Style | Spicy | No | Hot |

# SPICY SICHUAN BEEF

*I*n this dish the beef is finely shredded and cooked until nearly dry, thus it thoroughly absorbs the seasonings. You can make it as spicy as you like by varying the amount of chili peppers. Serve it with a large helping of Boiled Rice (page 167) and contrast it with a cooling Cucumber Salad (page 43).

## Marinade

**4 tablespoons dark soy sauce**
**1 tablespoon rice wine**
**1 teaspoon sugar**
**½ teaspoon finely minced fresh ginger**

**1 pound boneless beefsteak, cut into needlelike shreds**
**1½ cups very finely shredded carrots**
**1 cup very finely shredded celery**
**½ cup finely shredded hot green chili pepper**
**⅓ cup corn oil**
**8 dried hot red chili peppers**
**1 teaspoon oriental sesame oil**
**¼ teaspoon ground Sichuan peppercorns**

*1.* Combine the marinade ingredients with the meat and mix well. Set aside for 20 minutes. Place the remaining shredded ingredients separately on a work platter.

*2.* Heat a wok until hot and add 2 tablespoons of oil. Stir-fry the carrots, celery and fresh chili pepper for 1 minute, then transfer to a serving platter. Wipe out the wok and add the remaining oil. Add the dried chili peppers (breaking them open and releasing their seeds will make the dish even hotter) and lower the heat. Stir-fry until the peppers are dark brown, then add the beef. Turn the heat to high and stir-fry for about 5 minutes, or until the accumulated liquid evaporates. Lower the heat and continue to stir-fry for another minute. Add the cooked vegetables. Stir and add the sesame oil and Sichuan peppercorns. Mix well and transfer to the serving platter. Serve hot.

*Variation:* This beef can be put atop a bed of 2 cups of fried rice sticks, which can be found in the recipe for Duck Salad on page 39. Serve at room temperature.

Most dishes with curry have developed from Indian cuisine and have a characteristic Indian taste. This dish has a subtle taste of curry, yet it is distinctly Chinese. Cook it ahead, because it will taste better the next day after the flavors have had a chance to mellow and blend. The potatoes absorb the curry flavor and help thicken the sauce. Serve with Stir-Fried Spinach (page 146) and Boiled Rice (page 167)

*4 tablespoons corn oil*
*5 garlic cloves, peeled*
*2 onions, cut into 6 pieces*
*1 to 2 tablespoons curry powder, or to taste*
*2 pounds boneless beef foreshank or chuck, cut into 1½-inch cubes*
*3 tablespoons rice wine*
*¼ teaspoon kosher salt*
*2 tablespoons soy sauce*
*2 teaspoons granulated sugar or crushed rock sugar*
*1 cup beef broth, bouillon or water*
*2 medium potatoes, each cut into 6 pieces*

*1.* Heat a wok over medium heat until hot. Add 1 tablespoon oil, the garlic and the onions. Stir-fry until the onions become translucent, then transfer to a large heavy pot with a tight-fitting lid.

*2.* Reheat the wok until hot and add the remaining oil. Add the curry powder, stir a few seconds and add the beef. Stir-fry the beef until slightly brown, about 3 or 4 minutes. Add the wine around the side of the wok, stirring constantly as it sizzles. Transfer the contents of the wok to the pot with the garlic and onions.

*3.* Heat the wok again and add the salt, soy sauce, sugar and broth. Swirl them in the wok, then pour into the pot and bring to a boil. Turn the heat to medium and cook for 10 minutes. Turn down the heat to very low, cover and simmer gently for 1 hour or until tender. Stir several times during the cooking to be sure the beef does not stick to the bottom of the pot. Check the level of the liquid from time to time to be sure it does not dry out and add more liquid if necessary. There should be about 1 cup of sauce when done.

*4.* Add the potatoes and cook for 45 minutes, or until the meat is tender and the potatoes are soft. Serve hot.

# BRAISED BEEF WITH GARLIC

*Serves 6*

Garlic can be overpowering in any dish, but if it is first lightly browned in hot oil, it can be used copiously without a hint of its acrid taste. Be careful not to burn the garlic, for even slightly burnt garlic adds a strong and undesirable taste. In this recipe, garlic is gently braised with beef. You can substitute a whole piece of brisket for the beef shank and serve it like a pot roast, but you will have to increase the cooking time.

*4 tablespoons corn oil*
*10 garlic cloves*
*2½ pounds boneless beef foreshank or chuck, cut into 1½-inch cubes*
*3 tablespoons rice wine*
*¼ teaspoon kosher salt*
*2 teaspoons granulated sugar or crushed rock sugar*
*3 tablespoons soy sauce*
*1½ cups beef broth or bouillon*
*2 medium carrots, peeled and roll-cut (page 23) into 1-inch pieces*
*4 scallions, cut into 1-inch pieces*
*1 teaspoon cornstarch mixed with 2 tablespoons cold water*

**1.** Heat a wok over medium heat until hot. Add the oil, then add the garlic and stir-fry until lightly browned. Transfer the garlic to a large, heavy pot with a tight-fitting lid and set it aside. Turn the heat under the wok to high, then add the beef and stir-fry until brown, about 4 or 5 minutes. Splash the wine around the side of the wok, stirring constantly as it sizzles.

**2.** Transfer the beef to the pot with the garlic. Add the salt, sugar, soy sauce and broth. Bring to a boil, then turn down the heat to a simmer. Simmer uncovered for 10 minutes (this keeps the liquid clear and bright). Cover and simmer gently for 1½ hours, or until the beef is tender and the garlic is very soft. Stir several times during the cooking to be sure the beef does not stick to the bottom of the pot. Also, check the level of the liquid from time to time to be sure it does not dry out. Add more liquid if necessary. There should be about 1½ cups of sauce when done.

**3.** About 20 minutes before the beef is finished cooking, put the carrots and scallions on top. Do not mix the carrots in at this point or they will lose their bright color; the steam will cook them. Cover and cook for the remaining 20 minutes.

**4.** Stir the cornstarch mixture and add it to the pot. Stir in the carrots and cook until the sauce thickens slightly. Serve hot with Boiled Rice (page 167).

# STIR-FRIED BEEF WITH BEAN SPROUTS

*Serves 2 to 4*

$V$ery fresh bean sprouts should be pearly white, sweet and crunchy. Stir-frying at a high temperature for a few seconds enhances their flavor. They give a light quality to beef and are a good contrast in flavor and texture. The ginger and fresh hot pepper give added interest.

## Marinade

*2 tablespoons soy
  sauce*
*½ teaspoon cornstarch*
*¼ teaspoon sugar*
*1 tablespoon water*

*½ pound boneless
  beefsteak, shredded*
*1 pound fresh bean
  sprouts*
*5 tablespoons corn oil*
*1 teaspoon kosher salt*
*½ teaspoon sugar*
*1 scallion, shredded*
*1 hot green chili
  pepper, shredded
  (optional)*
*1 slice fresh ginger,
  shredded fine*

**1.** Combine the marinade ingredients with the beef, mix thoroughly and set aside for 20 minutes.

**2.** Place the bean sprouts in a large basin of water. Remove any seed hulls and loose roots that float to the surface. Pour the bean sprouts into a colander and shake several times to remove excess water.

**3.** Heat a wok over high heat until very hot and add 3 tablespoons oil. Swirl the oil around the wok. Take a large quantity of bean sprouts in both hands and carefully but quickly place the bean sprouts over the oil, covering the wok completely. (This keeps the oil from splattering on you.) Stir-fry until the bean sprouts are coated with oil. Add the salt, sugar, scallion and chili pepper and continue to stir-fry another 30 seconds. Transfer to a serving dish.

**4.** Wipe the wok with a paper towel and reheat until hot. Add the remaining oil and the ginger. Stir, then add the beef and stir-fry until it changes color. Return the cooked ingredients and stir-fry until blended. Turn off the heat, transfer the contents to a serving dish and serve.

# TOMATO BEEF

*Serves 2 to 4*

T omato Beef is an example of how the Chinese adapted New World vegetables, such as snow peas, corn and asparagus, to their varied cuisine. A favorite among Cantonese, this home-cooked dish is especially delicious in the summer when sun-ripened tomatoes are in season. The tomatoes make a wonderful sauce served on rice.

## Marinade

*2 tablespoons soy sauce*
*1/2 teaspoon cornstarch*
*1 tablespoon water*
*1/4 teaspoon sugar*

*1/2 pound boneless beefsteak, cut into 1 1/2 × 2 × 1/8-inch slices*
*3 plum tomatoes*
*2 scallions, cut into 2-inch lengths*
*5 tablespoons corn oil*
*1/2 teaspoon kosher salt*
*1/2 teaspoon sugar*
*1/2 teaspoon cornstarch mixed with 1 tablespoon water*

**1.** Combine the marinade ingredients with the meat and mix well to coat. Set aside for 20 minutes.

**2.** Bring a small pot of water to a boil and submerge the tomatoes in the water for a few seconds. Remove, drain and peel the tomatoes. Cut into 1/2-inch wedges. Set aside with the scallions.

**3.** Heat a wok over moderate heat and add 3 tablespoons of oil. When the oil is very hot, add the beef and stir-fry quickly over high heat to separate the pieces. Stir-fry 1 minute or until just done. Do not overcook. Transfer the beef to a serving dish and wash out the wok.

**4.** Reheat the wok and add the remaining 2 tablespoons oil. Add the scallions and stir a few seconds. Add the tomatoes. Stir and add the salt and sugar. Stir-fry until juice begins to run from the tomatoes, then return the cooked beef to the wok. Stir the cornstarch mixture and add it to the wok. Cook and stir until the sauce thickens. Turn off the heat, transfer the dish to a serving platter and serve hot.

**Note:** You may also add 1/2 cup of 1/2-inch diced bell pepper. Just stir-fry the peppers before adding the tomatoes and proceed with the recipe.

# STIR-FRIED BEEF WITH BROCCOLI

*Serves 2 to 4*

*T*his is typical home cooking in which a vegetable is stir-fried with a small quantity of meat. Vary the vegetable by picking the freshest available in the market. It could be cauliflower, zucchini, asparagus, string beans, peppers or snow peas. You can even parboil the vegetable and mix it in after you stir-fry the meat. Also, you can substitute chicken, veal or turkey for the beef. Serve it with a soup and rice to complete your meal.

*1 bunch fresh broccoli*
*½ pound boneless*
*beefsteak*

### Marinade

*1 teaspoon cornstarch*
*1 tablespoon soy sauce*
*¼ teaspoon sugar*
*1 tablespoon water*

*4 tablespoons corn oil*
*¾ teaspoon kosher*
*salt*
*½ teaspoon sugar*
*3 tablespoons water*
*1 teaspoon cornstarch*
*mixed with 2*
*tablespoons water*

**1.** Using a sharp paring knife, start from the bottom of each broccoli stem and peel back the tough outer skin until you reach the flowerets. Cut the skin away at the base of the flowerets and discard the skin. Separate the flowerets and their stems from the large stem. Cut flowerets into bite-size pieces and cut the stems into 1½ × ½ × ½-inch pieces.

**2.** Slice the beef thin across the grain, into ½ × 1½ × ¼-inch pieces. Combine the marinade ingredients with the beef and mix to blend thoroughly. Set aside for 20 minutes.

**3.** Before you begin stir-frying, have all the ingredients and measuring spoons near the stove. Heat a wok over medium heat until very hot and add 2 tablespoons of the oil. When the oil is hot, add the broccoli and stir-fry until all the pieces are coated with oil. Sprinkle on the salt and sugar. Stir and add the water. Cover immediately and turn down the heat to medium. Cook for about 2 minutes, or until the broccoli is bright green. Stir once or twice during cooking. Transfer to a warm serving platter. Wipe out the wok.

**4.** Reheat the wok over high heat. Add the remaining 2 tablespoons oil. When the oil is very hot, add the beef. Quickly stir-fry to separate the pieces of meat. Cook and stir 2 or 3 minutes over high heat until the beef loses its red color. Do not overcook. Turn down the heat to medium and add the broccoli. Stir to blend. Give the cornstarch mixture a stir and add it to the wok, stirring constantly until the sauce thickens and forms a glaze over the ingredients. Taste for salt. Turn off the heat and transfer the contents to a warm serving platter. Serve immediately.

*Note:*  If you are using string beans, parboil them for 5 minutes, rinse with cold water, then add to the wok as you stir-fry the beef.

# STIR-FRIED BEEF WITH ONIONS

*Serves 4*

*H*ere is an easy stir-fry dish. If you are a novice at stir-frying, try this— you'll be delighted with the results. If you're already experienced, you'll like the taste. Start the meal with Egg Drop Soup (page 155).

### Marinade
*2 tablespoons soy sauce*
*¼ teaspoon sugar*
*½ tablespoon cornstarch*
*1 tablespoon water*

*¾ pound boneless beefsteak, cut into 1½ × 2 × ¼-inch slices*
*4 tablespoons corn oil*
*3 medium onions, cut into ¼-inch wedges*
*½ teaspoon kosher salt*

*1.* Combine the marinade ingredients with the beef. Mix to coat evenly and set aside for 30 minutes.

*2.* Place all the ingredients near the stove. Heat a wok or a large skillet over medium heat until hot. Add 1 tablespoon oil. When the oil is hot, add the onions and stir-fry for 1 minute, or until they become translucent. Add the salt, mix briefly and transfer the mixture to a serving platter.

*3.* Reheat the wok over high heat until hot. Pour in the remaining oil. Add the beef and stir-fry quickly, separating the pieces of meat. Cook until the beef just turns color; do not overcook. Return the cooked onions to the wok. Stir to blend the beef and onions. Turn off the heat, transfer to platter and serve.

# ORANGE BEEF

*I*'m often asked how to make this orange-scented restaurant favorite, with its slightly sweet, slightly spicy taste. One reason for its popularity is that the slices of meat are lightly crisp around the edges yet remain tender in the middle. To accomplish this, heat the oil to a high temperature and stir-fry the beef twice.

*½ pound boneless beefsteak, sliced into 1½ × 2 × ¼-inch pieces*
*½ teaspoon baking soda*
*½ cup water*

### Marinade
*¼ teaspoon kosher salt*
*1 small egg*
*2 tablespoons cornstarch*
*1 tablespoon corn oil*

### Sauce
*2 tablespoons Chicken Broth (page 155)*
*1 teaspoon sugar*
*½ teaspoon cornstarch*
*1½ tablespoons rice wine*
*1½ teaspoons Chinkiang vinegar or mild rice vinegar*
*1 tablespoon soy sauce*
*1 teaspoon oriental sesame oil*

*2 cups corn oil, for frying*

**1.** Mix the beef with the baking soda and water; refrigerate for 1 hour. Rinse the beef thoroughly with cold water and dry well. The meat must be very dry. Mix the marinade ingredients, add the beef, mix well and refrigerate again for at least 1 hour.

**2.** Mix the sauce ingredients and set aside with all the other ingredients near the stove. Put a colander or stainless-steel Chinese strainer over a pot and place near the stove.

**3.** Heat a wok over high heat and add the oil. When the oil is hot and almost smoking, add the beef. Stir and fry until it just changes color, then remove the beef with a slotted spoon and drain in the colander.

**4.** Heat the oil again until very hot. Return the beef to the oil and stir and fry once more, until the beef is crispy around the edges. Pour the beef and oil into the colander over the pot and allow the oil to drain away.

**5.** Reheat the wok to medium hot. Heat 2 tablespoons of the drained oil, then add the tangerine peel, chili peppers, ginger, garlic and scallion. Stir-fry for a few seconds, or until the chili peppers brown, then add the beef. Stir for 30 seconds and add the sugar. Add the sauce to the beef, stirring constantly until it coats the meat

*1 large piece dried
tangerine peel,
in small pieces
4 to 5 dried hot red
chili peppers
2 tablespoons minced
fresh ginger
½ teaspoon minced
garlic
1 scallion, chopped
2 teaspoons sugar*

with a clear glaze. Turn off the heat and serve hot or at room temperature.

# STAR-ANISE BEEF

*Serves 6*

The star anise gives this dish its slightly licorice-like taste. This classic Shanghai recipe is an example of red cooking, which involves braising meat in soy sauce and spices. It can be prepared in two versions to make distinctly different dishes: the beef is cooked in one piece, sliced and served cold; or it is cut into chunks and braised in a stew.

*2 pounds boneless beef
foreshank, in 1 or 2
large pieces
2 tablespoons corn oil
2 slices fresh ginger
2 scallions, cut into
2-inch pieces
1 cup water
2 dried hot chili
peppers (optional)
1 star anise
4 tablespoons soy
sauce
3 tablespoons rice
wine
2 tablespoons crushed
rock sugar, or 1½
tablespoons sugar
2 medium carrots,
roll-cut (page 23), if
preparing stew*

**1.** Trim any membranes from the beef.

**2.** Heat a wok and add the oil. When the oil is hot, add the ginger and scallions. Stir, then transfer the ginger and scallions to a saucepan. If serving as an appetizer, leave the meat whole. If making the stew, cut into cubes. Add the beef and brown it on all sides, then transfer it to the same saucepan.

**3.** Add the remaining ingredients (except carrots) to the beef in the saucepan and bring to a boil. Turn the heat down to medium and cook for 5 minutes. Cover and turn down the heat. If meat is in 1 piece, simmer for 2 hours or until tender; if braising for stew, simmer for 1½ hours and add carrots during the last 30 minutes. Turn the beef a few times during the cooking.

**4.** If serving as an appetizer, cool the beef and refrigerate until firm. Cut into thin slices and arrange on a serving platter. Serve chilled.

# Jellied Lamb

**R**ecipes with aspic are normally summer dishes, and this one is a cool treat in hot weather. However, in the winter you can also serve it over a bed of hot rice, which will melt the aspic into a lovely sauce. The taste is unusual: lamb with anise. Agar-agar is the gelling agent in this dish.

*1 pound boneless lamb shank, cut into several large pieces, or a similar quantity of beef*
*2 scallions, cut into 4-inch lengths*
*2 garlic cloves*
*2 slices fresh ginger, cut ¼ inch thick*
*2 star anise*
*1 tablespoon crushed rock sugar or granulated sugar*
*4 tablespoons soy sauce*
*2 tablespoons rice wine*
*1½ cups beef broth*
*1 tablespoon agar-agar flakes*
*Several fresh lettuce leaves, for garnish*

**1.** Put the lamb or beef in a heavy pot, cover with water and boil for 3 minutes. Pour the contents of the pot into a colander. Rinse the meat and pot to remove any scum. Return the meat to the pot and add all the remaining ingredients except the agar-agar and lettuce. Bring the pot to a boil, turn the heat to medium and cook uncovered for 10 minutes. Cover the pot and turn to a low simmer; cook for 1½ hours or until tender.

**2.** Remove the lamb to cool. Discard the scallions, garlic, ginger and star anise but save the liquid. Cut the meat into ¼-inch pieces. Put the diced meat into a small loaf pan.

**3.** Strain the cooking liquid through a fine sieve and, if necessary, add enough water to make 1½ cups. Pour this liquid into a small saucepan, add the agar-agar and heat, stirring, until the agar-agar dissolves. Pour the liquid over the meat and refrigerate for 4 hours or until the liquid jells.

**4.** Remove any fat from the top of the jellied loaf. Use a knife to loosen from the pan, then unmold. Place an oblong serving platter over the pan and, holding the platter tightly to the loaf pan, turn mold upside down onto the platter. Cut the loaf into ½-inch-thick slices. Arrange slices on a platter with the lettuce around the lamb and serve cold.

**110** Beef and Lamb

# STIR-FRIED LAMB WITH SCALLIONS

*Serves 4*

*T*he Mongolians introduced lamb to the northern Chinese diet. Lamb has a strong flavor and can stand up to ginger and garlic. Here it is simply stir-fried with those seasonings and with scallions, another typical northern ingredient.

## Marinade

2 tablespoons soy
  sauce
½ teaspoon sugar
2 teaspoons cornstarch
1 tablespoon cold
  water

¾ pound boneless
  lamb shoulder, cut
  into 1½ × 2 × ⅛-
  inch slices

## Sauce

1 tablespoon soy sauce
2 tablespoons water
1 teaspoon distilled
  white vinegar
1 teaspoon oriental
  sesame oil

4 tablespoons corn oil
2 bunches scallions,
  roots and tips
  trimmed, cut
  diagonally into
  1½-inch lengths
3 thin slices fresh
  ginger, shredded
  fine
2 garlic cloves, sliced
  thin

*1.* Combine the marinade ingredients with the lamb in a mixing bowl. Stir to coat the meat evenly. Set aside for 30 minutes. Combine the sauce ingredients in a small bowl. Place the sauce and the remaining ingredients near the stove.

*2.* Heat a wok over medium heat until hot. Add 1 tablespoon oil and, when the oil is hot, add the scallions. Stir-fry about 1 minute, or until the scallions wilt. Transfer to a serving platter.

*3.* Reheat the wok over medium-high heat until hot and add the remaining 3 tablespoons oil. Add the ginger and garlic and stir-fry a few seconds. Turn the heat to high, add the lamb and stir-fry briskly until the lamb changes color, about 3 minutes. Return the cooked scallions to the wok and add the sauce. Stir once or twice to blend. Turn off the heat and transfer to a serving platter. Serve hot with Boiled Rice (page 167).

# Lamb Hunan Style

The strong taste of lamb contrasts well with potent chilies, so the Hunanese developed this hot dish. You can spice it to your preference.

## Marinade

1 small egg white
2 teaspoons cornstarch
¼ teaspoon kosher
    salt
1 teaspoon corn oil
1 tablespoon water

¾ pound lean boneless
    lamb shoulder, cut
    into 1½ × 2 ×
    ⅛-inch slices

## Sauce

3 tablespoons soy
    sauce
3 tablespoons rice
    wine
1 teaspoon sugar
1 teaspoon oriental
    sesame oil
2 teaspoons cornstarch
2 tablespoons water
1 to 2 teaspoons Hot
    Chili Sauce (page
    32), or to taste

1 cup shredded leeks,
    in 2-inch lengths
¼ pound fresh
    mushrooms, sliced
3 dried hot chili
    peppers, or
    to taste
3 garlic cloves, sliced
    thin
½ cup corn oil

**1.** Combine the marinade ingredients with the lamb in a mixing bowl. Mix with your hands to coat evenly. Refrigerate for at least 30 minutes or as long as several hours.

**2.** Mix the sauce ingredients in a small bowl and place near the stove. Put the leeks, mushrooms, chili peppers and garlic separately on a work platter, also near the stove.

**3.** Heat a wok over moderate heat until hot. Add the oil. Add the lamb and stir-fry briskly until the meat separates and changes color, about 3 minutes. Turn off the heat and transfer the lamb to a bowl, leaving as much oil as possible in the wok.

**4.** Reheat the wok over medium heat and add enough oil to make 2 tablespoons. Add the chili peppers and garlic and stir-fry for 30 seconds. Add the mushrooms and leeks and stir-fry about 1 minute. Add the lamb. Give the sauce ingredients a stir and add to the wok. Turn up the heat and stir-fry quickly until the sauce thickens and forms a glaze. Transfer the mixture to a serving platter and serve hot with Boiled Rice (page 167).

# FISH

$E$veryone knows we are supposed to eat more fish, and these tasty recipes will make it easier to do so. In general, Chinese like fish with firm flesh and a non-oily flavor, such as sea bass, red snapper, halibut and carp. These fish, along with flounder, gray sole and shad, are all excellent for steaming. And if you prefer fish fillets or pieces of fish, they are also excellent steamed; however, shorten the cooking time, depending on the size of the pieces. Whiting is especially good braised in soy sauce. And although salmon is not indigenous to China, it appears frequently on the menus of Chinese restaurants and I have used it with good results in this book. Try these recipes but feel free to substitute other fish available in your area.

For the freshest fish, look for clear bright eyes, a fresh smell, red gills and firm, resilient flesh when pressed.

| Recipes | | Prepare Ahead | Serving Temperature |
|---|---|---|---|
| Red-Cooked Whiting | | No | Hot |
| Puffed Fish Fillets in Mock Seaweed Batter | | No | Hot |
| Cantonese Steamed Fish | | No | Hot |
| Pan-Fried Peppers Stuffed with Pike | Spicy hot | No | Hot |
| Spicy Crispy Sea Bass | Spicy hot | No | Hot |
| Squirrel Fish | | No | Hot |
| Gray Sole Stir-Fried with Vegetables | | No | Hot |
| Steamed Fish with Ginger Sauce | | No | Hot |
| Stir-Fried Fishballs with Spinach | | No | Hot |
| Grilled Tile Fish | | No | Hot |
| Stir-Fried Halibut in a Basket | | No | Hot |
| Stir-Fried Salmon with Asparagus | | No | Hot |
| Sweet-and-Sour Steamed Yellow Pike | | No | Hot |
| Puffed Fish with Two Sauces | | No | Hot |
| Hunan Braised Fish | Spicy hot | No | Hot |

# RED-COOKED WHITING

$R$ ed-cooking" refers to the soy sauce in the cooking liquid, which adds color and rich flavor to the whiting. Try red-cooking with yellow pike, sea bass, or even winter carp. This dish goes well with Boiled Rice (page 167) and a stir-fried green vegetable.

*3 dried black
mushrooms*

*1 whiting, about 1½
pounds, cleaned but
with the head and
tail on*

*1 tablespoon flour, for
dusting*

*2 slices fresh ginger,
crushed with a
cleaver*

*2 garlic cloves, crushed
slightly with a
cleaver*

*2 scallions, cut into
2-inch lengths*

*¼ cup shredded
bamboo shoots*

*4 tablespoons soy
sauce*

*2 tablespoons rice
wine*

*1½ teaspoons sugar*

*¾ cup water*

*4 tablespoons corn oil*

*1.* Soak the mushrooms in warm water for 30 minutes. Remove stems and shred caps.

*2.* Rinse the fish inside and out. Dry with a paper towel. Dust evenly with the flour, shaking off any excess, and set aside on a plate.

*3.* Put the ginger, garlic and vegetables separately on a work platter and place near the stove. Keep the soy sauce, wine, sugar and water within easy reach.

*4.* Heat a 12-inch skillet, preferably nonstick, over moderate heat. Add the oil and heat. Then add the fish (cut the fish in half if it doesn't fit) and fry for about 2 minutes, shaking the skillet gently so that it doesn't stick. Add the ginger, garlic and scallions and continue to fry the fish for another 2 minutes, until lightly browned. Carefully turn the fish over and fry the other side for 1 minute. Sprinkle on the wine and cover for 30 seconds. Uncover and add the soy sauce, sugar, mushrooms, bamboo shoots and water. Turn the heat to medium-low, cover the pan again and cook over medium heat for about 5 minutes. Uncover and cook for another 5 minutes, frequently basting the fish with the sauce. There should be about ½ cup of sauce.

*5.* Transfer the fish to a large, oblong serving platter and pour the sauce with the mushrooms and bamboo shoots over the fish. Serve immediately.

# PUFFED FISH FILLETS IN MOCK SEAWEED BATTER

*Serves 2 to 4*

**D**eep-fried spinach, which the Chinese like to serve alone sprinkled with a bit of sugar, is turned into a mock seaweed. The spinach is incorporated into the batter for deep-fried fish cubes and the fish is served with a Sichuan peppercorn dip.

## Marinade

*1 teaspoon kosher salt*
*2 teaspoons rice wine*
*Dash of white pepper*

*1 pound gray sole, tile fish or scrod fillet, cut into 1½-inch cubes*
*3 cups corn oil, for deep-frying*
*2 cups fresh spinach (about ¼ pound), washed, stems removed and cut into needlelike shreds*

## Batter

*½ cup all-purpose flour*
*¼ cup cornstarch*
*2 teaspoons baking powder*
*¼ teaspoon kosher salt*
*⅔ cup cold water*

*Roasted Salt and Sichuan Peppercorns (page 37)*

**1.** Combine the marinade ingredients with the fish. Mix well and refrigerate for 1 hour.

**2.** Heat a wok and add the oil. When the oil is very hot, about 350° F., add the shredded spinach and deep-fry until the spinach turns dark green and is crisp. Remove with a skimmer and drain on paper towels. Set aside; you should have about ¾ cup.

**3.** Combine the batter ingredients and stir until smooth. Just before frying the fish, add the fried spinach and stir to blend.

**4.** Heat the oil again to 325° F. Dip the fish cubes into the batter and deep-fry as many pieces as will float freely in the oil until lightly browned and crisp, about 2 minutes. Remove and drain. Serve immediately with the roasted Sichuan peppercorn dip.

# CANTONESE STEAMED FISH

*Serves 2 to 4*

*T*his is an easy, delicious and nutritious way to cook fish. Steaming brings out the natural flavor of the fish, which is enhanced by the addition of ginger and scallions.

**1 sea bass or yellow pike (walleye), about 1½ to 2 pounds, cleaned but with head and tail on**
**½ teaspoon kosher salt**
**2 tablespoons rice wine**
**½ teaspoon sugar**
**2 tablespoons light soy sauce**
**2 tablespoons finely shredded fresh ginger**
**2 scallions, shredded fine**
**3 tablespoons corn oil**
**Few sprigs fresh coriander, for garnish**

**1.** Rinse and dry the fish with paper towels. At the thickest part of the fish, cut 2 diagonal slashes almost to the bone on both sides, about 1½ inches apart.

**2.** Place the fish on an oblong heatproof serving platter. Sprinkle both sides of the fish with salt and drizzle the rice wine on top.

**3.** Combine the sugar and soy sauce, stir and pour it over the fish. Sprinkle on the ginger and three-fourths of the scallions.

**4.** Bring at least 2 inches of water to a boil in a steamer large enough to accommodate the serving platter (a large roasting pan with cover can be used). Place the platter with the fish on a rack in the steamer. Cover and steam for 10 to 12 minutes or until done. The fish is done when you can easily pierce the thickest part with a chopstick.

**5.** Remove the fish from the steamer. Heat a small skillet until medium hot and add the oil. When the oil is near smoking, pour it over the fish. Stand back as you pour, since the hot oil will splatter slightly. Garnish with the remaining scallions and coriander. Serve immediately.

# PAN-FRIED PEPPERS STUFFED WITH PIKE

Choose either hot or sweet peppers and combine with yellow pike—you'll enjoy the contrasts in taste, color and texture.

*6 long, medium-hot Anaheim green chili peppers or a thin-skinned sweet green pepper*

*½ pound yellow pike (walleye), sea bass or red snapper fillet*

*3 tablespoons minced scallion, white part only*

*1 tablespoon cornstarch, plus extra for dusting*

*1 teaspoon kosher salt*

*½ teaspoon sugar*

*1 small egg white*

*1 tablespoon rice wine*

*3 tablespoons corn oil*

## Sauce

*1 tablespoon corn oil*

*1 tablespoon minced fresh ginger*

*2 garlic cloves, minced*

*4 tablespoons soy sauce*

*1 cup Fish or Vegetable Broth (pages 156, 159)*

*1 tablespoon cornstarch mixed with 2 tablespoons cold water*

**1.** Cut the peppers in half lengthwise and remove the seeds. If the peppers are very long, cut in half crosswise. Rinse and dry.

**2.** Chop the fish coarsely and mix it with the scallion, cornstarch, salt, sugar, egg white and wine. Stir in one direction until the mixture holds together.

**3.** Dust the inside of each pepper with a little cornstarch and fill each with the fish mixture.

**4.** Heat a flat-bottom skillet and add oil to coat the surface. Place the peppers, filling side down, in the skillet and cook over medium heat until lightly browned, about 2 to 3 minutes. Carefully turn each pepper over and cook the other side until lightly browned, another 2 minutes. Transfer to a warm serving platter.

**5.** Heat a saucepan, then add oil. Heat slightly, then add the ginger and garlic. Stir and add the soy sauce and broth. Bring to a boil, turn the heat to low, give the cornstarch mixture a stir and add it to the sauce. Cook and stir until the sauce thickens. Pour over the peppers and serve.

# SPICY CRISPY SEA BASS

*T*his recipe requires deep-frying a whole fish in a large quantity of hot oil. Strain the oil through a fine sieve after using, label it for fish and refrigerate for future use.

*1 sea bass, about 1½
pounds*
*½ cup all-purpose
flour, for dredging*

### Sauce

*3 dried black
mushrooms*
*2 tablespoons finely
minced fresh ginger*
*2 garlic cloves, minced
fine*
*¼ cup finely diced
bamboo shoots*
*¾ cup finely chopped
scallions*
*1 to 2 teaspoons Hot
Chili Sauce (page
32), or to taste*
*¼ cup rice wine*
*¼ cup Fish or
Vegetable Broth
(pages 156, 159)*
*1 tablespoon sugar*
*1 tablespoon white
distilled vinegar*
*3 tablespoons soy
sauce*
*1 teaspoon cornstarch
mixed with 2
tablespoons water*

*5 cups corn oil, for
deep-frying*

**1.** On both sides at the thickest part of the fish, cut 2 diagonal slashes nearly to the bone, about 1 inch apart. Dredge the fish in the flour, covering the entire surface including the insides of the slashes.

**2.** Soak the mushrooms for 30 minutes in warm water. Remove the stems and dice the caps fine. Meanwhile, place ingredients for sauce on a work platter next to the stove.

**3.** Heat the oil in a wok until very hot, almost smoking. Hold the fish firmly by the tail and carefully dip it into the hot oil once or twice, then gently lay the fish in the oil. Using a spatula, gently move it back and forth to be sure it is not sticking to the bottom. Ladle the hot oil over the fish. When the fish is golden and the bubbling and sizzling stops, in about 10 to 12 minutes, the fish is done. Transfer to a serving platter and keep warm.

**4.** Heat a small saucepan over medium-low heat and add 3 tablespoons of the frying oil. When the oil is hot, add the ginger and garlic. Stir a few seconds until the flavors are released, then add the mushrooms, bamboo shoots, scallions, chili sauce, wine, broth, sugar, vinegar and soy sauce. Cook, stirring, for 1 minute. Give the cornstarch mixture a stir and pour it into the sauce, stirring constantly. Continue to stir and cook until the sauce thickens. Pour the sauce over the fish and serve immediately.

# SQUIRREL FISH

$T$he Chinese can be very pragmatic about the names of things. For instance, a seasoning of five spices is called five-spice powder. On occasion, though, we indulge in more romantic, even symbolic names. In this dish, the fish is first boned and scored. When deep-fried, the scoring causes the flesh to curl, resembling a squirrel's tail. It's served with a sweet-and-sour sauce.

2 dried black
 mushrooms
2 sea bass, about 1½
 pounds each,
 cleaned with the
 heads removed
5 tablespoons
 cornstarch mixed
 with 5 tablespoons
 flour, for dusting

### Sauce

¼ cup sugar
¼ cup distilled white
 vinegar
1 tablespoon soy sauce
2 tablespoons catsup
¾ cup fish broth,
 made from the fish
 heads and bones, or
 recipe on page 156
1 teaspoon oriental
 sesame oil
1 tablespoon
 cornstarch mixed
 with 3 tablespoons
 water

2 tablespoons corn oil
1 garlic clove
1 small carrot, peeled
 and thinly sliced

**1.** Soak the mushrooms in warm water for 30 minutes.

**2.** Wash and dry the fish. Using a cleaver, cut along one side of the backbone as close as possible, then split the fish in half, leaving the tail attached. Turn the fish over and repeat the cutting on the other side. Cut off and remove the backbone and all other bones, leaving both sides connected at the tail. Score the inside flesh of the fillet (*not* the skinned outside) with crisscrossing diagonal cuts ½ inch apart. Cut deeply, but be careful not to cut all the way through. Repeat the same procedure with the second fish.

**3.** Dredge the fillets, including the insides of the scored cuts, with the cornstarch mixture. Drain mushrooms, remove stems and cut caps into quarters.

**4.** Combine the sauce ingredients in a small bowl and set aside.

**5.** Heat a small saucepan and add oil. Stir-fry the garlic until it is lightly browned, then remove and discard it. Add the carrot, onion, mushrooms, water chestnuts and peas. Stir-fry for a few seconds, then remove the vegetables for later use. Turn off the heat but leave the saucepan on the burner for further cooking.

1 small onion, cut into
   ¼-inch wedges,
   layers separated
2 fresh water
   chestnuts, peeled
   and sliced
2 tablespoons frozen
   peas, thawed
4 cups corn oil, for
   deep-frying

**6.** Heat a wok until very hot. Add the 4 cups oil and heat to about 385° F. Shake the fish to remove any excess flour and, one at a time, gently lower fish into the hot oil. Carefully ladle the hot oil over the fish, then gently shift the fish to be sure they fry evenly. Continue to fry until the fish are firm and lightly browned, about 10 minutes. Lift the fish with a stainless-steel strainer and place on a large, heated serving platter. Leave the oil in the wok, since the fish will be fried again just before serving, but turn off the heat.

**7.** Meanwhile, give the sauce ingredients in the bowl a stir and pour it into the saucepan. Turn the heat to medium and bring sauce to a boil while stirring constantly. Cook and stir until the sauce thickens. Add the cooked vegetables, cover and keep warm.

**8.** Reheat the oil in the wok. When it reaches about 385° F., refry the fish for 2 or 3 minutes or until crisp. Using the steel strainer, lift the fish out of the oil one at a time and place on a heated serving platter. Pour the warm sauce over and serve immediately.

# GRAY SOLE STIR-FRIED WITH VEGETABLES

*T*his is a delicate and delicious way to cook fish. Ask your fishmonger to fillet the fish, leaving the skin on so that the pieces stay together while being stir-fried.

## Marinade

1 extra-large egg
    white
¼ teaspoon salt
1 teaspoon rice wine
2 teaspoons cornstarch

1 pound gray sole or
    flounder fillets with
    the skin left on, cut
    into 2-inch cubes
¼ cup thinly sliced
    carrots
1 stalk broccoli
2 thin slices fresh
    ginger, each about
    the size of a quarter
¼ cup thinly sliced
    bamboo shoots
¼ cup canned straw
    mushrooms
1 tablespoon rice wine
½ teaspoon kosher
    salt
½ teaspoon sugar
1 cup corn oil, for
    poaching

**1.** Combine the marinade ingredients with the fish and refrigerate for at least 1 hour.

**2.** Parboil the carrots. Peel and cut the stalk of the broccoli into ¼-inch slices, and cut the flowerets small; parboil the broccoli. Place the ginger and vegetables separately on a work platter. Put the platter, wine, salt and sugar near the stove. Place a strainer over a pot and position near the stove.

**3.** Heat a wok over medium-low heat, add the oil and heat to about 280° F. Add the fish and gently stir. As soon as fish turns white, pour the contents of the wok into the strainer. Allow the oil to drain away.

**4.** Reheat the wok and add 2 tablespoons of the drained oil to it. Add the ginger. Stir and add the carrots, broccoli, bamboo shoots and mushrooms. Stir-fry for 1 minute, then add the salt, sugar and wine. Stir-fry for 1 more minute, then return the cooked fish to the wok. Stir gently to blend the ingredients. Taste for salt and transfer the fish to a large serving platter. Serve immediately.

*Note:* You can also serve this in a Taro-Root Basket (page 136).

# STEAMED FISH WITH GINGER SAUCE

### Serves 2 to 4

*T*his time the fish is steamed with just a little rice wine, and in the sauce the individual flavors of the ginger and scallions are released in the oil before the soy sauce and sugar are added. When the fish and sauce are brought together, the flavors are subtle yet complex.

*1 sea bass, about 1½ to 2 pounds, cleaned but with head and tail on*

*½ teaspoon kosher salt*

*2 tablespoons rice wine*

### Sauce

*3 tablespoons corn oil*

*2 tablespoons finely shredded fresh ginger*

*2 scallions, shredded fine*

*3 tablespoons soy sauce*

*½ teaspoon sugar*

*Few sprigs fresh coriander, for garnish*

**1.** Trim the fins off the fish. Rinse and dry with paper towels. On both sides of the fish cut 2 diagonal slashes almost to the bone, about 1½ inches apart. This permits more even steaming and also allows the seasonings to penetrate more of the fish. Place the fish on an oblong serving platter and sprinkle both sides with salt. Drizzle the rice wine on top.

**2.** Bring 2 inches of water to a boil in a steamer large enough to accommodate the serving platter. Place the platter with the fish on a rack in the steamer. Cover and steam for 12 minutes or until done. The fish is cooked when you can pierce through the center with a chopstick.

**3.** Heat a small skillet until medium hot and add the oil and shredded ginger. Turn the heat to low and cook the ginger for a few seconds. Turn off the heat and add the scallions, then stir in the soy sauce and sugar. Gently stir the sauce once, then remove the skillet from the heat.

**4.** Remove the platter with the fish from the steamer and carefully pour off any accumulated liquid. Pour the hot ginger and scallion sauce over the fish and garnish with the coriander. Serve immediately.

# STIR-FRIED FISHBALLS WITH SPINACH

*T*hese delicious balls of fish, with the sweetness of water chestnuts and the faint taste of coriander, are served on a platter of spinach. They can also be poached or deep-fried alone and served as an appetizer.

*1 pound fresh fish*
*fillets—scrod, cod,*
*yellow pike*
*(walleye) or pollack*
*—cut into cubes*

## Seasoning

*½ cup cold water*
*1 small egg white*
*1 ½-inch chunk fresh*
*ginger, pushed*
*through a garlic*
*press for juice*
*2 tablespoons minced*
*fresh water*
*chestnuts*
*1 tablespoon finely*
*chopped scallion,*
*white part only*
*1 teaspoon minced*
*fresh coriander*
*1 tablespoon finely*
*minced smoked*
*turkey*
*1 tablespoon rice wine*
*1½ teaspoons kosher*
*salt*
*¼ teaspoon sugar*
*1 tablespoon*
*cornstarch*
*1 tablespoon corn oil*

**1.** Put the fish cubes in the bowl of a food processor and, using the metal blade, process for 30 seconds. Add the water and the egg white and process for 2 seconds or so. Add the remaining seasoning ingredients and process until the mixture becomes well blended, about 20 seconds.

**2.** Pour 2 quarts of cold water into a pot. Wet one hand, take a handful of fish purée and squeeze your fingers into a fist, forcing the purée through the round opening between your thumb and forefinger to form a 1-inch ball. Catch the ball with a wet spoon in your other hand and drop it into the cold water. Repeat the procedure until all the fish purée is used.

**3.** Put the pot on the stove and bring the water almost to a boil. The fishballs are now cooked. Gently pour the fishballs into a colander and rinse with cold water.

**4.** Heat a wok over high heat until very hot and add the oil. When the oil is hot, add the garlic and stir-fry quickly to brown slightly. Add the spinach and stir-fry for a few seconds. Add the salt and sugar. Continue to stir-fry until the spinach is wilted. Remove and discard the garlic, turn off heat and, using a pair of chopsticks, transfer the spinach to a serving platter.

**5.** Turn the heat to medium and add the broth

3 tablespoons corn oil
1 garlic clove, crushed
    slightly with a
    cleaver
1 pound spinach,
    washed well and
    large stems removed
1 teaspoon kosher salt
½ teaspoon sugar
¼ cup Fish Broth
    (page 156)
2 teaspoons soy sauce
1 teaspoon cornstarch
    mixed with 2
    tablespoons cold
    water

and soy sauce to the liquid in the wok. Bring to a simmer, add the fishballs and stir-fry for a few seconds, or until the fishballs are heated through. Stir the cornstarch mixture and add it to the wok. Stir-fry until the sauce thickens, then place the fishballs over the spinach. Pour the sauce over all and serve immediately.

# GRILLED TILE FISH

*H*ere's a simple and delicious way to grill fresh fish in the summer. The medium-hot chili pepper gives it a touch of spiciness. Serve it with Fried Rice (page 169) and Peking Sweet-and-Sour Cabbage (page 145).

*3 tablespoons soy sauce*
*4 tablespoons corn oil*
*1¼ pounds tile fish, salmon or halibut fillets*
*⅛ teaspoon white pepper*
*2 teaspoons finely shredded fresh ginger*
*2 hot green chili peppers, seeded and shredded fine*

*1.* Rub the soy sauce and 2 tablespoons of oil over the fish fillets. Sprinkle the white pepper and ginger on the fish, then refrigerate for 1 hour.

*2.* Heat a small skillet. Add remaining 2 tablespoons oil and quickly stir-fry the chili peppers for about 1 minute. Set aside.

*3.* Heat an outdoor grill until very hot. Brush the grill with oil, then place fish on grill. Cook for 2 minutes, then carefully turn over and cook another 2 minutes or until just done. Transfer to a serving platter, garnish the top with the peppers and serve.

# STIR-FRIED HALIBUT IN A BASKET

*T*his is a delightful combination of the silky, smooth texture of halibut with the crispy crunchiness of a deep-fried taro-root or potato basket.

### Marinade
*½ small egg white*
*1 teaspoon cornstarch*
*¼ teaspoon kosher salt*
*1 teaspoon rice wine*

*1.* Combine the marinade ingredients with the fish and mix until the pieces are thoroughly coated. Refrigerate for at least 1 hour. Soak the mushrooms in warm water for 30 minutes. Remove stems, and quarter caps. Place the garlic, ginger and vegetables separately on a work plat-

Dash of white pepper
1 teaspoon oriental
	sesame oil

1 pound halibut fillets,
	cut into ½-inch
	chunks
3 dried black
	mushrooms
2 garlic cloves, peeled
	and slightly crushed
	with a cleaver
1 teaspoon finely
	shredded fresh
	ginger
1 scallion, cut into
	½-inch pieces
¾ cup snow peas,
	parboiled
½ cup corn oil, for
	poaching

### Sauce

2 teaspoons sugar
¾ teaspoon salt
1 teaspoon rice wine
1 tablespoon soy sauce
1 teaspoon cornstarch
1 teaspoon oriental
	sesame oil
3 tablespoons fish
	broth, made from
	the bones of the
	halibut, or
	Vegetable Broth
	(page 159)

Taro-Root or Potato
	Baskets (page 136),
	heated in the oven

ter near the stove. Combine the sauce ingredients and stir until the cornstarch dissolves. Place the sauce near the stove.

**2.** Put a strainer over a pot and place it near the stove. Heat a wok over moderate heat until hot. Add the oil. Swirl to coat the wok and add the fish; gently stir-fry until fish turns opaque. Pour the contents of the wok into the strainer and allow the oil to drain off. Wipe the wok clean.

**3.** Reheat the wok and add 2 tablespoons of the drained oil. Add the garlic, ginger and scallions. Stir-fry a few seconds to release the flavor, then add the mushrooms. Stir another few seconds and then add the snow peas. Stir sauce ingredients and add to the wok. As the sauce begins to thicken, add the halibut and stir-fry gently until the sauce forms a glaze over the ingredients.

**4.** Divide the fish mixture in half and put each half in one of the hot baskets. Serve at once.

---

**Note:** Scrod or cod, though not as delicate in taste or texture, can be substituted for the halibut. Also, you can use asparagus instead of snow peas when in season.

# STIR-FRIED SALMON WITH ASPARAGUS

**Serves 4**

## Marinade

*1 egg white*
*1 teaspoon cornstarch*
*¼ teaspoon salt*
*½ teaspoon oriental sesame oil*
**Dash of white pepper**

*¾ pound salmon fillet, skinned and cut into 1½ × ¾ × ½-inch pieces*
*3 tablespoons corn oil*
*½ teaspoon finely minced fresh ginger*
*1 pound fresh asparagus, cut on the diagonal into ½-inch pieces*
*1 teaspoon kosher salt*
*½ teaspoon sugar*
*2 tablespoons water*
*½ cup corn oil, for poaching*

## Sauce

*1 garlic clove, sliced thin*
*1 tablespoon minced scallion, both white and green parts*
*½ cup Fish Broth (page 156)*
*1 teaspoon rice wine*
*⅛ teaspoon white pepper*
*½ teaspoon kosher salt*
**(continued)**

**1.** Combine the marinade ingredients with the salmon and mix thoroughly. Refrigerate for at least 1 hour, or for as long as 4 hours.

**2.** Heat a wok over moderate heat until it is hot and add 3 tablespoons oil. Add the minced ginger, stir and add the asparagus. Stir until the asparagus is coated with oil, then add the salt and sugar. Add water and continue to stir-fry until the asparagus is tender-crisp. Transfer to a large serving platter. Clean out the wok.

**3.** Place a strainer over a pot and put near the stove. Reheat the wok and add the ½ cup oil. When the oil is about 280° F., add the salmon and stir gently but quickly to separate the pieces. As soon as the salmon turns opaque, pour the contents of the wok into the strainer. Allow the oil to drain off.

**4.** To make the sauce, reheat the wok over medium-low heat until hot. Add 2 tablespoons of the drained oil, heat and add the garlic and scallions. Stir and add the broth. Bring to a boil and add the wine, pepper, salt and sesame oil. Stir the cornstarch mixture and add it to the broth, stirring continuously. As the sauce begins to thicken, stir in the egg white. Return the salmon to the sauce and stir gently once or twice. Pour the salmon sauce over the asparagus and serve immediately.

1 teaspoon oriental
   sesame oil
1 teaspoon cornstarch
   mixed with 1
   tablespoon water
1 extra-large egg
   white, well beaten

# SWEET-AND-SOUR STEAMED YELLOW PIKE

*Serves 2 to 4*

*T*he mild and succulent yellow pike is enhanced with a sweet-and-sour sauce. Try it with sea bass or red snapper if yellow pike is not available.

1 yellow pike
   (walleye), sea bass
   or red snapper,
   about 1½ pounds,
   cleaned but with the
   head and tail on
1 tablespoon rice wine
½ teaspoon kosher
   salt

### Sauce

1 tablespoon corn oil
4 tablespoons sugar
4 tablespoons cider
   vinegar
1 tablespoon soy sauce
2 tablespoons catsup
¾ cup Fish or
   Vegetable Broth
   (pages 156, 159)
2 teaspoons cornstarch
   mixed with 2
   tablespoons water

4 scallion brushes
   (page 83), for
   garnish

*1.* Rinse the fish with cold water. Dry with paper towels. Place it on an oblong platter and sprinkle with the wine and salt.

*2.* Put 2 inches of water in an oblong enamel roaster. Place a rack in the bottom and bring the water to a boil. Put the plate with the fish on the rack, cover and steam for 10 to 12 minutes or until done. The fish is cooked when a chopstick easily pierces the thickest part.

*3.* While the fish is steaming, combine all the sauce ingredients except the cornstarch mixture in a small saucepan. Cook the sauce over low heat, stirring, until it begins to simmer. Stir the cornstarch mixture and pour it into the sauce, stirring constantly until the sauce thickens.

*4.* When the fish is cooked, transfer to a platter and pour the sauce over the fish. Garnish with scallion brushes and serve immediately.

# PUFFED FISH WITH TWO SAUCES

## Serves 2 to 4

*T*hese fish cubes puff up when deep-fried in a batter. This recipe gives you two sauce choices: a sweet-and-sour or a lemon sauce.

### Marinade

*½ teaspoon kosher salt*
*1 teaspoon soy sauce*
*1 teaspoon oriental sesame oil*
*⅛ teaspoon white pepper*
*1 pound gray sole, flounder, tile fish or scrod fillets, cut into 2-inch cubes*

### Sweet-and-Sour Sauce

*3 tablespoons sugar*
*3 tablespoons white distilled vinegar*
*⅓ cup water*
*1 tablespoon catsup*
*2 teaspoons light soy sauce*
*2 teaspoons cornstarch*

**1.** Combine the marinade ingredients with the fish. With your hands, mix to coat the fish well, then refrigerate for 30 minutes.

**2.** Combine ingredients for either sauce in a small saucepan and place on stove for cooking later. Combine the batter ingredients and stir until smooth.

**3.** Heat a wok over medium heat until hot and add the oil. As the oil is heating, add 1 tablespoon of the warm oil to the batter and mix well. When the oil reaches about 325° F., dip the fish pieces into the batter and then into the hot oil. Deep-fry as many pieces as can float freely in the oil until golden brown and crisp, about 2 minutes. Turn each piece several times during frying. Remove and drain; keep warm. Continue the procedure until all the pieces are cooked.

**4.** Stir the sauce ingredients until there are no cornstarch lumps. Over medium heat bring to a simmer, stirring constantly until the sauce thickens and becomes clear.

## Lemon Sauce

¼ *cup strained fresh lemon juice*

¼ *cup sugar*

¼ *cup mild Japanese rice vinegar (see Note)*

¾ *cup Fish or Vegetable Broth (pages 156, 159)*

1½ *tablespoons cornstarch*

## Batter

½ *cup all-purpose flour*

¼ *cup cornstarch*

2 *teaspoons baking powder*

¼ *teaspoon kosher salt*

⅔ *cup cold water*

2 *cups corn oil, for deep-frying*

*Few sprigs fresh coriander, for garnish*

*5.* Transfer the fish to a large serving dish and garnish with the coriander. Pour the sauce into a small serving bowl and serve as a dip.

---

*Note:* Marukan brand vinegar adds a pale yellow color. Distilled white vinegar can be used for a slightly sharper taste.

# HUNAN BRAISED FISH

*Serves 2 to 4*

*I*f you like your food hot and spicy, this fish will appeal to you.

3 dried black
  mushrooms
1 sea bass or yellow
  pike (walleye),
  about 1½ to 2
  pounds, cleaned but
  left whole
1 tablespoon all-
  purpose flour, for
  dusting
¾ cup corn oil
1 to 2 teaspoons Hot
  Chili Sauce (page
  32), or to taste
2 tablespoons finely
  minced fresh ginger
2 garlic cloves, minced
  fine
¼ cup bamboo shoots,
  minced fine
½ cup Vegetable or
  Fish Broth (pages
  159, 156) or water
¼ cup rice wine
1 tablespoon sugar
2 tablespoons soy
  sauce
1 tablespoon distilled
  white vinegar
2 tablespoons chopped
  scallions, green part
  only, for garnish

*1.* Soak the mushrooms for 30 minutes in warm water. Remove stems and mince caps fine. Wash and dry the fish and dust with the flour.

*2.* Heat a 12-inch skillet, preferably nonstick or well cured cast-iron, over moderate heat until hot but not smoking. Add the oil, then slip in the fish (cut in half if it doesn't fit) and fry until lightly browned, about 2 minutes. Carefully turn the fish over and brown the other side, about 2 minutes more. Transfer to a warm platter. Carefully pour the oil into a bowl.

*3.* Reheat the same skillet and add 3 tablespoons of the drained oil. Add the chili sauce, ginger and garlic. Stir and add the bamboo shoots, mushrooms, broth, rice wine, sugar, soy sauce and vinegar. Turn the heat to low, return fish to the skillet, cover and simmer for 5 to 8 minutes. Carefully turn the fish over, cover and simmer for another 5 to 8 minutes, or until the fish is done. The fish is cooked when a chopstick easily pierces the thickest part.

*4.* Transfer the fish to a warm serving platter. Pour the sauce remaining in the skillet over the fish and garnish with the scallions. Serve immediately.

# VEGETABLES

**Y**ou'll be delighted to learn how easy and delicious a simple vegetable stir-fry can be. Imagine a dinner of broiled chicken and roast potatoes enlivened with Spicy Eggplant (page 137) or Stir-Fried Bok Choy with Mushrooms (page 135). Even children will eat their veggies stir-fried.

The details will be useful, too. You'll learn the Chinese way to peel broccoli so that the delicious stem can be eaten, and you'll serve unpeeled eggplant, more nutritious than the peeled version.

| Recipes | | Prepare Ahead | Serving Temperature |
| --- | --- | --- | --- |
| Stir-Fried Bok Choy with Mushrooms | | Yes | Hot |
| Taro-Root Basket | | Yes | Hot |
| Spicy Eggplant | Spicy | Yes | Hot or room temp. |
| Braised Bean Curd | Spicy | No | Hot |
| Vegetarian Lettuce Packages | | Yes | Hot |
| Stir-Fried Potatoes | | Yes | Hot or cold |
| Fried String Beans | | No | Hot |
| Stir-Fried Asparagus | | No | Hot or room temp. |
| Stir-Fried Green Cabbage | | No | Hot |
| Deep-Fried Eggplant | | No | Hot |
| Braised Dried Mushrooms | | Yes | Hot |
| Seasoned Pressed Bean Curd | | Yes | |
| Peking Sweet-and-Sour Cabbage | | Yes | Hot or room temp. |
| Braised Chinese Cabbage with Chestnuts | | Yes | Hot |
| Stir-Fried Spinach | | No | Hot or room temp. |
| Deep-Fried Bean Curd | | Yes | Hot |
| Buddha's Delight | | Yes | Hot |
| Stir-Fried Broccoli | | No | Hot |
| Stir-Fried Snow Peas with Ginger | | Yes | Hot |

# STIR-FRIED BOK CHOY WITH MUSHROOMS

*T*his is a basic stir-fry recipe for many vegetables, such as mustard greens, Chinese broccoli and Chinese cabbage. In this recipe, bok choy is combined with braised dried mushrooms. You'll enjoy the visual contrast of white and green leaves topped by the dark brown mushroom caps.

*10 large dried black mushrooms*
*1 cup warm water*
*4½ tablespoons corn oil*
*¾ teaspoon sugar*
*1 tablespoon dark soy sauce*
*1 pound bok choy*
*1 teaspoon kosher salt*
*½ teaspoon sugar*
*2 tablespoons water*

*1.* Wash and soak the mushrooms in the warm water for at least 2 hours, or until they are soft. Squeeze the mushrooms dry; strain and reserve the liquid. Cut off and discard the stems and leave the caps whole.

*2.* Combine the mushroom caps and the reserved mushroom liquid in a saucepan. Bring the liquid to a boil and skim off the scum. Add 1½ tablespoons of oil and simmer over low heat for 1 hour. Add the sugar and soy sauce. Continue cooking until very little sauce remains. Set aside.

*3.* Separate the stalks and leaves of the bok choy and wash both in warm water. Cut the stems on the diagonal into 1-inch pieces. Cut the leaves separately into 1-inch pieces.

*4.* Heat a wok over moderate heat until hot and add remaining 3 tablespoons of oil. Add the bok choy stems and stir-fry for 1 minute. Add the leaves and stir-fry for another minute. Add the salt, sugar and water, and stir-fry for a few seconds to blend the ingredients.

*5.* Cover the wok and cook over medium heat for about 2 minutes, or until the stems are translucent. Stir several times and transfer the bok choy to a serving platter, making a flattened mound. Place the mushroom caps top side up in the center on top, allowing the green and white cabbage to show at the edges. Serve hot.

# TARO-ROOT BASKET

*Makes 4 baskets*

Deep-fried baskets of taro root turn an ordinary stir-fry dish into an elegant banquet presentation. Available year-round in Latin American and oriental markets, taro root is a tuber with the delicate flavor of chestnuts. The baskets are delicious and can be made in advance and reheated in the oven. If taro root is not available, baskets can be made from another tuber, the potato. I recommend Idaho potatoes; the cooking directions are the same as for the taro root. To make the basket, you need two metal strainers, 6 inches in diameter, one to fit into the other.

*½ pound taro root*
*1 teaspoon kosher salt*
*2 tablespoons*
*all-purpose flour*
*2 tablespoons*
*cornstarch*
*3 cups corn oil, for*
*deep-frying*

**1.** Cut the taro root into matchstick-size shreds or shred in a food processor. Mix the shreds with the salt, then rinse several times to remove the salt and surface starch. Dry the taro root with paper towels, then coat with the flour and cornstarch.

**2.** Select a deep pot. If necessary, bend the handles of the strainers straight up so the strainer baskets will touch the bottom of the pot. Line one of the strainers with a layer of shredded taro root and press the other strainer over, to sandwich it. Heat pot and add the oil; heat it to 350° F. Lower the strainers into the hot oil, which should cover the taro-root shreds. Deep-fry until the basket is crisp and lightly golden, about 2 or 3 minutes. Remove the strainers from the oil, lift off the top strainer and tap the bottom one gently to loosen the taro-root basket. Carefully remove and put on a paper towel to drain. Deep-fry the remaining taro-root baskets in the same way.

*Note:* The baskets can be made as far as a day in advance and reheated in a preheated 350° F. oven for 10 minutes.

# SPICY EGGPLANT

Serve this Sichuan dish cold as an appetizer or hot as the main dish in a vegetarian meal—both are equally delicious. You can vary the spiciness to taste. As an appetizer, the spiciness is best balanced with the blandness of unsalted crackers. As a hot entrée, accompany with Boiled Rice (page 167). In Chinese cooking the eggplant is almost never peeled, which makes it as nutritious as it is delicious.

1½ pounds eggplant,
   preferably oriental,
   cut into ½-inch
   cubes

### Sauce

¾ teaspoon kosher
   salt
2 teaspoons sugar
2 tablespoons soy
   sauce
¼ cup Chicken Broth
   (page 155)
2 teaspoons Hot Chili
   Sauce (page 32), or
   to taste

½ cup corn oil
1 tablespoon minced
   fresh ginger
1 garlic clove, sliced
1 hot green chili
   pepper, Anaheim
   type, diced into
   ⅛-inch cubes
2 teaspoons distilled
   white vinegar
1 teaspoon oriental
   sesame oil

**1.** Soak the eggplant pieces in cold water for 10 minutes. This keeps them from soaking up too much oil while cooking. Pour the eggplant into a colander and shake several times to remove water. Blot with paper towels to dry thoroughly. Combine the sauce ingredients in a small bowl, then put near the stove along with all other ingredients.

**2.** Heat a wok over medium heat until moderately hot. Add the oil and then the eggplant. Stir-fry the eggplant until it is soft, about 4 or 5 minutes. Remove with a slotted spoon, leaving as much of the oil in the wok as possible.

**3.** Add more oil if necessary to have about 2 tablespoons in wok. Add the ginger, garlic and chili pepper. Stir for a few seconds, then add the sauce. Stir, and then add the eggplant; continue stirring to blend. Add the vinegar and sesame oil, then transfer to a serving dish. Serve hot or at room temperature.

# BRAISED BEAN CURD

## Serves 2 to 4

*I*n most cuisines, there is a difference between home and restaurant cooking. Home cooking generally is simpler while restaurant dishes should be more complex and showy. This bean-curd dish certainly is home cooking. It is simple to make and uses very modest ingredients. Use the freshest bean curd you can find, for its taste is highlighted here.

*1 pound soft bean curd*

### Sauce

*½ teaspoon kosher salt*
*3 tablespoons soy sauce, or to taste*
*1 tablespoon rice wine*
*1 teaspoon Hoisin Sauce (page 31)*
*1 to 2 teaspoons Hot Chili Sauce (page 32; optional)*
*1 teaspoon cornstarch*

*2 tablespoons corn oil*
*3 scallions, cut into ⅛-inch rounds, white and green parts in separate mounds*
*2 teaspoons oriental sesame oil*

1. Place the bean curd in a bowl, pour in boiling water to cover and allow to set for 15 minutes. This firms up the bean curd, making it easier to handle. Carefully remove the bean curd and drain it. Cut into ¼-inch cubes.

2. Combine the sauce ingredients in a bowl and place near the stove.

3. Heat a wok over medium heat until hot. Add the corn oil, then the white part of the scallions. As they sizzle, add the bean curd to the wok. Slide a spatula along the bottom of the wok and gently turn the curd up and over to blend with the oil. Lower the heat and cook for 4 minutes. Stir the sauce ingredients and add to the wok. Gently stir the bean curd while the sauce simmers. When the sauce thickens, add the sesame oil, stir once and gently transfer the bean curd to a warm serving platter. Sprinkle the chopped green scallion parts on top and serve piping hot.

# VEGETARIAN LETTUCE PACKAGES

*Serves 6*

*H*ere is a vegetarian version of the popular meat-filled Lettuce Packages (page 91). You'll find it delicious, colorful and low in calories.

*6 dried black mushrooms*
*1 head iceberg lettuce*
*3 tablespoons corn oil*
*1½ cups minced Seasoned Pressed Bean Curd (page 144)*
*2 tablespoons soy sauce*
*1 red bell pepper, stem removed, seeded and minced fine*
*10 fresh water chestnuts, peeled and minced fine*
*1 cup bamboo shoots, minced fine*
*1 teaspoon kosher salt*
*½ teaspoon sugar*
*2 tablespoons Hoisin Sauce (page 31)*

*1.* Soak the mushrooms in warm water for 30 minutes. Remove the stems and mince caps fine. Cut out the core of the lettuce and soak the head in lukewarm water for about 5 minutes. Separate the leaves. Using a pair of scissors, cut the leaves in the shape of cups 6 inches in diameter. Dry the leaves, put them in a plastic bag and refrigerate until ready to use.

*2.* Heat a wok and add the oil. Add the bean curd and stir, then add the soy sauce and stir-fry a few seconds. Add the red pepper, stir-fry a few more seconds, then add the water chestnuts and bamboo shoots. Add the salt and sugar and continue to stir-fry for 2 minutes. Add the Hoisin Sauce, stirring several times to blend. Taste for salt, then transfer the mixture to the center of a large platter. Surround it with the lettuce-leaf cups and serve. Each guest takes a leaf cup, puts 1 heaping tablespoon of the bean-curd mixture in it, wraps the lettuce in a cylindrical package and eats it by hand.

*Note:* You can add ¼ cup minced fresh hot chili peppers if you like it spicy.

# STIR-FRIED POTATOES

Potatoes are served in many well-known forms and tastes in the West: mashed, french-fried, scalloped, and so on. My husband came home from a recent trip to Beijing with this potato recipe. It gives the potato a unique, clean taste that is delicious served hot as part of a Chinese or Western meal, or cold at a picnic.

*1 pound potatoes, peeled and cut into julienne strips*
*3 tablespoons corn oil*
*2 tablespoons minced scallions*
*½ teaspoon Roasted Sichuan Peppercorns (page 34)*
*2 tablespoons soy sauce*
*¾ teaspoon kosher salt*
*2 tablespoons distilled white vinegar*

**1.** In a pot bring 2 quarts of water to a boil and add the shredded potatoes. Boil for 1 minute or until cooked yet still firm. Drain and rinse with cold water. Drain again and pat dry with paper towels.

**2.** Heat a wok over moderate heat until hot, then add the oil. When the oil is hot, stir in the scallions and the Sichuan peppercorns. Add the shredded potatoes and stir-fry for a few seconds, then add the soy sauce, salt and vinegar. Stir well, then transfer to a serving platter. Serve hot or cold.

# FRIED STRING BEANS

In this Sichuan dish, string beans are deep-fried without batter until they wrinkle. They are then stir-fried briefly with ground meat, dried hot chili peppers and just a little soy sauce.

*1 pound string beans*
*2 cups corn oil, for deep-frying*
*8 dried hot chili peppers*

**1.** Remove both tip ends of the string beans and the strings. Wash and dry well. Heat the oil in a wok until hot, about 325° F. Meanwhile, place a strainer over a pot and place near the stove. Carefully add the string beans to the hot oil. Stirring

¼ pound ground beef
  or veal
2 tablespoons soy
  sauce
½ teaspoon kosher
  salt
1½ teaspoons sugar
1 tablespoon rice wine
1 tablespoon distilled
  white vinegar

frequently, fry until the beans wrinkle, then care-fully ladle or pour the contents of the wok into the strainer and allow the oil to drain away com-pletely.

**2.** Reheat the wok and add 2 tablespoons of the drained oil. Add the chili peppers. If you want a really spicy taste, expose the seeds by breaking the peppers open with the edge of a spatula. Stir-fry until peppers turn brown, then add the ground meat and stir-fry until the pieces separate and change color. Return the string beans to the wok and add the soy sauce, salt, sugar, wine and vinegar. Stir until all is well blended. Trans-fer contents of wok to a serving platter and serve hot.

# STIR-FRIED ASPARAGUS

*Serves 4 to 6*

In the short asparagus season, we look for ways to serve this delightful vegetable. Here's asparagus with a hint of ginger. Serve this with any meat dish, Chinese or Western style.

2 tablespoons corn oil
½ teaspoon finely
  minced fresh ginger
1 pound fresh
  asparagus, tough
  ends removed and
  discarded, stems
  cut on the diagonal
  into ½-inch pieces
1 teaspoon kosher salt
½ teaspoon sugar

Heat a wok over medium heat until hot. Add the oil and, when it is hot, add the ginger. Stir-fry a few seconds, add the asparagus and stir-fry for a few more seconds. Add the salt and sugar and continue to stir-fry until the asparagus is tender yet crisp, about 3 minutes. Serve hot or at room temperature.

*Note:* Snow peas and string beans can be substituted for asparagus. Par-boil them first, the snow peas for about 1 to 2 minutes until tender and crisp, and the string beans for 5 minutes.

# STIR-FRIED GREEN CABBAGE

*Serves 4*

**G**reen cabbage is a different vegetable when simply stir-fried with a little salt and sugar. It is wonderfully sweet and delicious.

*3 tablespoons corn oil*
*1 small carrot, sliced thin (optional)*
*½ cup fresh mushrooms, sliced thin (optional)*
*1 small head green cabbage, about 1 pound, shredded*
*1 teaspoon kosher salt, or to taste*
*½ teaspoon sugar*

Heat a wok over high heat until hot. Add the oil, carrot and mushrooms. Stir-fry a few seconds, then add the cabbage. Sprinkle on the salt and sugar and continue to stir-fry until the cabbage wilts and becomes translucent, about 2 minutes. Turn off the heat, transfer to a serving platter and serve hot.

# DEEP-FRIED EGGPLANT

*Serves 4*

**E**ggplant is absolutely delicious when batter-dipped and deep-fried. The moist, flavorful texture of the vegetable contrasts with the crispy batter, making it one of my family's favorites. Serve it with Soy Sauce Dip (page 36), as an appetizer or a first course.

*1 medium eggplant, about 1 pound*

**Batter**
*1 cup all-purpose flour*
*½ cup cornstarch*
*4 teaspoons baking powder*

**1.** Trim off the stem and cut eggplant crosswise into ¼-inch slices. Cut the slices into 2 × 1½-inch pieces. Put the pieces in a large mixing bowl, cover with cold water and soak for 10 minutes. Drain and shake to remove water. Blot with paper towels to dry thoroughly.

**2.** Combine the batter ingredients and mix until

½ teaspoon kosher
 salt
1¼ cups cold water

2 cups corn oil, for
 deep-frying

smooth. Heat a wok and add the oil. While the oil is heating, add 1 tablespoon of warm oil to the batter and stir it in. When the oil reaches 325° F., dip the eggplant pieces into the batter and place in the oil. Deep-fry as many pieces as will float freely until lightly golden, about 2 minutes. Turn the pieces once or twice while frying. Remove and drain on paper towels. Keep fried pieces warm in a low oven—up to 30 minutes—while you fry remainder or prepare to serve. Serve hot.

# BRAISED DRIED MUSHROOMS

*Serves 4*

*T*hese mushrooms have an almost meatlike quality. They can be combined with any stir-fried vegetable, such as broccoli or snow peas, or served as an appetizer. The quality of the mushrooms is defined by the price: the higher the price, the better the mushrooms.

12 large dried black
 mushrooms, of good
 quality
1½ tablespoons corn
 oil
¾ teaspoon sugar
1 tablespoon dark soy
 sauce

**1.** Wash and soak the mushrooms in 1½ cups of warm water for at least 2 hours, or until they are soft. Squeeze the mushrooms dry; strain and reserve the liquid. Cut off and discard the stems and leave the caps whole.

**2.** Combine the mushroom caps and the reserved mushroom liquid in a saucepan. Bring the liquid to a boil and skim off the scum. Add the oil and simmer over very low heat for 1 hour.

**3.** Add the sugar and soy sauce to the mushrooms. Continue cooking until the sauce is reduced to 2 or 3 tablespoons. Serve the braised mushrooms as an appetizer or add to other stir-fried vegetables.

 VEGETABLES 143

# SEASONED PRESSED BEAN CURD

*Makes 1 pound*

*S*easoned Pressed Bean Curd is an excellent meat substitute; I have used it in Vegetarian Spring Rolls (page 204). You can get it in oriental markets or you can make your own.

**1 pound fresh firm or super-firm bean curd**

### Marinade
**1½ cups water**
**½ cup soy sauce**
**1 star anise (8 pods)**
**2 tablespoons sugar**
**½ teaspoon kosher salt**

*1.* Wrap the bean curd in a layer of cheesecloth. Put in a shallow dish and cover with a small, flat baking pan. Place a heavy weight, about 5 pounds, on top and allow the bean curd to sit overnight or at least 8 hours in the refrigerator. Discard the accumulated water.

*2.* In a small saucepan, combine the marinade ingredients and bring to a boil. Turn the heat to low and simmer for 10 minutes.

*3.* Add the bean curd; the marinade should cover it completely. Cover the saucepan and simmer for 20 minutes. Be careful not to let the liquid boil or the pressed bean curd will become spongy. Remove saucepan from the heat and let cool. Leave the bean curd in the marinade overnight. It is now ready to use.

*Note:* For a more intensely flavored taste, slice or shred the pressed bean curd following the directions of the recipe you are using. Then place the slices back in the marinade for several hours before proceeding with the recipe. Store the pressed bean curd in the refrigerator, in a covered container, for up to 2 weeks.

# PEKING SWEET-AND-SOUR CABBAGE

*T*his is a popular, simple and delicious way to cook cabbage. It tastes best if prepared a day in advance, is allowed to marinate in the refrigerator, and then is served, either at room temperature or hot. It's a great dish to serve when entertaining large groups or to serve as a salad in a Western meal.

*1 small head green cabbage*

**Sauce**
*2½ tablespoons sugar*
*½ teaspoon cornstarch*
*2 tablespoons soy sauce*
*2 tablespoons distilled white vinegar*

*4 tablespoons corn oil*
*1 garlic clove, slightly crushed with a cleaver and peeled*
*¼ cup thinly sliced carrots and/or sweet or medium-hot green or red chili peppers, cut into 1-inch cubes*
*1 teaspoon kosher salt, or to taste*

*1.* Cut the cabbage into 8 equal wedges. Cut away and discard the core. Separate the leaves in the center of each wedge and cut into 1-inch squares. Cut the remaining leaves at the outside of each wedge into 1-inch squares. Separate the leaves and sprinkle with a little cold water.

*2.* Combine the sauce ingredients in a small bowl and place it near the stove.

*3.* Heat a wok over moderate heat until hot, then add the oil. When the oil is hot, add the garlic, stir-fry until it is lightly browned, then remove and discard it.

*4.* Add the carrots and/or chili peppers to the hot oil. Stir and add the cabbage. Add salt. Stir-fry the ingredients over high heat for a few seconds, then lower the heat to medium and continue to stir-fry until the cabbage is tender, crisp and translucent, about 2 to 3 minutes.

*5.* Add the sauce to the wok and stir-fry until ingredients are thoroughly coated. Serve hot or at room temperature.

# BRAISED CHINESE CABBAGE WITH CHESTNUTS

*Serves 4*

*I*n this dish, chestnuts (real chestnuts, not water chestnuts) enhance the sweetness of the cabbage. Prepare this in the fall, when chestnuts are in season; when no chestnuts are to be found, try braising the Chinese cabbage by itself.

*¼ pound fresh chestnuts*
*3 tablespoons corn oil*
*1 pound Chinese cabbage, cut into 1 × 2-inch pieces*
*1 teaspoon kosher salt*
*2 tablespoons soy sauce*
*¼ teaspoon sugar*
*¼ cup Chicken Broth (page 155)*

**1.** With a paring knife, cut an **X** on the flat side of each chestnut, then boil in water for 10 minutes. Remove a few at a time from the hot water and, using a sharp knife, shell and peel the chestnuts starting at the **X**. There should be about ½ cup nut meats.

**2.** Heat a wok over medium heat until hot and add the oil. Add the cabbage and stir-fry until it is coated with oil. Add the salt, soy sauce and sugar, and stir for a few seconds. Add the chestnuts and broth, cover and simmer for about 10 minutes, or until the cabbage is soft and the chestnuts are cooked. Serve hot.

# STIR-FRIED SPINACH

*Serves 4*

*S*tir-fried spinach is delicious, warm or at room temperature. You can also substitute romaine lettuce or watercress.

*1 pound fresh spinach*
*3 tablespoons corn oil*
*1 garlic clove, lightly crushed with a cleaver and peeled*

**1.** Remove the tough stems from the spinach. Rinse several times in warm water until sand is removed. (Warm water is more effective than cold in cleaning the leaves of sand.) Drain and shake several times to remove most of the water.

1 teaspoon kosher salt,
  or to taste
1/2 teaspoon sugar
1 teaspoon oriental
  sesame oil
  (optional)

**2.** Heat a wok over high heat until very hot. Add the oil and then the garlic. Stir the garlic quickly to release its flavor, being careful not to let it burn, since burned garlic gives an undesirable, harsh flavor. Remove and discard.

**3.** Add the spinach and stir-fry quickly to mix with the oil. Add the salt and sugar, and stir-fry until the spinach just wilts, about 30 seconds. Stir in the sesame oil. Remove the spinach with a pair of tongs or chopsticks, draining off the liquid into the wok to be discarded. Serve hot or at room temperature.

# DEEP-FRIED BEAN CURD

*Makes 24 1 × 1¾ × ¼-inch slices*

When bean curd is deep-fried, its texture changes from soft and custard-like to firm and spongy; its taste, always subtle, is more defined. It is then used as an ingredient in stir-fried dishes such as Buddha's Delight (page 148), or served hot with Hoisin Sauce (page 31) as a dip.

1 pound firm bean
  curd
2 cups corn oil, for
  deep-frying

**1.** Cut the bean curd crosswise into ¼-inch slabs. Cut each slab into quarters. Rinse and dry on paper towels.

**2.** Heat a wok and add the oil. When the oil is very hot, about 400° F., carefully slide the bean curd into it. Stand back a bit, since the oil will splatter. Deep-fry the bean curd, stirring and turning it with a pair of tongs or chopsticks, until golden, about 4 or 5 minutes. Remove the slices from the hot oil with a strainer and drain on paper towels. Deep-fried bean curd can be stored, covered, in the refrigerator for 2 to 3 days.

# BUDDHA'S DELIGHT

*Serves 4*

In China, this is a favorite vegetarian dish. A complete meal, it is a delightful combination of fresh vegetables, dried ingredients, cellophane noodles and soybean products. Prepare this dish in advance; it gets better when the flavors have time to blend.

*5 large dried black mushrooms*
*1 cup warm water*
*2 ounces cellophane noodles*
*4 tablespoons corn oil*
*12 slices Deep-Fried Bean Curd (page 147)*
*¾ cup sliced carrots*
*½ pound Chinese cabbage*
*1 teaspoon kosher salt, or to taste*
*2 teaspoons sugar*
*1 cup sliced bamboo shoots*
*1 tablespoon tree ears, soaked and washed*
*2 to 3 tablespoons soy sauce*
*1 cup Vegetable Broth (page 159) or water*

**1.** Soak the mushrooms in warm water for 30 minutes. Remove the stems, and cut the caps into quarters. Strain and reserve the soaking liquid. Soak the noodles for 15 minutes in warm water, then cut into 4-inch lengths. (It is easier to cut them when they are soft.)

**2.** Heat a wok over medium heat until moderately hot. Add 2 tablespoons of oil and, after the oil is hot, add the bean curd and mushrooms. Stir-fry gently for 2 minutes, then transfer to a bowl.

**3.** Add remaining 2 tablespoons of oil to the wok, allow the oil to heat, then add the carrots and cabbage. Stir-fry until the cabbage is coated with oil, then sprinkle on the salt and sugar. Stir-fry for a few minutes, then add the cellophane noodles, bamboo shoots and tree ears. Stir-fry for a few more minutes, then add the bean curd, soy sauce, broth and reserved mushroom water. Bring to a boil and cover the wok. Turn the heat to very low and simmer for about 20 minutes, or until the cabbage is tender. Taste for salt. Serve hot.

# STIR-FRIED BROCCOLI

*T*his is a basic stir-fry recipe for nonleafy vegetables such as cauliflower, zucchini, squash, carrots or broccoli. Broccoli is a bit more complicated because it must be properly trimmed and cut. (See step 1, below.) Preparation of the other vegetables is simple: cut them into bite-size pieces. All will have a fresh, lightly cooked taste that is a widely admired characteristic of Chinese cuisine.

*1 bunch broccoli*
*2 tablespoons corn oil*
*1 teaspoon kosher salt,*
*    or to taste*
*½ teaspoon sugar*
*3 tablespoons water*
*1 tablespoon soy sauce*

**1.** Using a sharp paring knife, start from the bottom of each broccoli stem and peel back the tough outer skin until you reach the flowerets. (The broccoli will peel more easily if it is at room temperature.) Cut the skin away at the base of the flowerets and discard. Separate the flowerets and their stems from the large stem. Cut the flowerets into small, bite-size pieces. Cut the stems into 1½ × ½ × ½-inch pieces. Put the broccoli pieces in a colander and rinse. Shake several times to remove water.

**2.** Heat a wok over medium heat until hot. Add the oil and, when the oil is hot, add the broccoli. Stir-fry about 1 minute. Sprinkle on the salt and sugar, stir and add the water. Cover quickly, turn the heat to medium-low and cook until the stalk pieces are bright green, about 2 minutes. Stir several times during the cooking. Taste for salt, then transfer broccoli to a serving platter, drizzle on the soy sauce and serve.

# STIR-FRIED SNOW PEAS WITH GINGER

*Serves 4*

*T*he snow peas in this simple recipe are enhanced with minced ginger. For a more elaborate dish, serve Braised Dried Mushrooms (page 143) on a bed of these snow peas. Fresh snow peas do not stir-fry evenly, so blanch them first, then stir-fry them.

*1 pound fresh snow peas, washed and strings removed*
*2 tablespoons corn oil*
*½ teaspoon finely minced fresh ginger*
*1 teaspoon kosher salt*
*½ teaspoon sugar*

*1.* Bring 2 quarts of water to a boil. Add the snow peas and cook for 1 minute, or until the peas are tender yet crisp. Drain and immediately rinse with cold water to cool them.

*2.* Heat a wok until moderately hot and add the oil. Add the ginger, stir and then add the snow peas, salt and sugar. Stir for a few seconds, or until the snow peas are heated through. Serve hot.

*Note:* String beans can be substituted for snow peas. Remove the strings from the beans, break in half and parboil for 5 minutes.

# SOUPS AND HOT POTS

**U**nlike Western meals, soup is not served as a first course in China. Traditionally, it is served simultaneously with other dishes in a daily meal, almost as a beverage. Usually it is a clear chicken broth with some vegetables and a little meat. On the other hand, when soup is included in a banquet it is served midway through many courses and is a rich broth with many, often expensive ingredients. Feel free to adapt Chinese soups to your own style of eating. In fact, try substituting Fishball Soup (page 155) for gefilte fish or have Corn Flower Soup (page 162) as a light supper with bread and a salad. Wonton Soup (page 156) or Sizzling Rice Soup (page 154) also makes a satisfying yet light one-dish meal.

A hot pot, or fire pot, is a festive meal designed for a cold winter night. For centuries Chinese have used hot pots—ornate brass containers fueled with burning charcoal—to cook many ingredients right at the table, like a Chinese fondue. Diners sit around the hot pot both for warmth and to dip their food into the boiling broth. Many ingredients that can be used in a hot pot, and included is a recipe that will give you the authentic experience while remaining kosher.

Today, cooking with charcoal or alcohol at the table is impractical, so use an electric wok or electric hot pot. Though not as charming as a charcoal hot pot, they maintain a constant heat without producing fumes. The electric hot pot can be purchased in Chinatown grocery stores.

| Recipes | | Prepare Ahead | Serving Temperature |
|---|---|---|---|
| Hot-and-Sour Soup | Spicy | Yes | Hot |
| Sizzling Rice Soup | | No | Very Hot |
| Chicken Broth | | Yes | Hot |
| Fishball Soup | | Yes | Hot |
| Wonton Soup | | Yes | Hot |
| Fish Broth | | Yes | Hot |
| Winter Melon Soup | | Yes | Hot |
| Hot Pot | Spicy | No | Hot |
| Vegetable Broth | | Yes | Hot |
| Egg Drop Soup | | Yes | Hot |
| Bean Curd and Fish Chowder | | No | Hot |
| Corn Flower Soup | | Yes | Hot |
| Watercress and Meatball Soup | | No | Hot |

# HOT-AND-SOUR SOUP

*Serves 8*

This pungent soup from northern China has become one of the more popular dishes in Chinese restaurants. White pepper and vinegar give it its sour, peppery taste. The soup is hearty, filling and easy to make.

### Marinade

*½ teaspoon cornstarch*
*1 tablespoon water*

*½ cup finely shredded raw chicken breast*
*2 tablespoons tree ears*
*20 tiger lily buds*
*2 cakes soft bean curd (3 × 4 × 1½ inches)*
*6 cups Chicken Broth (page 155)*
*3 tablespoons soy sauce*
*3 tablespoons distilled white vinegar, or to taste*
*½ to 1 teaspoon white pepper, or to taste*
*2 tablespoons cornstarch mixed with ¼ cup water*
*2 extra-large eggs, beaten lightly*
*2 teaspoons oriental sesame oil*
*2 tablespoons chopped scallions*

**1.** Combine the marinade ingredients in a small bowl with the chicken and set aside.

**2.** Soak the tree ears and tiger lily buds separately in warm water for 30 minutes. Wash and rinse the tree ears several times. Discard the water and cut the tree ears into small pieces. Wash and rinse the lily buds several times. Stack buds in a neat pile lengthwise, cut off the hard knots, if any, at the base of their stems and cut the pile in half crosswise. Place the tree ears and lily buds separately on a work platter.

**3.** Gently slice the bean curd into thin slabs, then cut the slabs into thin julienne strips. Place the strips on the work platter with the tree ears and lily buds.

**4.** In a large pot bring the broth to a boil. Turn the heat to a simmer and add the chicken. Stir immediately to separate the pieces, then add the tree ears and lily buds, stirring once or twice. Stir in the soy sauce, vinegar and pepper. Taste for seasonings and add more if necessary. Give the cornstarch mixture a stir and add to the simmering pot while stirring constantly. Continue to simmer and stir until the soup thickens, about 1 to 2 minutes.

**5.** Add the bean curd and bring the soup to a boil. Stir once gently, then turn off the heat and slowly pour in the eggs in a thin stream, stirring in a circular motion. Drizzle on the sesame oil and garnish with the scallions. Serve hot.

# SIZZLING RICE SOUP

$T$his is a showpiece recipe—a dish that tastes, looks and *sounds* good. With guests seated, you bring a platter of fried rice patties and a cook-and-serve pot of soup to the table, then slide the very hot patties into the simmering soup. The sizzling sound made when the patties meet the soup is guaranteed to bring applause. But timing is the key. Two tasks—the heating of the rice patties (which can be made in advance) and the making of the soup—proceed simultaneously, so that they are both completed at precisely the same time. It's easy and it's fun!

---

**6 dried black mushrooms**

### Coating

**1 teaspoon cornstarch**
**¼ teaspoon sugar**

**½ boneless chicken breast or 6 ounces boneless turkey breast, diced**
**6 to 8 Rice Patties (page 171)**
**6 cups Chicken Broth (page 155)**
**1 tablespoon rice wine**
**2 tablespoons soy sauce**
**¼ cup diced bamboo shoots**
**3 water chestnuts**
**½ cup frozen peas, thawed**
**Kosher salt**
**White pepper**

*1.* Soak the mushrooms in warm water until soft, about 30 minutes. Remove the stems and dice caps. Preheat the oven to 475° F.

*2.* Mix the coating ingredients, combine with the diced chicken or turkey and set aside.

*3.* Put the Rice Patties on a heatproof serving plate and heat in the oven for about 8 minutes. Immediately proceed to next step.

*4.* Put the broth in a large flameproof bowl or a cook-and-serve pot. Place the pot on the stove and bring broth to a boil. Reduce heat to low; add the wine, soy sauce, bamboo shoots, water chestnuts and mushrooms. Simmer the soup for 5 minutes, then add the chicken or turkey. Simmer for 3 minutes more. Add the peas. Add salt and pepper to taste. This entire step should take 8 minutes, finishing just as the Rice Patties are heated through. (This simultaneous finish ensures that both patties and soup will be at their hottest temperatures.)

*5.* Remove the Rice Patties from the oven. To retain heat, transfer the hot patties to a hot platter. Carry the hot Rice Patties and hot soup to the dinner table. Gently slide the patties from their platter into the soup. Enjoy the sizzle, then serve immediately.

# CHICKEN BROTH

*P*ure, rich chicken broth is the basis for most Chinese soups. It is also used in small quantities to flavor many dishes, so it is worth the time it takes to prepare your own. Make a large amount and freeze some in ice-cube trays so you have easy access to small amounts.

*1 stewing fowl, about 5 pounds, or bones and carcasses of 2 chickens*
*3½ quarts cold water, or enough to cover*
*1 scallion*
*1 slice fresh ginger, ½ inch thick*
*2 tablespoons rice wine*
*2 teaspoons kosher salt, or to taste*

**1.** Rinse the chicken. Put the chicken or carcasses in a large heavy pot and add the water. Bring to a boil and remove any foam that collects on top. Add the scallion, ginger slice, wine and salt.

**2.** Turn the heat to very low, cover and simmer gently for 3 hours. If the stock is maintained at a low simmer, it will remain clear; however, once it is allowed to boil, it becomes cloudy. Pour the broth through a fine sieve, chill and then remove the fat. Freeze or store in the refrigerator.

# FISHBALL SOUP

*T*his soup has a wonderful clear, clean taste.

*3 cups water*
*24 Stir-fried Fishballs (page 124)*
*2 tablespoons soy sauce*
*2 teaspoons minced scallions*
*Kosher salt*
*White pepper*
*1 teaspoon oriental sesame oil*

**1.** Put the water into a 2-quart saucepan and bring to a boil. Add the fishballs and turn the heat to very low. Simmer gently for 4 to 5 minutes, or until the fishballs are heated through.

**2.** Add the soy sauce and scallions, and season to taste with salt and pepper. Add the sesame oil and serve hot.

# Wonton Soup

**W**onton soup is a Chinese classic, best when homemade. Cooked egg noodles can be combined with the wontons for a more substantial meal.

*7 cups Chicken Broth
(page 155)*
*Kosher salt and white
pepper to taste*
*1 teaspoon oriental
sesame oil*
*½ recipe freshly boiled
hot Wontons, about
40 (page 194)*
*¼ pound boiled egg
noodles (optional)*
*Soy sauce to taste*
*¾ cup sliced
Cantonese Roast
Veal (page 97;
optional)*
*2 tablespoons minced
scallions*

**1.** Bring the broth to a boil in a large pot. Add the salt, pepper and sesame oil to taste.

**2.** Distribute several wontons in equal number (and boiled noodles, if desired) among individual soup bowls. To each bowl add a dash of white pepper, a little soy sauce, a few slices of Cantonese Roast Veal and a pinch of minced scallions. Ladle the hot broth over the contents of each bowl and serve immediately.

# Fish Broth

**F**ish broth is easy to make and good to have on hand, because it is used in several fish dishes in this book. The Chinese usually substitute chicken broth, but I find that the fish dishes are tastier if a well-seasoned fish broth is used instead.

*2 fish heads—sea bass,
yellow pike, or red
snapper (ask your
fishmonger to save
the heads for you)*

**1.** Rinse the fish heads in cold water and set aside. Heat a large saucepan over medium heat until hot. Add the oil and ginger, and stir-fry for a few seconds to release the flavor.

1 tablespoon corn oil
1 large slice fresh
   ginger
5 cups cold water
1 scallion, cut into
   2-inch lengths
1 tablespoon rice wine
2 teaspoons kosher
   salt, or to taste

**2.** Add the water and fish heads and bring to a boil, then remove any scum that rises to the surface with a slotted spoon. Turn the heat to low, add the scallion and simmer for 30 minutes.

**3.** Add the wine and salt. Strain the broth through a sieve, and store in the refrigerator for up to 3 or 4 days or freeze it for future use.

# WINTER MELON SOUP

### Serves 8

*I*f winter melon is not available, substitute peeled cucumber and shorten the cooking time.

3 dried black
   mushrooms
1½ pounds winter
   melon
5 cups Chicken Broth
   (page 155)
½ cup diced bamboo
   shoots
Kosher salt to taste
Dash of white pepper
½ cup diced uncooked
   chicken breast
2 tablespoons
   cornstarch mixed
   with 3 tablespoons
   water
1 extra-large egg
   white, beaten
   lightly

**1.** Soak mushrooms in warm water for 30 minutes. Discard stems and dice caps. Cut off the rind and remove and discard seeds and pith from the winter melon.

**2.** Place broth in a 5-quart saucepan and bring to a boil. Reduce heat and add the winter melon. Simmer gently until the melon becomes almost translucent, about 5 minutes. Add the bamboo shoots and mushrooms. Stir and add salt and pepper to taste. Simmer for another 5 minutes.

**3.** Add the chicken and stir. Stir the cornstarch mixture and slowly add it to the simmering broth, stirring until the soup thickens. Taste for salt.

**4.** Turn off the heat and slowly add the beaten egg white while stirring in a circular motion. Serve hot in individual bowls.

# HOT POT

**A** hot pot is a traditional winter meal first introduced to northern China by the Mongols. Cooked at the table by your guests in a special fire pot, it is the centerpiece of an entertaining and festive evening of dining.

*1 pound boneless chicken breast*
*1 pound boneless beefsteak*
*½ pound chicken livers, large ones cut into halves or quarters*
*2 ounces cellophane noodles*
*1 teaspoon kosher salt*
*¼ teaspoon white pepper*
*2 teaspoons rice wine*
*2 teaspoons corn oil*
*36 Wontons (page 194), cooked*
*1½ pounds Chinese cabbage heart, bok choy or spinach, cut into 3 × 1½-inch pieces*
*2 Steamed Egg-Crêpe Rolls (page 54)*

## Sauce

*4 extra-large eggs*
*1 teaspoon sugar*
*6 tablespoons soy sauce*
*4 tablespoons rice wine*
*2 tablespoons minced scallions*

**1.** Freeze the chicken, thaw until semifrozen, then cut into thin 2-inch squares. Freeze the steak, thaw until semifrozen, then cut into thin 2-inch squares. Sprinkle the chicken livers with salt and broil for 2 minutes on each side; cut into halves or quarters if the pieces are large. Soak the cellophane noodles in hot water for 20 minutes until soft; cut into 4-inch lengths.

**2.** Arrange the chicken, beef and livers on separate platters, the pieces slightly overlapping each other in an attractive arrangement. Sprinkle on the salt, pepper, wine and corn oil. Cover with plastic wrap and refrigerate until ready to serve. Put the Wontons, cellophane noodles, and greens into separate serving bowls. Cut the Egg-Crêpe Rolls into diagonal ¼-inch thick slices and arrange attractively on a serving platter.

**3.** To make the sauce, beat the eggs thoroughly, then mix in the remaining ingredients. Pour the sauce into 6 individual rice bowls, to be used as a dip before or after cooking the raw ingredients. Put a bowl of sauce at each place setting.

**4.** Place a traditional charcoal fire pot, high-powered electric wok or electric skillet on the dining table. (Though less romantic, the electric pots are cleaner, safer and more reliable.) Pour in the broth and bring to a boil, then lower the heat. The broth should be kept at a continuous gentle boil during the meal while cooking the raw ingredients.

2 tablespoons oriental
 sesame oil
1 teaspoon Hot Chili
 Sauce (page 31), or
 to taste (optional)
10 cups Chicken Broth
 (page 155)

**5.** Place the platters and bowls of ingredients on the table around the fire pot. Each person takes a few pieces of the raw ingredients with chopsticks or fondue forks and dips them into the boiling broth until cooked to the desired doneness. The guests use the sauce as a dip before or after cooking. The whole meal proceeds in this way, with each guest alternating cooking with eating. Generally, the meat is consumed first, then the vegetables and remaining ingredients, however there is no set rule; the ingredients may be consumed in any order desired and the quantity of ingredients can vary according to the appetite of the diners. At the end of the meal, ladle the broth, now rich with varied tastes, into individual soup bowls and serve.

# VEGETABLE BROTH

*Makes 1 quart*

$A$lways keep some of this broth on hand. It adds flavor to dishes in which you cannot use chicken or fish broth; it is also delicious on its own.

3 tablespoons corn oil
1 medium onion, diced
3 cups chopped green
 cabbage, in 1-inch
 cubes
1 carrot, sliced thin
3 fresh mushrooms,
 quartered
1 small potato, diced
5 cups water
1 teaspoon kosher salt
White pepper

**1.** Heat a large saucepan until moderately hot. Add the oil and stir-fry the onion for 1 minute. Add the remaining vegetables and continue to stir-fry for 3 to 4 minutes.

**2.** Add the water to the pot and bring to a boil. With a slotted spoon, remove any scum that rises to the surface. Turn the heat to low and simmer partially covered for 1½ hours. Add salt and pepper to taste. Serve the broth as it is; or strain and store it in the refrigerator for a few days, or freeze it for future use.

**Note:** Other vegetables, such as celery, zucchini and cauliflower, can be used in addition or substituted.

# EGG DROP SOUP

T his is probably the most familiar Chinese soup, and also the easiest to prepare.

**5 cups Chicken Broth (page 155)**
**1½ teaspoons kosher salt, or to taste**
**1 tablespoon soy sauce**
**1 tablespoon rice wine**
**2 tablespoons cornstarch dissolved in ½ cup water**
**2 extra-large eggs, well beaten**
**2 teaspoons oriental sesame oil**
**2 teaspoons finely chopped scallions**

**1.** In a large saucepan bring the broth to a boil. Add the salt, soy sauce and wine, reduce the heat and simmer the broth for a few seconds. Stir the cornstarch mixture and gradually add it to the broth, stirring until the broth thickens. Bring the broth back to a boil.

**2.** Turn off the heat and immediately but slowly add the beaten eggs in a thin stream, stirring gently and constantly in a circular motion. That's it! Ladle the soup into individual bowls and garnish with the sesame oil and chopped scallions. Serve immediately.

# BEAN CURD AND FISH CHOWDER

A fish stock is the base for this soup. Ask your fishmonger for fish heads to make the broth. The delicate flavor of the broth is enhanced with a dash of sesame oil and a garnish of coriander and scallions.

**Fish Stock**
**2 fish heads—sea bass, yellow pike or any non-oily fish**
**1 tablespoon corn oil**

**1.** To make the stock, rinse the fish heads in cold water and set aside. Heat a large saucepan over medium heat until hot. Add the corn oil and ginger, and stir-fry a few seconds to release the flavor. Add the cold water and fish heads and bring

*1 slice fresh ginger
about the size of a
quarter*
*5 cups cold water*
*1 scallion*
*1 tablespoon rice wine*
*Kosher salt*

### Marinade
*½ teaspoon cornstarch*
*½ teaspoon kosher
salt*
*Dash of white pepper*

*½ pound gray sole,
white snapper or
scrod fillet, cut into
¼-inch cubes*
*1 teaspoon kosher salt,
or to taste*
*⅛ teaspoon white
pepper, or to taste*
*1 tablespoon
cornstarch mixed
with 3 tablespoons
water*
*1 pound soft bean
curd, cut into
½-inch cubes*
*2 teaspoons oriental
sesame oil*
*1 tablespoon minced
fresh coriander*
*1 tablespoon minced
scallions, green part
only*
*1 slice ginger, shredded
very fine*

to a boil, then remove the scum. Turn the heat to low, add the scallion and simmer for 30 minutes. Add the wine and salt to taste. Strain the broth through a sieve and set aside.

**2.** Combine the marinade with the fish cubes and set aside.

**3.** Pour the fish stock into a 2-quart saucepan. Bring to a boil and add the salt and white pepper. Give the cornstarch mixture a stir and slowly add to the boiling soup while stirring gently. Add the fish cubes and bean curd. Turn down the heat and simmer until the soup thickens, stirring gently once or twice. Ladle soup into individual soup bowls and garnish each with a drop of sesame oil, a pinch of coriander and scallion, and a few shreds of ginger. Serve hot.

# CORN FLOWER SOUP

*H*ere is a nourishing, slightly sweet soup that is very satisfying on a cold winter's night. All you need are Scallion Pancakes (page 201) and Cucumber Salad (page 43) for a light, delicious meal.

*2 extra-large eggs*
*½ boneless chicken breast, shredded fine*

**Marinade**

*1 teaspoon cornstarch*
*½ teaspoon kosher salt*

*2½ cups Chicken Broth (page 155)*
*1 17-ounce can cream-style corn*
*Kosher salt and white pepper*
*2 tablespoons minced smoked turkey, for garnish (optional)*

*1.* Break 1 of the eggs and combine ½ of the egg white with the shredded chicken. (Save the rest of the egg for later use.) Add the cornstarch and salt. Using a pair of chopsticks or your hands, mix the chicken thoroughly with the marinade. Set aside. (If prepared several hours in advance, refrigerate.)

*2.* Combine the remaining egg white and yolk with the whole egg and beat slightly. Set aside.

*3.* Bring the broth and the corn to a boil. Turn the heat to a low simmer and add the salt and pepper to taste. Add the chicken while stirring vigorously to separate the pieces and continue to simmer until done. The chicken is cooked as soon as it turns white; do not overcook. Turn off the heat and pour the beaten egg into the soup in a thin stream while stirring in a circular motion. Taste for salt. Serve the soup in individual bowls garnished with smoked turkey.

# WATERCRESS AND MEATBALL SOUP

*Serves 6*

**A** clear chicken broth containing a leafy vegetable and meat is frequently served as the beverage for a home-style meal. Spinach, bok choy or Chinese cabbage can be substituted for watercress, and thin slices of uncooked chicken or turkey can be substituted for the meatballs. Serve this instead of matzoh-ball soup at your next holiday meal.

### Meatballs
*½ pound ground veal or turkey*
*2 tablespoons finely minced water chestnuts*
*½ teaspoon kosher salt*
*1 tablespoon soy sauce*
*½ teaspoon sugar*
*1 teaspoon rice wine*
*⅛ teaspoon white pepper*
*1 tablespoon cornstarch mixed with 3 tablespoons water*

*2 bunches fresh watercress*
*6 cups Chicken Broth (page 155)*
*Kosher salt to taste*
*White pepper to taste*

*1.* Combine the ingredients for the meatballs and stir in one direction until well blended. Wet the palms of your hands, place a dab of meat mixture between both palms and roll a small meatball about 1 inch in diameter. Repeat until all the mixture is used. There should be about 25 meatballs.

*2.* Rinse the watercress; pinch off and discard the larger stems, if any.

*3.* In a 3-quart saucepan, bring the broth to a boil. Turn the heat to a simmer and add the meatballs. Stir once or twice. Bring the broth back to a boil; taste for salt and pepper and add if necessary. Add the watercress and, as soon as it wilts, serve the soup.

# RICE AND NOODLES

*T*wo kinds of rice are commonly used in Chinese cooking. Long-grain rice is used for cooking the plain rice served with daily meals at home and in Chinese restaurants. Glutinous rice is used as a stuffing. When it is ground into flour, it is used for making sweet pastries.

For the Chinese the sweet fragrance of rice cooking is comparable to the Westerner's delight in the aroma of bread baking. Plain boiled rice is the center of a Chinese meal. Along with the rice, several well-seasoned dishes are served and as one eats the flavorful sauces of these dishes mingle with the rice.

The Chinese have created many different kinds of noodles, made from a variety of ingredients. There are noodles made from wheat, rice and even beans; and their texture, color and taste vary accordingly. Some are chewy, others are slick and smooth, while still others are transparent and soft.

| Recipes | | Prepare Ahead | Serving Temperature |
|---|---|---|---|
| Boiled Rice | | Yes | Hot |
| Rice Congee | | Yes | Hot |
| Fried Rice | | Yes | Hot |
| Rice Sticks Singapore Style | | No | Hot |
| Rice Patties | | Yes | Hot |
| Egg Sheets | | Yes | |
| Two-Sided Brown Noodles | | Yes | Hot |
| Sesame Noodles | Spicy hot | Yes | Room temp. |
| Noodles with Brown Sauce | | Yes | Hot |
| Cold Noodles with Scallion Sauce | Spicy hot | Yes | Room temp. |
| Cold Noodles with Ginger Sauce | | Yes | Room temp. |
| Roast Veal Lo Mein | | Yes | Hot |
| Vegetarian Lo Mein | | Yes | Hot |
| Ants on the Tree | Spicy hot | Yes | Hot |
| Rice Noodle Sheets | | Yes | |
| Beef with Wide Rice Noodles | | No | Hot |

# BOILED RICE

$P$lain, boiled rice is the main dish of an everyday meal in China, with other dishes adding flavor and variety to the primary fare. This is less true in the West, where prosperity has made variety affordable. Nevertheless, most Chinese feel a meal is incomplete without a serving of rice. Long-grain rice is preferred because it holds together, which makes it easy to eat with chopsticks, and it can be cooked to the texture of an individual's preference. Leftover rice is easily reheated in a microwave oven or in a steamer. It's also ideal for Fried Rice (page 169). Instant rice, or any rice that has been processed, will not stick together and does not have the texture or flavor the Chinese prize.

---

*2 cups long-grain rice*
*3 cups cold water*

**1.** Rinse the rice several times and drain. Place in a heavy saucepan with a tight-fitting lid and add the cold water. Put the uncovered saucepan over high heat and bring to a boil. Boil for 4 or 5 minutes, or until the water is absorbed by the rice.

**2.** Cover the saucepan, turn the heat to very low and cook for 20 minutes. Turn off the heat, but do not remove the pan from the stove or lift the cover for at least another 10 minutes. When ready, fluff the rice with wet chopsticks and serve in individual rice bowls.

---

**Note:** 1 cup of raw rice makes 3 cups cooked rice. For larger quantities, for each additional cup of rice, add 1 cup of water.

# RICE CONGEE

*R*ice Congee is rice cooked in water or broth to the consistency of gruel. It is usually served as a Chinese breakfast, but can be offered anytime as a light meal and is particularly satisfying and warming in winter. The congee is first cooked plain, and can be served plain, or other ingredients such as fish or cooked beef or chicken can be added. The plain version and two variations are given here. Since Rice Congee is bland in taste, texture and color, side dishes of highly seasoned condiments, such as salty preserved vegetables, roasted peanuts, salted fish or preserved eggs are usual accompaniments. At the table, guests mix these condiments into the hot congee.

*10 cups water*
*1 cup long-grain rice*
*2 teaspoons kosher salt*

**Plain Rice Congee:**   Pour the water into a 3-quart pot and add the rice. Bring to a boil, stir thoroughly once, then turn the heat to very low and simmer gently, covered, for about 2 hours. Stir occasionally to be sure the rice does not stick to the pot. When the congee is done, add the salt and stir. The mixture will be a thick, smooth gruel with barely visible cracked rice kernels, like cooked oatmeal.

**Chicken Congee:**   Shred and marinate ½ boneless chicken breast in 1 teaspoon cornstarch and ½ teaspoon kosher salt. Bring the plain congee to a simmer and add the chicken, stirring constantly. Simmer for a minute or two, or until the chicken turns white. Remove the congee from the stove and ladle into large, individual soup bowls. Garnish with a little shredded lettuce, minced scallions, minced fresh coriander, finely shredded ginger and a drop of oriental sesame oil.

**Fish Congee:**   Cut very thin slices of ½-pound yellow pike, gray sole or sea bass fillet and season with ⅛ teaspoon white pepper, 1 teaspoon kosher salt and ½ teaspoon oriental sesame oil. Place the seasoned fish slices in the bottom of individual serving bowls. Bring the plain congee to a boil, then ladle it over the fish. The hot congee will cook the fish in the bowls. Garnish with a little shredded lettuce, minced scallions, minced fresh coriander, finely shredded ginger and a drop of oriental sesame oil.

# FRIED RICE

### Serves 4 to 6

*F*ried Rice must be made with cold, leftover rice; when cooking rice, make enough for this dish the following day. This is a great way to use leftover meat or chicken. You can also vary the vegetables. Fried Rice can be kept warm in a low oven or reheated very successfully. If prepared in advance, cook the peas separately and add just before serving.

**4 cups cold cooked rice**
**5 tablespoons corn oil**
**¾ cup diced cooked chicken, veal, turkey or beef**
**¼ cup chopped celery**
**1 teaspoon kosher salt, or to taste**
**3 tablespoons soy sauce**
**2 extra-large eggs**
**¼ cup chopped scallions**
**¾ cup frozen peas, thawed**
**½ cup shredded lettuce or bean sprouts (optional)**

*1.* In a bowl, separate the grains of rice with your hands and set aside. Heat a wok over medium heat until hot. Add 2 tablespoons oil and swirl to coat wok. Add the meat and stir-fry for a few seconds or until heated through. Add the celery and continue stir-frying for another minute. Dish out and set aside.

*2.* Reheat the wok until hot and add 2 more tablespoons oil and the rice. Stir-fry the rice until it is thoroughly heated, about 4 to 5 minutes. Return the cooked ingredients to the wok; add the salt and soy sauce. Stir several times to blend, then make a well in the center and add the remaining tablespoon of oil. Place eggs in well and as the eggs set, stir them into the hot rice. Add the scallions and peas, as well as the lettuce or bean sprouts, if desired. Continue to stir-fry until blended. Taste for salt and serve.

# RICE STICKS
# SINGAPORE STYLE

**Serves 4**

*I*f you like curry, this dish is for you. Usually served in teahouses, it is a favorite of Chinese everywhere.

*1 extra-large egg, well beaten*
*1 medium onion, shredded*
*½ cup shredded green bell peppers*
*½ cup shredded celery or bamboo shoots*
*½ pound dried thin rice sticks*

### Sauce

*1 teaspoon kosher salt*
*1 teaspoon sugar*
*2 tablespoons soy sauce*
*1 cup Chicken Broth (page 155)*

*½ cup corn oil*
*1½ cups Cantonese Roast Veal (page 97) or cooked chicken, cut into matchstick strips*
*1 tablespoon Madras curry powder, or to taste*
*2 scallions, shredded fine*
*Sprigs of fresh coriander, for garnish*

**1.** Heat an 8-inch nonstick or well-cured skillet over medium heat until hot, then coat lightly with a little oil. Add half the egg and tip the pan so the egg spreads in a thin, even layer. As soon as the egg sets and the edges begin to curl, turn the egg over and cook on the other side for a few seconds. Remove the egg from the pan and cool. Cut into thin shreds. Repeat with remaining egg and set aside.

**2.** Place the shredded vegetables separately on a work platter.

**3.** Soak the rice sticks in hot water for a few minutes or until just pliable. Drain.

**4.** Combine the sauce ingredients in a small bowl and place near the stove.

**5.** Heat a wok until hot, but not smoking, and add 3 tablespoons oil. Add the onion and stir-fry for a few seconds. Add the peppers and celery and stir-fry a few seconds more. Add the veal and stir-fry until heated through. With a slotted spoon, remove the ingredients from the wok, leaving as much oil in wok as possible. Set ingredients aside near the stove.

**6.** Reheat the wok and add 3 more tablespoons oil. Stir in the curry and let it sizzle for a few seconds. Add the sauce, then the rice sticks. Lightly toss the rice sticks in the wok until they absorb all the sauce, then add the remaining 2 tablespoons oil around the sides of the wok to prevent the rice sticks from sticking. Return the other cooked ingredients, scallions and egg shreds to the wok, then toss and mix with the rice sticks until blended. Transfer mixture to a warm serving platter and garnish with the coriander sprigs. Serve immediately.

# RICE PATTIES

*Makes 20 patties*

Chinese cuisine has many snacks and this is one of them that's easy to make. They're also the sizzle in Sizzling Rice Soup (page 154).

*2 cups long-grain rice*
*3 cups water*
*2 cups corn oil, for*
  *deep-frying*
*Kosher salt (optional)*

**1.** Rinse the rice several times. Spread it in an even layer over the entire surface of an approximately 12 × 15-inch jelly-roll pan. Slowly add the water. Be sure the grains of rice are touching each other and are evenly distributed. Let stand for 30 minutes. Preheat the oven to 350° F.

**2.** Cover the jelly-roll pan with a large sheet of aluminum foil. Bake for 30 minutes. Remove the foil and turn oven to 300° F. Continue to bake, uncovered, for 1 hour more. Remove the pan from the oven and allow the rice to dry undisturbed overnight.

**3.** The next day, cut the rice into 3-inch squares. Store in an airtight container for up to 2 months until needed.

**4.** When ready to use patties, heat the oil in a wok to about 375° F. Deep-fry the rice patties a few at a time on both sides until they puff up. Sprinkle with salt while hot if they are to be eaten as a snack, or store in an airtight container to be used in Sizzling Rice Soup.

# EGG SHEETS

*Makes 4 sheets, 8 inches in diameter*

*E*gg Sheets are often cut into shreds, to serve as a tasty and colorful garnish, as in Cold Noodles with Scallion Sauce (page 176).

**2 extra-large eggs**
**Pinch of kosher salt**
**1 teaspoon rice wine**
**½ teaspoon corn oil**

**1.** Beat the eggs lightly, then add the salt, wine and oil. Beat again and set aside for 10 minutes.

**2.** Heat an 8-inch skillet over medium heat until hot, then turn the heat to low. Lightly oil the pan. Pour one-fourth of the beaten egg mixture into the pan. Tip the pan around so the egg spreads in a thin even layer. Cook over low heat until the egg sets into a crêpe and, as the edges begin to curl, turn the crêpe over. Cook briefly on the other side. Transfer to a plate.

**3.** Repeat the procedure to make 3 more sheets. Allow to cool, then shred into very fine 2-inch-long strips.

# TWO-SIDED BROWN NOODLES

*Serves 2 to 4*

*T*hese noodles are fried in the form of a cake with a slightly crunchy outside and a soft inside. The noodles are then topped with shredded vegetables, chicken and enough tasty sauce to soak into the noodles. It's a light meal in itself and a real family favorite.

**4 dried black**
   **mushrooms**

### Marinade

**1 tablespoon soy sauce**
**1 teaspoon cornstarch**

**1.** Soak the mushrooms in warm water for 30 minutes. Remove stems and shred caps. Preheat oven to low (200° F).

**2.** Combine marinade ingredients with the chicken in a bowl. Mix with your hands until

1 tablespoon water

1/2 pound boned and
skinned chicken
breast, semifrozen
and shredded
2 cups finely shredded
Chinese cabbage
1/4 cup shredded
bamboo shoots
2 scallions, shredded
1/2 pound fresh or
dried egg noodles
1 1/2 teaspoons kosher
salt
1/2 cup corn oil
1/4 teaspoon sugar

### Sauce
1 cup Chicken Broth
(page 155)
2 tablespoons soy
sauce
1 tablespoon
cornstarch

well coated, then refrigerate until ready to cook.

**3.** Place the shredded ingredients separately on a work platter near the stove.

**4.** Bring a large pot of water to a boil. Separate the noodles as you add them to the boiling water. Stir and cook for 3 minutes, then drain and rinse with cold water. Sprinkle with 1 teaspoon kosher salt and toss.

**5.** Heat a 10-inch skillet over medium heat until hot and add 1/4 cup of the oil. When the oil is hot, spread the noodles evenly in the skillet. Cook without stirring until the bottom turns brown and holds together in the form of a cake, about 4 minutes. Carefully turn the cake over and brown the other side. Transfer to a large, round, warm serving platter. With a pair of scissors, cut the noodle cake into 6 pie-shape pieces (cutting the noodles makes for easier serving). Keep warm in oven.

**6.** Heat a wok over medium heat until hot and add 2 tablespoons of oil. Add the chicken and stir-fry until it turns white, about 3 minutes. Add the mushrooms and stir-fry a few seconds. Transfer to a bowl. Wash out the wok.

**7.** Reheat the wok to medium and add remaining 2 tablespoons of oil. Add the shredded cabbage. Stir and add the remaining 1/2 teaspoon salt and the sugar. Add the bamboo shoots and half the scallions and stir-fry for 2 minutes. Return the chicken and mushrooms to the wok and stir-fry until the chicken is heated through. Make a well in the center of the chicken mixture. Stir the sauce ingredients together and add them to the well. Continue cooking and stirring until the sauce thickens and forms a glaze over the ingredients. Ladle mixture over the warm noodles, garnish with the remaining scallions and serve immediately.

# Sesame Noodles

Sesame noodles are very popular with my students. They are easy to make and can be prepared in advance, making them perfect for a party.

*1 pound fresh or dried
thin egg noodles
1 tablespoon corn oil
1 cucumber*

### Sauce

*2 tablespoons warm
water
3 tablespoons soy
sauce
1 tablespoon distilled
white vinegar
1 tablespoon oriental
sesame oil
2 teaspoons Hot Chili
Sauce (page 32), or
to taste
2 teaspoons sugar
3 tablespoons creamy
peanut butter or
sesame paste*

*1 tablespoon finely
minced garlic
2 tablespoons finely
chopped scallions*

**1.** Bring 2 quarts of water to a boil. Add the noodles, stir and boil for 3 minutes or until tender. Drain the noodles in a colander and rinse with cold water. Shake to remove excess water. Transfer noodles to a serving platter and toss with the corn oil. With a pair of scissors, make several random cuts through the mound of noodles (cutting the long strands makes them easier to serve). Spread the noodles on a serving platter.

**2.** Peel the cucumber, then cut crosswise into 2-inch sections. Place each section flat on a cutting board and cut thin slices from one edge until you reach the seeds, which will be discarded. Rotate the section one-quarter turn and continue to cut thin slices until you reach the seeds. Rotate and slice the 2 remaining sides until the center section containing the seeds is left in a solid piece; discard. Stack the cucumber slices and cut into lengthwise shreds. Continue until all the cucumber is shredded. Chill.

**3.** Combine the sauce ingredients in a bowl by adding the liquid ingredients first, 1 tablespoon at a time, and mixing after each addition until smooth. Continue with thicker ingredients, blending well.

**4.** Just before serving, arrange the shredded cucumber, reserving a little for garnish, on top of the noodles. Stir the garlic and scallions into the sauce, then drizzle half the sauce evenly over all and toss. Garnish with the remaining shredded cucumbers and serve at room temperature. Serve the remaining sauce in a small bowl on the side.

# NOODLES WITH BROWN SAUCE

*Serves 6*

*T*his is a popular noodle dish from northern China. Prepare its tasty sauce in advance, then cook the noodles when you're ready to serve.

*1 cucumber, or 1 cup blanched bean sprouts*
*5 tablespoons corn oil*
*1 garlic clove, minced*
*1 pound ground veal or turkey*
*1 tablespoon rice wine*
*4 tablespoons soy sauce*
*4 tablespoons Hoisin Sauce (page 31)*
*2 teaspoons sugar*
*½ cup Chicken Broth (page 155)*
*¼ cup minced scallions*
*2 teaspoons cornstarch mixed with 2 tablespoons water*
*1 teaspoon kosher salt*
*1 pound fresh or dried egg noodles*

**1.** Peel the cucumber, then cut it crosswise into 2-inch sections. Place each section flat on a cutting board and cut thin slices from one edge until you reach the seeds, which will be discarded. Rotate the section one-quarter turn and continue to cut thin slices until you reach the seeds again. Rotate and slice the 2 remaining sides until the center containing the seeds is left in a solid piece; discard. Stack the slices of cucumber and cut into lengthwise shreds. Set aside.

**2.** Heat a wok over medium heat and add 4 tablespoons of the oil. Add the garlic and stir until it browns lightly. Add the ground meat and stir-fry until it separates and changes color. Splash the wine around the edge of the wok, then add the soy sauce, Hoisin Sauce and sugar. Stir and add the broth. Bring to a boil, turn the heat to low and cook for 3 or 4 minutes. Add the scallions and cornstarch mixture, then cook and stir until the sauce thickens. Transfer to a large serving bowl and keep hot.

**3.** Bring 4 quarts of water to a boil and add the salt. Separate the noodles as you add them to the boiling water and cook for about 3 minutes. Drain, and add remaining 1 tablespoon oil to the noodles. Toss to prevent sticking.

**4.** Serve the noodles in large individual soup bowls with several tablespoons of meat sauce on top. Garnish with the shredded cucumbers.

# COLD NOODLES WITH SCALLION SAUCE

**Serves 4 to 6**

1 teaspoon kosher salt
1 pound fresh or dried
   egg noodles
2 tablespoons corn oil

### Scallion Sauce

2 tablespoons corn oil
¼ cup finely chopped
   scallions
½ teaspoon kosher
   salt
2 tablespoons soy
   sauce
⅛ teaspoon white
   pepper
2 tablespoons Chicken
   Broth (page 155)

**1.** Bring 4 quarts of water to a rolling boil in a large pot. Add the salt. Separate the noodles while adding them to the boiling water, stir and cook for 3 minutes or until desired tenderness; they should be springy to the bite. Drain in a colander, rinse with cold water and shake colander several times to remove excess water. Add oil and toss. Set aside to cool to room temperature.

**2.** For the sauce, heat a small saucepan over medium heat and add the oil. When oil is hot, remove the pan from the heat and add the scallions and remaining sauce ingredients. Mix, then pour the sauce over the noodles. Toss to coat evenly.

# COLD NOODLES WITH GINGER SAUCE

**Serves 4 to 6**

1 teaspoon kosher salt
1 pound fresh or dried
   egg noodles
2 tablespoons corn oil

### Ginger Sauce

2 tablespoons corn oil
2 tablespoons finely
   shredded fresh
   ginger
2 tablespoons soy
   sauce
1 teaspoon sugar
2 tablespoons Chicken
   Broth (page 155)

**1.** Bring 4 quarts of water to a rolling boil in a large pot. Add the salt. Separate the noodles while adding them to the boiling water, stir and cook for 3 minutes or until desired tenderness; noodles should be springy to the bite. Drain in a colander, rinse with cold water and shake colander several times to remove excess water. Add oil and toss. Set aside to cool to room temperature.

**2.** For the sauce, heat a small saucepan over medium heat and add the oil. When oil is hot, add the remaining sauce ingredients and cook for 2 minutes. Pour the sauce over the cooled noodles. Toss to coat evenly.

# ROAST VEAL LO MEIN

This noodle dish includes Cantonese-style roast veal, a very versatile meat used to add a slightly sweet, roasted taste to many dishes. This lo mein is great for large groups because it can be made in advance and re-heated without losing flavor.

*3 dried black
   mushrooms
½ pound fresh or
   dried egg noodles
4 tablespoons corn oil
¼ cup shredded
   bamboo shoots
2 scallions, shredded
2 cups shredded
   Chinese cabbage
   or bean sprouts
½ pound Cantonese
   Roast Veal (page
   97), cut into
   matchstick strips
1 teaspoon kosher salt
4 tablespoons soy
   sauce
Sprigs of fresh
   coriander, for
   garnish*

**1.** Soak the mushrooms in warm water for 30 minutes. Remove the stems and shred the caps.

**2.** Bring 2 quarts of water to a boil. Separate the noodles as you add them to the boiling water and cook for 3 minutes. Drain and rinse with cold water. Shake the noodles dry and spread them out on a shallow baking pan. With scissors, make several random cuts through the noodles (cutting the long strands of noodles makes them easier to handle). Add 1 tablespoon of oil, then toss and mix well. Set aside near the stove.

**3.** Place the shredded vegetables separately on a large work platter and also place near the stove.

**4.** Heat a wok over medium heat until hot and add the remaining 3 tablespoons oil. Add the veal and stir-fry over medium heat for a few seconds. Add the Chinese cabbage or bean sprouts, bamboo shoots, mushrooms and scallions. Stir-fry for 2 minutes, then spread the noodles on top of this mixture. Sprinkle on the salt and soy sauce, turn up the heat and continue stir-frying with a tossing and mixing motion until ingredients are thoroughly blended and noodles are heated through. Turn off the heat and transfer to a warm serving platter. Garnish with the coriander sprigs and serve.

# VEGETARIAN LO MEIN

*T*hose who don't eat meat will find many choices in this book because Chinese cuisine relies predominantly on vegetables. Serve this light and tasty combination of noodles and vegetables as a complete meal.

8 dried black
    mushrooms
2 tablespoons tree ears
½ pound fresh or
    dried egg noodles
7 tablespoons corn oil
1 teaspoon minced
    fresh ginger
½ pound minced fresh
    mushrooms
4 tablespoons soy
    sauce
½ cup shredded carrots
2 cups shredded green
    cabbage
2 scallions, shredded
1 teaspoon kosher salt
½ teaspoon sugar
2 teaspoons oriental
    sesame oil

**1.** Soak the mushrooms in warm water for 30 minutes. Remove stems and shred caps. Strain and reserve ½ cup of the mushroom soaking water for later. Soak the tree ears in warm water until they swell, about 5 minutes, then rinse and shred; there should be about ½ cup after soaking.

**2.** Bring water to a boil in a large pot. Separate the noodles as you add them to the boiling water, then stir and cook for 3 minutes. Drain in a colander and shake several times to remove excess water. Add 1 tablespoon corn oil and toss the noodles. Transfer to a flat pan and, using a pair of scissors, make several random cuts through the noodles. Set aside.

**3.** Heat a wok over medium heat until hot. Add 2 tablespoons of corn oil. Add the ginger and fresh mushrooms, and stir-fry for about 1 minute or until the mushrooms are wilted. Transfer the mushrooms, ginger and any liquid to a large bowl. Reheat the wok and add 2 more tablespoons oil. Add the shredded black mushrooms and tree ears, and stir-fry for a few seconds. Add 2 tablespoons soy sauce and ¼ cup of the reserved mushroom liquid. Stir and cook for about 1 minute. Transfer the contents of the wok to the bowl containing the mushrooms and ginger.

**4.** Reheat the wok for the third time and add the remaining 2 tablespoons of oil. Add the carrots, cabbage and scallions, and stir-fry for a few seconds. Add the salt, sugar and cooked noodles.

Stir and pour the remaining soy sauce and remaining ¼ cup of mushroom liquid on top of the noodles. Stir and add the cooked ingredients. Continue to stir and toss until ingredients are well blended. Taste for salt and stir in the sesame oil. Serve.

*Note:* This dish can be kept warm in a low oven or reheated without losing flavor.

# ANTS ON THE TREE

*Serves 4*

Don't be put off by the name of this dish. A chef with a vivid imagination conjured up this image for bits of meat clinging to cellophane noodles. You'll find it deliciously spicy and easy to make.

*2 ounces cellophane noodles*

**Marinade**

*2 tablespoons soy sauce*
*2 teaspoons cornstarch*
*1 tablespoon water*
*1 tablespoon corn oil*

*½ pound ground veal, turkey or beef*

*3 tablespoons corn oil*
*2 tablespoons minced scallions*
*2 tablespoons Hot Chili Sauce (page 32), or to taste*
*1 teaspoon sugar*
*1 cup Chicken Broth (page 155)*

*1.* Soak the cellophane noodles in water for 5 minutes or until soft. Drain and, using scissors, cut into 4–inch lengths. Set aside.

*2.* Combine the marinade ingredients with the ground meat. Mix until the meat absorbs the marinade.

*3.* Heat a wok over medium heat until hot. Add the oil, then the meat and scallions. Use your spatula to break up the meat and stir-fry until the meat separates. Add the sauce and sugar, stir and add the noodles. Stir again and add the broth.

*4.* As the broth begins to boil, turn the heat to low, cover and cook for a few minutes or until the liquid is absorbed. Stir once or twice during cooking. Serve hot.

*Note:* This dish can be prepared in advance, if you like, and reheated just before serving.

# RICE NOODLE SHEETS

*Makes 12 sheets, 9 inches in diameter*

*T*his recipe is for those who prefer to make their own rice noodle sheets, to be used in dishes such as Beef with Wide Rice Noodles (page 181). Make it ahead and keep at room temperature for up to 24 hours. The special rice flour for these sheets is not readily available so I have substituted cake flour. Ready-made rice noodles are sold by the sheet in bean-curd factories or in packages in supermarkets in Chinatowns.

*2 cups cake flour (do not substitute all-purpose)*
*¼ cup cornstarch*
*2 tablespoons tapioca flour (optional)*
*1 teaspoon kosher salt*
*⅓ cup corn oil*
*2 ⅔ cups cold water*

**1.** Put the dry ingredients and the oil in a large mixing bowl. With a wire whisk, beat in half the water until mixture is smooth. Beat in the remaining water and blend well.

**2.** Oil a 9-inch round cake pan and pour in just enough batter to cover the bottom of the pan. Place the pan in a steamer and steam for 3 minutes. Remove and allow to cool thoroughly.

**3.** Brush the surface of the cooked noodle sheet with a little corn oil and roll up jelly-roll fashion. Transfer the rolled sheet to a lightly oiled platter and unroll.

**4.** Continue making noodle sheets until all the batter is used. Be sure to stir the batter before each addition, since the flour can settle to the bottom of the bowl. The rice noodle sheets can be stacked without sticking.

*Note:* To speed the cooking, use two 9-inch pans, so that while you steam one sheet, the other is cooling. The pans should be washed, dried and re-oiled after each use.

# BEEF WITH WIDE RICE NOODLES

### Serves 6

*I*n Cantonese, this dish is called *chow fun,* and it is very popular among Chinese. *Fun* is a snow-white, velvety slick, slightly chewy noodle made from rice flour. Its texture may not appeal to everyone, but those who like it enjoy it with a passion.

*½ pound boneless beefsteak, cut into slices ⅛ inch thick and 2 inches long*

### Marinade

*1 teaspoon minced fresh ginger*
*2 tablespoons soy sauce*
*2 teaspoons cornstarch*
*1 tablespoon rice wine*
*1 tablespoon corn oil*

*4 tablespoons corn oil*
*1½ Rice Noodle Sheets (page 180), cut into ½-inch-wide strips (about 1 pound)*
*½ teaspoon kosher salt*
*½ teaspoon sugar*
*2 tablespoons soy sauce*
*2 cups fresh bean sprouts or shredded Chinese cabbage*
*2 scallions, split and cut into 2-inch-long sections*

**1.** Combine the beef and marinade ingredients in a mixing bowl. Mix well and let stand for 30 minutes.

**2.** Heat a wok until hot, then add 3 tablespoons of the oil. When the oil is hot, add the beef. Stir-fry quickly to separate the pieces and until the meat just loses its redness. Transfer to a large platter.

**3.** Reheat the wok over low heat and add the remaining 1 tablespoon oil. Add the rice noodles and gently stir until heated through; the noodles will soften as they heat. Sprinkle the salt, sugar and soy sauce on top of the noodles, then toss gently to mix.

**4.** Return the beef to the wok and scatter the bean sprouts and scallions over all. Using the same gentle tossing motion, lift the noodle mixture from the bottom to the top, being careful not to scorch the noodles. Continue to cook and turn the noodles until the bean sprouts are just tender-crisp. Transfer noodles to a large serving platter and serve immediately.

# DIM SUM

**Y**es, you can actually make these—even in a kosher kitchen! Literally translated, *dim sum* means "dot the heart," and these delicious morsels will capture your heart and your taste buds, and unlike the typical shared dish, they are your very own. Various steamed, braised or deep-fried savories or dumplings known as dim sum are served with tea in Chinese teahouses only in the morning and early afternoon. Since teahouses are not kosher, the only way you'll be able to enjoy these dumplings is to make them yourself. I have used ground veal and turkey in place of pork and have adjusted the seasonings and developed a curried chicken filling for the steamed buns. You might want to experiment with some of the fillings yourself once you have become familiar with the recipes. After all, what is a kreplach if not a distant relative of a dumpling?

Many of these dim sum can be prepared ahead and frozen. This method can fit your daily or festive holiday meals because all you need do is put them in a heated oven to warm up.

| Recipes | | Prepare Ahead | Serving Temperature |
| --- | --- | --- | --- |
| Yeast Dough | | Yes | |
| Lotus Leaf Buns | | Yes | Hot |
| Steamed Cantonese Roast Veal Buns | | Yes | Hot |
| Pan-Fried Meat Buns | | No | Hot |
| Steamed Curried Chicken Buns | | Yes | Hot |
| Steamed Vegetable Buns | | Yes | Hot |
| Pearl Balls | | Yes | Hot |
| Cantonese Egg Rolls | | Yes | Hot |
| Egg-Roll and Wonton Wrappers | | Yes | |
| Wontons | | Yes | Hot |
| Curried Wontons | Spicy | Yes | Hot |
| Taiwan Fried Dumplings | Mildly spicy | Yes | Hot |
| Steamed Veal Dumplings | | Yes | Hot |
| Fried Dumplings, Northern Style | | Yes | Hot |
| Peking Pancakes | | Yes | Hot |
| Scallion Pancakes | | Yes | Hot |
| Spring-Roll Wrappers | | Yes | Hot |
| Vegetarian Spring Rolls | | Yes | Hot |
| Shanghai Spring Rolls | | Yes | Hot |

# YEAST DOUGH

*B*ecause there are so few ovens in China, the Chinese developed a method for steaming bread. These steamed breads are called buns. They do not brown or form a crust, but they do have the texture of bread. If you've never had steamed bread before, the white color may seem unusual, but you'll become a fan in no time as many of my students have. What makes this recipe so simple is that the dough only has to rise once.

*1 package active dry yeast*
*¾ cup plus 2 tablespoons warm water*
*1 tablespoon sugar*
*2 tablespoons corn oil*
*2 ½ cups all-purpose flour*

*1.* Dissolve the yeast in the warm water. Let stand for 1 minute. Add the sugar and oil and mix well. Measure the flour into a large mixing bowl. If you are mixing the dough by hand, proceed with steps 2 and 3; if using a food processor, skip steps 2 and 3 and proceed with step 4.

*2.* Stir the yeast mixture into the flour. Mix with your hands to form a ball of dough. Transfer the dough to a lightly floured surface and knead until smooth. Place dough back in the mixing bowl and cover with plastic wrap. Set bowl in a warm place and let dough rise until it is double its original bulk, about 30 minutes.

*3.* Punch dough down with your fist. Transfer to a lightly floured surface and knead for 10 minutes. Dough is ready to shape into buns.

*4.* If using a food processor, fit it with the metal blade and add flour to the bowl. Turn on the machine and pour in the yeast mixture in a steady stream through the feed tube. After the dough forms a ball, about 10 seconds, process for 30 seconds. Turn off the machine, uncover the bowl and turn the ball of dough over. Cover and continue to process another 30 seconds. Dough does not require rising and is ready to shape into buns.

# LOTUS LEAF BUNS

*Makes 20 buns*

*T*his steamed bun is in the shape of a lotus leaf. The bun opens easily so you can fill it with slices of roast veal or duck and serve it as a sandwich, as in Steamed Cantonese Roast Veal Buns (page 187).

*1 recipe Yeast Dough*
  *(page 185)*
*Corn oil, for brushing*

**1.** Transfer the dough to a lightly floured surface and knead for a few seconds. Roll the dough into a cylinder 14 inches long, then cut the cylinder into 20 equal pieces. With the palm of your hand, flatten each piece into a disk. With a rolling pin, roll each disk into a round measuring 3½ inches in diameter.

**2.** Brush half of each disk with oil and fold the other half over to make a half-moon shape. With the sharp edge of a cleaver, make light impressions at ⅛-inch intervals across the half-moon, creating lines resembling the veins of a leaf. To complete the leaf's shape, place your thumb and forefinger at the straight edge and pinch the dough to form a stubby stem at one end. At the same time, push the ends of 2 chopsticks into the round edge of the half-moon to form 2 indentations like the serrations of a leaf. Place each bun on a 3-inch square of parchment or wax paper and put in a warm place to rise for 30 minutes or until doubled in size.

**3.** Transfer the buns, with the papers, to a steamer. Place buns about 1 inch apart and steam for 15 minutes. Serve immediately.

*Note:* These buns freeze and reheat easily. Cool them after steaming, then place in a plastic bag and freeze. To reheat, just steam again or put several in a plastic bag and microwave for 1 minute at high power.

# STEAMED CANTONESE ROAST VEAL BUNS

*Makes 16 buns*

### Filling

2 tablespoons corn oil
1 cup minced onions
5 tablespoons soy
  sauce
1 tablespoon light
  brown sugar
2 tablespoons
  granulated sugar
1 teaspoon honey
1 teaspoon oriental
  sesame oil
¼ teaspoon
  **Five-Spice Powder**
  **(page 35)**
3 tablespoons
  cornstarch mixed
  with ½ cup water
2 cups chopped
  **Cantonese Roast**
  **Veal (page 187)**
¼ cup minced
  scallions

1 recipe Yeast Dough
  (page 185)

*1.* Slightly heat a heavy saucepan and add the oil. Add the minced onions and cook, stirring until the onions are translucent. Stir in the soy sauce, both sugars, honey and sesame oil. Sprinkle on the Five-Spice Powder. Pour the cornstarch mixture into the saucepan, stirring constantly until the sauce thickens, then add the chopped veal and scallions. Continue to cook, stirring, for 2 minutes, then remove the pan from the heat and spread the filling on a platter to cool. (The filling can now be refrigerated or frozen. Bring it to room temperature before filling the buns.)

*2.* To shape the buns, transfer the dough to a lightly floured surface and knead for a few seconds. Roll the dough into a cylinder 16 inches long. Cut the cylinder across into 1-inch sections. Turn each section on its side and flatten slightly into a disk. With a rolling pin, roll each disk into a 3-inch circle, rolling the edges thinner than the center.

*3.* Place a disk in the palm of your hand and put about 1 tablespoon filling in the center. Draw up the edges of dough over the filling, then twist to close. Fill and shape remaining buns.

*4.* Place each filled bun on a 2-inch square of parchment or wax paper. Put the buns with the paper on a steamer rack about 1 inch apart. Let the buns rise, covered, in a warm place for about 30 minutes or until doubled in size.

*5.* Bring at least 2 inches of water to a boil in a steamer. Place the buns in the steamer, cover and steam for 15 minutes.

*Note:*   Steamed buns freeze well. Reheat by steaming again for 15 minutes.

# PAN-FRIED MEAT BUNS

*H*ere is a tasty, juicy variation on the steamed bun. Because these buns are pan-fried with a moist filling, they are crusty on the bottom yet juicy on the inside.

## Filling

1 pound ground veal,
    turkey or beef
2 teaspoons finely
    minced fresh ginger
½ cup finely chopped
    scallions
1 teaspoon kosher salt
2½ tablespoons soy
    sauce
1 tablespoon oriental
    sesame oil
¼ cup Chicken Broth
    (page 155)
1 tablespoon corn oil

1 recipe Yeast Dough
    (page 185)
2 tablespoons corn oil
1 cup water

*1.* Combine the filling ingredients in a large bowl. Stir in one direction until the meat holds together, then refrigerate for at least 30 minutes.

*2.* Place the dough on a lightly floured surface and knead for a few seconds. Shape the dough into a cylinder 16 inches long, then cut the cylinder across into 1-inch sections. Turn the sections on their sides and flatten each with the palm of your hand. With a rolling pin, lightly roll each disk into a 3-inch diameter, rolling the edges thinner than the center.

*3.* Place a disk on the palm of your hand and put 1½ tablespoons filling in the center. Using the fingers of the other hand, draw up the edges of the disk over the filling toward the center and twist to close. Set aside on a lightly floured surface until all the buns are made. Cover with a dish towel and let rise for 30 minutes.

*4.* Have one 12-inch or two 10-inch nonstick skillets with fitted lids ready. Heat the skillet or skillets over medium heat until very hot. Add oil to coat pan, then arrange the buns, twisted side up, about 1 inch apart. Fry until lightly browned on the bottom, then hold the lid in your hand m21 and add the water to the skillet. Cover immediately and cook for 8 minutes, or until the water evaporates. Remove the cover and continue cooking until a crust forms on the bottom of the buns. (Be careful not to burn the bottoms.) Serve hot. Warn your guests to bite carefully since the filling can be hot and juicy.

# STEAMED CURRIED CHICKEN BUNS

2 cups diced boneless
chicken, part white
and part dark meat,
in ⅛-inch cubes

### Marinade

1 tablespoon soy sauce
1 teaspoon kosher salt
2 teaspoons cornstarch

3 tablespoons corn oil
1 tablespoon rice wine
½ cup minced onions
2 teaspoons Madras
curry powder, or to
taste
½ teaspoon kosher
salt
¼ teaspoon sugar
2 teaspoons cornstarch
mixed with 3
tablespoons
Chicken Broth
(page 155)
1 recipe Yeast Dough
(page 185)

**1.** Combine the chicken with the marinade.

**2.** Heat a wok over moderate heat, then add 2 tablespoons oil. When the oil is hot, add the chicken and stir-fry quickly until the chicken changes color, about 2 minutes. Splash wine around the edge of the wok, then remove the chicken with a slotted spoon, leaving as much oil in the wok as possible.

**3.** Reheat the wok and add the remaining tablespoon of oil. Add the onions and stir-fry until translucent. Add the curry and mix with the onions. Add the cooked chicken, salt and sugar. Stir-fry a few seconds, then stir in the cornstarch mixture and add to wok. Stir until the sauce thickens, then spread filling on a dish to cool.

**4.** Knead the dough on a lightly floured surface a few seconds. Roll into a 16-inch cylinder, then cut the cylinder into 1-inch sections. Turn each section on its side and flatten slightly into a disk. With a rolling pin, roll each disk into a 3-inch circle, rolling the edges thinner than the center.

**5.** Place a disk in the open palm of your hand and put about 1 tablespoon of filling in the center. Draw up the edges of the dough over the filling toward the center, then twist to close.

**6.** Place each bun on a 2-inch square of parchment or wax paper. Put the buns with the paper on a steamer rack about 1 inch apart. Let buns rise, covered, in a warm place for about 30 minutes or until doubled in size.

**7.** Bring at least 2 inches of water to a boil in a steamer. Place buns in the steamer, cover and steam for 15 minutes.

# Steamed Vegetable Buns

*H*ere is a steamed bun for vegetarians. The pressed bean curd gives the filling substance and the cellophane noodles keep it light.

## Filling

4 dried black
 mushrooms
1 ounce cellophane
 noodles (cut a
 2-ounce package
 in half with
 scissors)
½ 10-ounce package
 frozen leaf spinach,
 thawed and chopped
 fine
2 tablespoons corn oil
½ cup finely chopped
 Seasoned Pressed
 Bean Curd (page
 144)
¼ cup minced bamboo
 shoots
2 tablespoons soy
 sauce
½ teaspoon kosher
 salt
½ teaspoon sugar
1 teaspoon cornstarch
 mixed with 1
 tablespoon water
1 teaspoon oriental
 sesame oil

1 recipe Yeast Dough
 (page 185)

**1.** Soak the mushrooms in warm water for 30 minutes. Remove stems and mince caps.

**2.** Put the cellophane noodles in a saucepan, cover with cold water, place on medium heat and bring to a boil. Turn heat down and simmer for 2 minutes. Turn off heat and let stand for 10 minutes. Turn off heat and let stand for 10 minutes. Drain and chop coarsely.

**3.** Put the spinach in a strainer and rinse with very hot water. Squeeze out most of the water. Set aside.

**4.** Heat a saucepan and add the corn oil. Add the bean curd, mushrooms and bamboo shoots. Stir and add the soy sauce, salt, sugar, spinach and cellophane noodles. Cook and stir for a few minutes. Re-stir the cornstarch mixture and add to the saucepan while stirring constantly. Finally, add the sesame oil. Cook and stir filling for a few more minutes, then set aside to cool.

**5.** Transfer dough to a lightly floured surface and knead for a few seconds. Roll the dough into a cylinder 16 inches long, then cut the cylinder across into 1-inch sections. Turn each section on its side and flatten slightly into a disk. With a rolling pin, roll each disk into a 3-inch circle, rolling the edges thinner than the center.

**6.** Place a disk in the open palm of your hand and put about 2 tablespoons of filling in the center. Draw up the edges of the disk over the filling toward the center, then twist to close. Fill and shape remaining buns.

**7.** Place each filled bun on a 2-inch square of parchment or wax paper. Put the buns with the paper on a steamer rack about 1 inch apart. Let buns rise, covered, in a warm place for about 30 minutes or until doubled in size.

**8.** Bring at least 2 inches of water to a boil in a steamer. Place buns in the steamer, cover and steam for 15 minutes.

*Note:* Steamed buns freeze well. Reheat by steaming again for 15 minutes.

# PEARL BALLS

*Makes 30 pearl balls*

Small meatballs are rolled in grains of white glutinous rice so that after cooking they resemble pearls. Minced fresh water chestnuts add crunch.

*¾ cup glutinous rice*
*1 pound finely ground veal or turkey*
*1 small egg*
*1 teaspoon kosher salt*
*¼ teaspoon sugar*
*1 tablespoon light soy sauce*
*1 tablespoon cornstarch mixed with 2 tablespoons water*
*5 water chestnuts, minced fine*
*1 tablespoon minced scallions*

**1.** Wash the rice and soak in cold water for 1 hour.

**2.** Combine the meat, egg, salt, sugar, soy sauce and cornstarch mixture. Mix in one direction until the meat holds together, then add the water chestnuts and scallions. Continue to mix until the mixture is sticky. Refrigerate for 30 minutes.

**3.** Drain and dry the rice completely. Spread out on a clean towel.

**4.** Lightly oil a steamer rack or plate. Take 1½ tablespoons of the meat mixture and roll it into a ball about 1 inch in diameter. Roll the ball evenly in the grains of rice until it is completely covered. Place on the steamer rack or platter. Continue this procedure until all the meat is used. Place the pearl balls ½ inch apart on the rack.

**5.** Bring 2 inches of water to a boil in the base of a steamer. Put the rack with the balls over the boiling water, cover and steam for 20 minutes. Serve hot as an appetizer.

# CANTONESE EGG ROLLS

Make your own egg rolls and serve them with homemade Hoisin Sauce (page 31), Hot Mustard Sauce (page 32), or Duck Sauce (page 33), each of which is also available commercially.

*6 dried black
mushrooms*

**Marinade**

*3 tablespoons soy
sauce*
*1 teaspoon cornstarch*
*1 tablespoon water*
*1 tablespoon corn oil*
*¼ teaspoon sugar*

*¾ pound ground
chicken or veal*
*4 tablespoons corn oil*
*1 tablespoon rice wine*
*½ teaspoon sugar*
*5 cups shredded green
cabbage*
*¾ teaspoon kosher
salt*
*½ cup shredded
bamboo shoots*
*2 scallions, shredded*
*1 tablespoon
cornstarch mixed
with 3 tablespoons
Chicken Broth
(page 155)*
*1 extra-large egg,
beaten*
*24 homemade
Egg-Roll Wrappers
(page 193) or
store-bought*
*2 cups corn oil, for
deep-frying*

1. Soak mushrooms in warm water for 30 minutes. Remove stems and shred caps.

2. Combine the marinade ingredients, add the meat, mix and set aside. Heat a wok and add 2 tablespoons of the oil. When the oil is hot, add the meat and stir-fry until it changes color. Add the mushrooms and splash the wine around the edge of the wok. Add the sugar and stir-fry for 2 more minutes, then transfer to a bowl and set aside. Wipe the wok clean with a damp cloth.

3. Reheat the wok and add the remaining 2 tablespoons oil. Add the cabbage and stir-fry until it is wilted. Add the salt and mix well, then add the bamboo shoots and scallions. Return the meat and mushrooms to the wok and continue to stir-fry until all is thoroughly blended. Make a well in the center. Re-stir the cornstarch mixture and pour it into the well, then cook until the sauce thickens and forms a glaze over the ingredients. Spread the filling on a large platter to cool.

4. Place a pastry brush and the beaten egg near the work area. Put a wrapper on the counter with one corner pointing toward you. Put 1½ tablespoons of filling in the lower half of the wrapper, then bring the bottom corner of the wrapper over the filling and roll upward one turn. Brush some egg on the exposed edges of the wrapper and fold the 2 side corners toward the center, envelope style. Continue to roll the wrapper into a cylinder. The egg seals the wrapper closed.

**5.** Heat a skillet and add the 2 cups oil. When the oil is 325° F., add the egg rolls and deep-fry until golden brown and crispy, about 5 minutes. Turn them over occasionally for even frying. Drain.

---

*Note:* The egg rolls can be frozen after frying. To reheat, heat the oven to 350° F. and place the frozen egg rolls in a single layer on a rack over a shallow baking pan. Heat for 20 minutes.

# EGG-ROLL AND WONTON WRAPPERS

*Makes 24 egg-roll wrappers, or 96 wonton or steamed-dumpling wrappers*

Wrappers for wontons are also available commercially.

---

*2 ½ cups all-purpose flour*
*1 teaspoon kosher salt*
*1 extra-large egg*
*½ cup water, approximately*
*Cornstarch, to keep wrappers separate*

**1.** Put the flour and salt in a large mixing bowl. Make a well in the center and pour in the egg and water. With your fingers, combine the ingredients until they adhere into a dough. Add more water, 1 tablespoon at a time, if the dough is dry. Knead the dough until smooth and soft, cover with plastic wrap and let rest for 30 minutes.

**2.** Divide the dough in half. Keep half the dough covered and roll out the other half on a heavily floured surface into a very thin (1/32-inch) sheet, about 36 × 12 inches. With a sharp knife, cut 6-inch squares for egg-roll wrappers or 3-inch squares for wonton wrappers. Do the same with the remaining half of the dough.

**3.** Sprinkle cornstarch between each wrapper and stack them. They are now ready to use. To store fresh wrappers, wrap in foil and put in a plastic bag. They will keep in the refrigerator for up to 3 days or in the freezer for up to a month.

---

*Note:* If you have a pasta machine, use it to roll out the dough. Start with the thickest setting and work up to the thinnest.

# WONTONS

*Makes about 80 wontons*

**W**ontons are a great favorite among my students—the Chinese version of kreplach. To serve boiled wontons, arrange them on a platter and serve with a dip made of 2 tablespoons soy sauce, 1 teaspoon oriental sesame oil and Hot Chili Sauce (page 32) to taste. You can also deep-fry and serve them as an appetizer with Sweet-and-Sour Sauce (page 34). Freeze uncooked wontons ahead of time and store in plastic bags. Just add 3 minutes to the cooking time when you use them.

## Filling

1 pound ground veal
  or turkey
1 tablespoon minced
  scallions
1 teaspoon finely
  minced fresh ginger
2 tablespoons soy
  sauce
1 teaspoon salt
½ teaspoon sugar
1 tablespoon oriental
  sesame oil
1 teaspoon cornstarch
2 teaspoons rice wine
1 egg
⅛ teaspoon white
  pepper
1 tablespoon corn oil
1 pound homemade
  Wonton Wrappers
  (page 193) or
  store-bought

2 cups corn oil, for
  deep-frying
  (optional)

*1.* Combine the filling ingredients and mix in one direction until the mixture is light and sticky.

*2.* Keep the wonton wrappers covered with a damp cloth to prevent drying. Place a wrapper on the counter with one corner pointing toward you. Put ½ teaspoon of the filling on this corner. Roll the corner over the filling to form a roll about halfway up the wrapper. Moisten the left corner of the rolled wrapper with water, bring around the right corner and stick it on top of the moistened corner. Press the corners to seal. Repeat this until all the filling is used. Cover the finished wontons with a moist dish towel to prevent drying. For boiling, see step 3; for deep-frying, proceed to step 4.

*3.* To boil the wontons, bring 2 quarts of water to a boil. Turn off the heat and add the wontons. Return the heat to high and bring the pot back to a boil. Then lower the heat to a simmer and cook gently for 10 minutes. Transfer wontons with a slotted spoon to soup bowls or a serving plate.

*4.* To deep-fry the wontons, heat a wok and add the 2 cups of oil. When the oil reaches 325° F., slip in no more than 10 to 12 wontons. Fry until lightly browned, turning them frequently. Remove and drain.

# CURRIED WONTONS

*T*his is a great appetizer to serve with cocktails.

## Filling

1 medium potato
5 tablespoons corn oil
1 pound ground beef,
   turkey or veal
2 tablespoons soy
   sauce
½ teaspoon kosher
   salt
1½ teaspoons sugar
1 cup minced onions
1 tablespoon Madras
   curry powder, or to
   taste

1 pound (96)
   homemade Wonton
   Wrappers (page
   193) or store-bought
2 cups corn oil, for
   deep-frying

*1.* Wash and steam the potato in its skin until done, about 15 minutes. Peel, place in a bowl and mash until smooth. You should have ½ packed cup. Set aside.

*2.* Heat a wok until hot and add 4 tablespoons of the oil. Add the meat and stir-fry until it separates, then add the soy sauce, salt and sugar. Stir well and transfer to a bowl. Set aside.

*3.* Reheat the wok until hot and add the remaining tablespoon of oil. Add the onions and stir-fry until they are translucent. Add the curry powder and continue to stir-fry for another minute. Return the cooked meat to the wok and add the mashed potato. Cook and stir until well blended, then transfer to a plate to cool.

*4.* Keep the wonton wrappers covered with a damp cloth to prevent drying. Place a wrapper on the counter with one corner pointing toward you. Place ¾ teaspoon of the filling on this corner. Roll the corner over the filling to form a roll about halfway up the wrapper. Moisten the left corner of the rolled wrapper with water and bring around the right corner and stick it on top of the moistened corner. Press the corners to seal. Repeat this until all the filling is used. Cover the finished wontons with a slightly damp dish towel to prevent drying.

*5.* Heat a wok and add the 2 cups oil. When the oil reaches 325° F., slip in 10 to 12 wontons, or as many as will float freely in the hot oil. Fry the wontons until lightly browned, turning them frequently as they fry. Remove and drain. Serve hot.

# TAIWAN FRIED DUMPLINGS

*Makes 20 dumplings*

*I*f you like a slightly spicy fried dumpling, this one from Taiwan has the sharp taste of ginger to balance the flavor of lamb. It has a rounder shape and is fried on both sides.

## Dough

2 cups all-purpose
   flour
¾ cup cold water

## Filling

1 pound ground lamb
   (about 2 cups)
1½ tablespoons finely
   minced fresh ginger
½ clove garlic, minced
   fine
¾ cup finely chopped
   scallions
½ teaspoon kosher
   salt
⅛ teaspoon white
   pepper
3 tablespoons dark soy
   sauce
1 tablespoon oriental
   sesame oil
¼ cup Chicken Broth
   (page 155)

2 tablespoons corn oil,
   for pan-frying

**1.** Put the flour in a large mixing bowl. Add the water gradually and stir with chopsticks to make soft dough. Turn out the dough onto a lightly floured surface and knead until smooth and elastic. Cover and let rest for 30 minutes while you make the filling.

**2.** Combine the filling ingredients in a mixing bowl and stir in one direction until the filling is sticky and holds together. Set aside.

**3.** Divide the dough in half. Keep one half covered and knead the other half on a lightly floured surface for a few seconds. Roll the dough in a cylinder about 10 inches long. Cut the dough into 10 equal pieces, then flatten each piece with your palm. With a rolling pin, roll each piece into a 3-inch disk, rolling the edges thinner than the center. Keep the disks covered to prevent drying.

**4.** Place 1½ tablespoons of filling in the center of a disk. Hold the disk in the palm of one hand and, with the other, bring together the edges of the disk and twist the dough over the filling to close the dumpling completely. Place the dumpling on a flat surface seam side down and gently press to flatten into a 3-inch dumpling about ½ inch thick. Set aside and keep covered with a dish towel. Continue the process until all the dough is used. You should have 20 dumplings.

**5.** Heat 1 or 2 large skillets over medium heat until hot. Lightly coat the pan with oil, then put the dumplings in the frying pan fairly close together and fry for 1 minute. Put 2 to 3 drops of oil on each dumpling and fry another minute, or until the bottoms are lightly brown. Turn the dumplings over and fry another 2 minutes. The dumplings will puff slightly when they are done. Serve hot.

# STEAMED VEAL DUMPLINGS

*T*hese tasty steamed dumplings are easy to make and can be prepared in advance. They are wonderful served as a snack, first course, light lunch or at any other time.

### Filling

**6 dried black mushrooms**
**1 pound ground veal or turkey**
**¾ cup finely minced bamboo shoots**
**2 tablespoons finely minced scallions, white part only**
**1 teaspoon finely minced fresh ginger**
**1 teaspoon kosher salt**
**½ teaspoon sugar**
**1 tablespoon rice wine**
**2 teaspoons oriental sesame oil**
**Dash of white pepper**

**40 store-bought or homemade Wonton Wrappers (page 193)**

*1.* Soak mushrooms in warm water for 30 minutes. Remove stems and mince caps fine. Combine with the rest of the filling ingredients in a large mixing bowl and stir in one direction until the filling is light and sticky.

*2.* Trim and round off the 4 corners of each wrapper so that wrapper is nearly a circle. Place about 1 tablespoon of filling in the center of the wrapper. Moisten one edge of the wrapper and gather the wrapper around the filling, forming little pleats as you squeeze the dumpling around the middle to form a waist. Make sure the wrapper adheres firmly to the filling. Leave the filling exposed at the top. Press the bottom of the dumpling on a flat surface so that it stands upright. Sprinkle the top edge of the wrapper with cold water, since the wrappers tend to remain dry during steaming.

*3.* Oil the rack of a bamboo steamer or a heat-proof platter. Place the dumplings on the rack or platter about ½ inch apart. Bring 2 inches of water to boil in the base of a steamer. Cover and steam over boiling water for 15 minutes. Serve the dumplings on the bamboo steamer or the platter.

# FRIED DUMPLINGS, NORTHERN-STYLE

*Makes 32 dumplings*

These dumplings are sometimes called Peking ravioli or, in California, pot stickers. They are fried and steamed so they become both crispy and moist, then served with Soy Sauce Dip (page 36).

## Dough

2 cups all-purpose
  flour
¾ cup water

## Filling

½ 10-ounce package
  frozen leaf spinach,
  thawed, chopped
  fine and pressed dry
1 pound very lean
  ground beef
½ cup chopped
  scallions
1 tablespoon finely
  minced fresh ginger
6 tablespoons Chicken
  Broth (page 155)
3 tablespoons soy
  sauce
1 tablespoon rice wine
1 teaspoon kosher salt
⅛ teaspoon white
  pepper
1 tablespoon oriental
  sesame oil
1 tablespoon corn oil

*1.* Put the flour in a mixing bowl. Bring the water to a boil, let it cool slightly, then slowly add it to the flour. Stir with a wooden spoon until the dough is firm and smooth. Do not overwork. Add another tablespoon of water if the dough seems too dry.

*2.* Turn the dough onto a lightly floured surface and knead until very smooth, about 3 or 4 minutes. Put the dough into a plastic bag and close tightly. Let rest for 15 minutes while you prepare the filling.

*3.* Combine the filling ingredients in a large mixing bowl. Stir together in one direction until filling holds together.

*4.* Place the dough on a lightly floured surface. Knead a few seconds, then divide in half. Return half the dough to the plastic bag and shape the other half into a cylinder 12 inches long. Cut into 16 equal pieces and, with the palm of your hand, flatten each piece. With a rolling pin, roll each piece into a 3-inch disk, rolling the edges thinner than the center. Repeat until all the dough is used. Keep disks covered to prevent drying.

*5.* Place a disk in the open palm of your hand and put 1 tablespoon of filling in the center. Bring opposite edges together over the filling to make a half-circle. Pinch the edges together with your index finger and thumb to make pleats on the back side of the dumpling. The dumpling should be crescent shaped. Place the finished dumplings on a lightly floured tray. Repeat this procedure with the remaining disks. The dumplings can be frozen at this point.

**6.** Heat a large nonstick or well-cured cast-iron skillet until hot. Have the lid within easy reach. Add enough oil to just coat the pan, then swirl the oil in the pan, turn down the heat and carefully place the dumplings in a circular pattern to cover the surface of the skillet. Fry the dumplings until the bottoms are lightly browned, then add 1/2 cup water and immediately cover the skillet. Cook, covered, over medium heat for 5 minutes. Uncover and continue to cook undisturbed for another 2 minutes, or until the bottoms are dark brown and the dumplings puff slightly.

**7.** Transfer dumplings, bottom side up, to a serving platter and serve hot.

# PEKING PANCAKES

*T*hese pancakes are served with Peking Duck (page 82) or Mu Shu Chicken (page 64). They are soft, bland and slightly chewy to contrast with the duck or chicken. Make them in advance and freeze them for later use.

*⅞ cup water,*
   *approximately*
*2 cups all-purpose*
   *flour*
*1 tablespoon corn oil*

**1.** Bring the water to a boil. Put the flour in a large mixing bowl and make a well in the center. Gradually add all but a few tablespoons of the boiling water to the center of the flour while stirring the flour with a wooden spoon. Stir until most of the flour is moist. If the dough seems too dry, add a little more hot water. Gather and press the dough into a ball. It should be firm and not sticky. Cover the dough and let rest for 15 minutes.

**2.** Turn out the dough onto a lightly floured surface and knead for a few minutes. Divide in half. Keep one half covered to prevent drying and roll out the other half evenly into a large pancake about ¼ inch thick. Using a 2-inch cookie cutter, cut as many disks as possible. Add the leftover dough to the reserved dough.

**3.** Brush half the disks with oil. Place an unoiled disk on top of an oiled one. Roll the 2 disks together with even pressure; do not bear down on the edges. Rotate the disks as you roll to keep them round and turn them over once or twice while rolling so both disks remain the same diameter. Roll the disks into 6-inch pancakes then dust lightly with flour. Set aside and cover with a towel while you roll out the remaining dough.

**4.** Heat a dry heavy 10- or 12-inch skillet over medium heat until hot. Place as many pancakes as possible without touching in the skillet. Cook on one side until pancakes begin to bubble; this should take only a few seconds. Be careful not to

overcook them; they should not brown. Turn pancakes over to cook for a few seconds on the other side, then remove and let cool slightly. Pull the 2 pancakes apart while still hot, and keep covered and warm until ready to serve.

---

*Note:* To prepare pancakes for freezing, stack in a pile of 15 or more and wrap in plastic and foil. To heat, wrap a stack in a light, slightly damp towel and steam over very low heat for 30 minutes.

# SCALLION PANCAKES

*Makes 4 pancakes*

*S*callion Pancakes are a delicious appetizer or accompaniment to soup.

*⅔ cup plus 1 tablespoon hot water, approximately*
*2 cups all-purpose flour*
*½ cup corn oil*
*2 teaspoons kosher salt*
*4 tablespoons chopped scallions*

*1.* Bring the water to a boil. Put the flour in a large mixing bowl and make a well in the center. Turn the heat off under the water, let it stand about a minute, then slowly pour into the well as you stir with a wooden spoon until all the flour is damp. Form the dough into a ball. Transfer the ball to a floured surface and knead until smooth. Divide the dough into quarters, cover with plastic wrap and set aside for 15 minutes.

*2.* With even pressure on a rolling pin, roll one portion of the dough into an oblong sheet 8 × 6 inches. Brush the dough with ½ tablespoon oil, then sprinkle with a scant ½ teaspoon salt and 1 tablespoon chopped scallions. Gently roll over the salt and scallions to press into the dough.

*3.* With your fingers and starting with the longer side, roll the sheet into a thin cylinder, like a jelly roll. Press the long edge against the roll to seal it, then place the roll on the counter and coil it in a spiral, keeping the pinched edge on the inside. Tuck the end underneath the center. Press the coil gently to flatten it, cover and let rest for 30 min-

(continued)

 DIM SUM **201**

utes. Repeat the procedure with the remaining portions of dough. With the rolling pin, roll each flattened patty into an 8-inch pancake.

**4.** Heat a 10-inch skillet until very hot. Turn the heat to medium-high and add enough oil to cover the bottom of the skillet, about 2 tablespoons. When the oil is hot, add a pancake. Shake the skillet to make sure the pancake does not stick. Cover it and let fry for 2 minutes or until lightly brown and crisp. The heat should be hot enough for the pancake to form a crisp crust in about 2 minutes without burning; adjust the heat, if necessary. Uncover and carefully turn pancake over with spatula. Cover and fry another 2 minutes. Fry the remaining pancakes in the same manner, adding oil to skillet as needed. Cut each pancake into 6 wedges and serve hot.

---

*Note:* Scallion Pancakes are best made fresh, but you can also stack, wrap well and refrigerate or freeze. To reheat, place on a rack over a shallow baking pan in a single layer and heat in a 450° F. oven for 5 minutes.

# SPRING-ROLL WRAPPERS

*Makes approximately 40 wrappers*

---

*I*f you have difficulty finding a kosher brand, here is a recipe for Spring-Roll Wrappers. It takes patience, trial and error, and dexterity to make these. The challenges are to have the skillet at the proper temperature, and to handle a sticky, flowing dough with one hand and the wrappers with the other hand.

---

*3½ cups all-purpose flour*
*2 teaspoons kosher salt*
*1⅔ cups water*

**1.** Put the flour in a large mixing bowl. Add the salt to the water. Gradually stir the water into the flour while you mix, knead and pull the dough with your hands in the bowl. If the dough seems dry, add more water, 1 tablespoon at a time—the dough should be very soft. Continue to knead and pull the soft dough with your fingers and fists for about 5 minutes, until the dough is tof-

feelike, homogenized and free of lumps.

**2.** Cover the dough with plastic wrap and refrigerate for at least 2 hours or as long as overnight. Before making the wrappers, remove the dough from the refrigerator and let stand at room temperature for about 20 minutes.

**3.** To make the wrappers, heat a large, greasefree griddle or electric skillet to about 300° F. The temperature of the griddle is critical. If the heat is too high the dough will not stick to the griddle, and if too low the crêpe will be too thick. You want a very thin crêpe, so you may have to experiment with the temperature until you get the desired results. Place a large plate with a large, high lid near the griddle. (The high lid is to cover the crêpes as they are made.)

**4.** With one hand, grasp a large handful of dough about the size of a small grapefruit. Because the dough is very soft, it tends to flow out of your hand. To avoid this, rotate your wrist in a continuous scooping motion to keep the dough centered in your palm. This takes practice, so repeat the motion until you are comfortable with it. When you feel ready, turn your palm down and, as the dough begins to flow out of your hand, press the dough onto the hot griddle. Quickly pull the dough away from the griddle with your hand and fingers. A thin layer of dough will stick to the griddle to make a 7-inch crêpe. Flatten any lumps with the fingertips of your free hand, all the while rotating the dough ball in the first hand to keep it from dripping. As the crêpe cooks, the edges will begin to separate and curl. Using your free hand, carefully peel the crêpe off the griddle and put it on the plate, bottom side up. Cover the crêpe. Repeat the procedure until all the dough is used.

---

*Note:* Wrap crêpes in plastic wrap and put in a plastic bag. They can be stored in the refrigerator for a week and frozen for up to a month.

# VEGETARIAN SPRING ROLLS

8 dried black
   mushrooms
1 pound Seasoned
   Pressed Bean Curd
   (page 144), or ½
   package presliced
   seasoned pressed
   bean curd
¾ pound Chinese
   cabbage, shredded
   (about 5 cups)
1 cup finely shredded
   bamboo shoots
2 scallions, shredded
5 tablespoons corn oil
2 tablespoons soy
   sauce
1 tablespoon rice wine
1½ teaspoons kosher
   salt
1 teaspoon sugar
1½ tablespoons
   cornstarch mixed
   with 2 tablespoons
   mushroom liquid
1½ teaspoons
   oriental sesame oil
1 extra-large egg
30 Spring-Roll
   Wrappers,
   store-bought or
   homemade
   (page 202)
2 cups corn oil, for
   deep-frying

**1.** Soak the mushrooms in warm water until soft, about 30 minutes. Remove stems and shred caps. Strain and reserve the soaking liquid.

**2.** Cut the bean curd into thin slices and the slices into thin shreds. If using presliced bean curd, pile several slices together and cut into shreds. You should have about 2 cups. Set aside on a work platter with the other shredded ingredients.

**3.** Heat a wok over medium heat until hot. Add 2 tablespoons corn oil and stir-fry the bean curd and mushrooms for about 2 minutes. Add the soy sauce and wine, mix well, then transfer to a dish. Wipe the wok clean.

**4.** Reheat the wok and add 2 more tablespoons of corn oil. Add and briefly stir-fry the Chinese cabbage, bamboo shoots and scallions. Add the salt and sugar. Stir until the cabbage wilts, about 1 minute, then return the bean curd and mushrooms to the wok. Stir-fry to blend the ingredients, then re-stir and add the cornstarch mixture. Stir-fry until the sauce thickens, then stir in the sesame oil and transfer to a platter to cool.

**5.** Beat the egg and set aside. Have a pastry brush handy. Separate the wrappers and cover with a slightly damp cloth to soften and prevent drying.

**6.** Place a wrapper on a flat surface with one corner pointing at you. (The folding procedure is the same as for a round crêpe.) Put 1 large tablespoon of filling in the center of the lower half of the wrapper. Starting with the bottom corner, fold the wrapper over the filling and turn over once more to make the shape of a triangle. Brush the edge of the top two sides with egg. Then fold the side corners toward the center envelope style.

Continue to roll up to form a cylinder. The egg will seal the edges closed.

**7.** Heat a clean wok or skillet and add the 2 cups oil. When the oil reaches 325° F., deep-fry the spring rolls a few at a time. Turn them over immediately and then occasionally until they are light brown. Drain and serve hot with the dip for Shanghai Spring Rolls (page 205).

*Note:* Spring rolls can be frozen after frying. Reheat on a rack set in a shallow baking pan in a preheated 450° F. oven for 10 minutes.

# SHANGHAI SPRING ROLLS

*Makes 30 spring rolls*

Spring rolls are a northern Chinese version of egg rolls. The basic difference is in the wrapper. A spring-roll wrapper is made with a thin, soft wheat crêpe; an egg-roll wrapper is a soft noodle dough. Spring rolls are so named because they are traditionally served during Chinese New Year, which coincides with the Spring festival. Honey-brown in color, they are thought to resemble gold bars, which symbolize prosperity and good luck.

**5 dried black mushrooms**
**¾ pound ground chicken breast or veal**

### Marinade
**1 tablespoon soy sauce**
**¼ teaspoon sugar**
**1 teaspoon cornstarch**
**1 teaspoon water**
**1 tablespoon corn oil**

**½ cup shredded bamboo shoots**
**1 pound Chinese cabbage, shredded**
**2 scallions, shredded**

**1.** Soak the mushrooms in warm water until soft, about 30 minutes. Remove stems and shred caps.

**2.** Mix the chicken or veal with the marinade ingredients. Place the shredded ingredients separately on a large work platter.

**3.** Heat a wok over medium heat until hot and add 2 tablespoons oil. Add the meat and quickly stir-fry until it turns white and separates. Add the mushrooms, then splash the wine around the edge of the wok. Stir to blend, then transfer to a large platter. Rinse out the wok.

**4.** Reheat the wok until hot. Heat 3 tablespoons oil, then add the bamboo shoots, Chinese cab-

(continued)

 **DIM SUM 205**

*5 tablespoons corn oil*
*1 tablespoon rice wine*
*1½ teaspoons kosher salt*
*½ teaspoon sugar*
*1½ tablespoons cornstarch mixed with 3 tablespoons water*
*1 extra-large egg, well beaten*
*30 Spring-Roll Wrappers, store-bought or homemade (page 202)*
*2 cups corn oil, for deep-frying*

### Sauce

*3 tablespoons soy sauce*
*1 tablespoon distilled white vinegar*
*½ teaspoon sugar*
*½ teaspoon Hot Chili Sauce (page 32), or to taste*

bage and scallions. Stir several times until the oil coats the vegetables, then add the salt and sugar and continue to stir-fry until the cabbage wilts, about 1 minute. Return the meat to the wok. Give the cornstarch mixture a stir and add to wok. As the mixture begins to bubble, cook and stir until the sauce thickens and coats the ingredients. Spread the filling onto a large platter to cool.

**5.** In a small bowl, beat the egg and set aside. Have a pastry brush handy. Carefully separate the wrappers and cover with a damp towel to prevent drying.

**6.** Place a wrapper on a flat surface with a corner pointing at you. (The folding procedure is the same for a round crêpe.) Put 1½ tablespoons of filling in the center of the lower half of the wrapper and spread it out 4 inches wide. Starting with the bottom corner, fold the corner up over the filling, tucking it in. Roll up one turn and fold in the side flaps, making sure all folded sides are straight. Brush the edges of the remaining flap with egg and continue to roll up into a 5-inch cylinder; the egg will seal the edges. Repeat the procedure until all the wrappers are used.

**7.** Heat a clean wok and add the oil; the wok should be about half-full. When the oil reaches about 325° F., deep-fry as many spring rolls as will float freely. Turn them immediately and then occasionally until they are crisp and lightly browned, about 3 to 4 minutes. Remove and drain.

**8.** Combine the sauce ingredients. Serve the spring rolls hot, with the sauce as a dip.

---

*Note:* These spring rolls can be made in advance. In one method, deep-fry them partially to a light brown, then refrigerate or freeze. When you want to serve, deep-fry again to a golden brown. In a second method, freeze after complete frying. To reheat, place on a rack over a shallow baking pan in a preheated 450° F. oven for 10 minutes.

# DESSERTS

Chinese desserts often are soothing warm or cold fruit or else nut soups thickened with rice flour, tapioca or cornstarch. I offer several here, along with other adaptations of Chinese desserts. Make one of these desserts ahead of time and surprise everyone on a boring Tuesday. An ending like this can lift any meal out of the realm of the ordinary into another dimension.

| Recipes | Prepare Ahead | Serving Temperature |
| --- | --- | --- |
| Almond Cream/Almond Float | Yes | Warm or cool |
| Firecrackers | Yes | Room temp. |
| Hot Tapioca Pudding | Yes | Warm |
| Candied Ginger | Yes | Room temp. |
| Sweet Walnut-Date Soup | Yes | Warm |
| Crispy Bows | Yes | Room temp. |
| Almond Cookies | Yes | Room temp. |
| Caramelized Apples | No | Hot |
| Glacéed Oranges | Yes | Chilled |
| Sweet Red Bean Paste | Yes | |
| Orange Sponge Cake | Yes | Room temp. |
| Steamed Pears with Candied Ginger | Yes | Chilled |

# ALMOND CREAM/ ALMOND FLOAT

1 cup large blanched
  almonds
2 tablespoons
  long-grain rice
5 cups cold water
7 tablespoons sugar
1 tablespoon almond
  extract

**1.** Rinse the almonds and rice several times. Soak together in 2 cups of water for 4 hours. Put the almonds and rice with the soaking water in a blender and add 2 cups of water. Blend for 5 minutes or until the liquid is no longer grainy.

**2.** Cover a large mixing bowl with 4 layers of cheesecloth, 12 × 14 inches, overlapping the edges of the bowl. Put the remaining cup of water in a separate bowl. Slowly pour the almond cream through the cheesecloth, bringing up and closing the edges of the cloth. Twist the cloth to wring the almond cream into the bowl. Dip the cloth, with the almond paste tightly enclosed, into the bowl with the clear water, and swirl it around to soak up some of the water. Repeat the squeezing process into the first bowl. Combine the liquid from both bowls and discard the almond residue.

**3.** Pour the almond cream into a saucepan, heat it slightly, then add the sugar and almond extract. Slowly, taking about 15 minutes, bring the liquid to a boil over medium-low heat, stirring constantly. (It is important the cream be heated slowly to avoid curdling.) If serving Almond Cream, serve hot or cold in individual bowls.

**4.** To make Almond Float, pour the almond cream into a rectangular casserole and chill until jelled. Cut the jelled almond cream into 1-inch diamond pieces. Make diagonal cuts 1 inch apart in one direction and diagonally 1 inch apart in the other direction. Transfer the pieces to a glass serving bowl and add chilled fruit such as lychees or mandarin oranges and their syrup. Serve cold.

# FIRECRACKERS

Chinese have always enjoyed firecrackers, believing that their bangs and pops ward off evil spirits. Here's a dessert shaped like a firecracker, and whenever I serve it, it gets as big a bang as any real firecracker. It has a lot going for it: it's absolutely delicious, easy to make, looks smashing and can be made in advance and kept in an airtight container. The Cointreau isn't a part of authentic Chinese cuisine, but the results are tasty.

## Filling

1 10-ounce package pitted dates

½ cup finely chopped walnuts

2 tablespoons apricot preserves

1 tablespoon grated orange rind

1 teaspoon Cointreau (optional)

80 store-bought or homemade Wonton Wrappers (page 193)

2 cups corn oil, for deep-frying

Confectioner's sugar, for dusting

*1.* If using a food processor, chop the dates until fine. Add the walnuts and process a few seconds more. Scrape the sides of the work bowl, add the preserves, orange rind and Cointreau, and process a few seconds more until the filling holds together.

*2.* If working by hand, chop the dates, walnuts and orange rind separately, then mix in a bowl. Spread the mixture on a chopping board, add the preserves and chop all the ingredients together.

*3.* Transfer the filling to the center of a large square of plastic wrap. Fold the plastic wrap over the mixture (this keeps your hands from touching the very sticky filling) and mold it into a flat 6-inch square about ¼ inch thick. Unwrap the filling and wet the blade of a small knife. Cut the filling into strips 1 inch long × ¼ inch wide.

*4.* Put a strip of filling in the corner of a wonton wrapper and roll to form a cylinder. Wet the free corner of the wrapper and press against the roll to seal. Twist both ends of the roll to enclose the filling and to create the look of a firecracker. Continue making the firecrackers until all the filling is used.

*5.* Heat the oil in a wok until it reaches 325° F. Add as many firecrackers as will float freely, then deep fry, stirring frequently until they're golden brown and crisp. Drain the firecrackers on paper towels. Allow to cool, then dust with confectioner's sugar.

# HOT TAPIOCA PUDDING

*Serves 4*

*T*apioca is a natural thickener made from yucca, a starchy root, which can be made into puddings. This pudding uses a nondairy creamer, but cream and butter can be substituted if you are serving a dairy meal.

*2 cups water*
*6 tablespoons*
   *small-pearl tapioca*
*4 tablespoons*
   *margarine, at*
   *room temperature*
*1 cup nondairy*
   *creamer*
*2 small eggs*
*Dash of kosher salt*
*3 tablespoons sugar*
*1 teaspoon vanilla*
   *extract*

### Topping
*1 tablespoon sugar*
*1/2 teaspoon margarine*

*1.* Put the water into a large saucepan and bring to a boil. Add the tapioca and cook until pearls are translucent and only a small white dot remains in the center. Cool slightly, then add the margarine. Stir well and set aside.

*2.* In a small saucepan, heat the nondairy creamer until hot. Beat the eggs in a mixing bowl, then add the salt, sugar and vanilla and blend. Add 2 tablespoons of the hot creamer to the egg mixture and stir, and then slowly pour the egg mixture into the saucepan of creamer, stirring constantly.

*3.* Put the saucepan with the tapioca over moderate heat. Cook, stirring, until the mixture bubbles around the edges of the pan. Add the creamer mixture and stir well. Pour mixture into a 7-inch Pyrex pie plate or 4 individual heatproof dessert cups.

*4.* Sprinkle the top with sugar and dot sparingly with bits of margarine.

*5.* Place pudding under the broiler until the sugar turns golden brown and the margarine melts. Serve warm.

# CANDIED GINGER

*C*andied Ginger is easy to make and will keep for weeks in an airtight jar. The homemade version has a sharper, stronger taste than the commercial variety.

*4 ounces fresh ginger*
*½ cup water*
*¾ cup sugar*
*Additional sugar, for*
*dusting*

**1.** Peel and cut the ginger into ⅛-inch-thick slices, each about the size of a quarter.

**2.** Put the ginger in a saucepan and add ¼ cup cold water or enough to cover the ginger. Bring liquid to a boil, turn down the heat to a bare simmer and cook for 20 minutes. Drain and pat dry with paper towels.

**3.** Sprinkle a layer of ¼ cup of sugar on a plate and place it and the sugar bowl near the stove.

**4.** Combine the remaining ½ cup sugar and ¼ cup water in a saucepan and bring to a boil. Turn the heat to medium and cook the syrup for a few minutes until sugar is completely dissolved. Add the ginger and when the syrup begins to boil again, turn the heat to low. Cook for 5 minutes. Turn the heat back up to medium-high and cook until the sugar reaches 230° F. on a candy thermometer.

**5.** Put a strainer over a wide-mouth jar and pour the ginger with the syrup into the strainer. Quickly put the drained ginger on the sugared plate and sprinkle more sugar on top of the ginger pieces. Toss to coat the ginger, being careful not to burn your fingers. Store the ginger in an airtight container layered in its own sugar. It will keep for months.

*Note:* Save the ginger syrup and add several spoonfuls to Steamed Pears (page 219) or to a fruit salad.

# SWEET WALNUT-DATE SOUP

### Serves 6

**U**se a Chinese ceramic spoon to experience the smoothness of this soup.

*2 cups shelled walnuts*
*¼ cup rice flour*
*4 tablespoons sugar*
*5 dates, chopped*
*4 cups water*

*1.* Place the walnuts, rice flour, sugar, dates and 2 cups of the water in a blender and blend them until mixture is smooth.

*2.* Pour the mixture and the remaining 2 cups of water into a heavy saucepan. Put the saucepan over medium heat and bring to a boil. Reduce the heat to a simmer, stir frequently to prevent sticking and cook for 10 minutes. Ladle into small bowls and serve warm.

# CRISPY BOWS

### Makes 80 bows

**W**onton wrappers are very versatile. This time they appear as an easy, delicious dessert. Serve them with a mixture of cut-up fresh fruit, Glacéed Oranges (page 216) or Steamed Pears with Candied Ginger (page 212).

*80 store-bought or homemade Wonton Wrappers (page 193)*
*2 cups corn oil, for deep-frying*
*Confectioner's sugar, for dusting*

*1.* Twist each wrapper in the center to form a bow.

*2.* Heat a wok and add the oil. When the oil reaches about 325° F., add the bows 8 or so at a time; do not crowd them. Stir frequently while they fry to a light brown. Remove and drain on paper towels. Let cool, then sprinkle both sides with confectioner's sugar.

*Note:* The bows will keep for several weeks in an airtight container.

# ALMOND COOKIES

Chinese cuisine has very few cookies, but here is a winner. They're not too sweet and have a subtle taste of almonds. Easy to make, they keep well in a cookie tin.

1½ cups all-purpose
  flour
½ cup sugar
¼ teaspoon baking
  soda
¼ teaspoon kosher
  salt
½ cup solid vegetable
  shortening
2 extra-large eggs, 1
  beaten
1 teaspoon almond
  extract
½ cup blanched
  almond halves

**1.** In a large mixing bowl, combine the dry ingredients. Cut in the shortening with a pastry blender or 2 knives until the mixture resembles coarse meal.

**2.** Add the unbeaten egg and almond extract. Knead only until the egg is absorbed, then chill the dough for about 1 hour.

**3.** Preheat the oven to 300° F. Break off bits of dough and shape each into a disk about 2 inches in diameter and ½ inch thick. Alternatively, roll the dough until ½ inch thick and cut out 2-inch rounds with a cookie cutter. Place the cookies on an ungreased cookie sheet about ½ inch apart. Brush the tops with the beaten egg and press an almond half in the center of each.

**4.** Bake the cookies for 5 minutes, then increase oven temperature to 350° F. and bake 15 minutes longer, or until cookies are light brown and crisp. Remove the cookies and cool on a rack.

# CARAMELIZED APPLES

This Chinese dessert requires organization, dexterity and timing. The challenge is fun and the results are delicious. First, the batter-coated apples are deep-fried until crisp. At the same time some sugar is caramelized quickly in hot oil. Then the fried fruit is coated with the syrup. Finally, at the table, the coated fruit is dipped in ice water to harden the glaze. The effect is spectacular and the taste delectable.

---

### Batter
1 cup all-purpose flour
¼ cup cornstarch
2 teaspoons baking powder
⅛ teaspoon kosher salt
1 cup plus approximately 3 tablespoons water

2 firm apples, such as Delicious or Rome
Flour, for dusting
2 cups corn oil, for deep-frying
7 tablespoons corn oil, for caramelizing
¾ cup sugar

1. Combine the dry ingredients for the batter in a large mixing bowl and gradually add the 1 cup of water, stirring until smooth. Add the remaining water, one tablespoon at a time, and only as many as it takes for the batter to reach the consistency of thick cream.

2. Peel the apples. Cut each apple into 6 equal wedges and remove the cores. Cut each wedge into 3 equal pieces. Sprinkle each piece with a little flour and set aside.

3. Place an oiled platter near the stove and have a bowl of ice water with many ice cubes in it ready to take to the table. Put a large saucepan on one burner and a wok on the burner next to it. Add the 2 cups of oil to the saucepan and heat to about 325° F. Dip the apple pieces into the batter and then place them in the hot oil. Deep-fry as many apple pieces as will float freely until golden brown. Turn frequently while frying, then remove and drain. Continue until all the apple pieces are fried.

4. As soon as the apples are fried, heat the wok and add the 7 tablespoons oil. Heat the oil until almost smoking, then add the sugar, stirring constantly. Cook and stir until the sugar begins to turn light brown. Pour in the apple pieces and toss until apples are coated with the caramelized sugar. Transfer the apples to the oiled platter and quickly take the platter with the hot caramelized apples and the bowl of ice water to the dining table. Dip the pieces of apple into the ice water and serve immediately.

---

*Note:* The oil from caramelizing the sugar and from deep-frying the apples can be saved and re-used for other cooking.

# GLACÉED ORANGES

Chinese often serve oranges after dinner. Here they are dressed up for company. Serve with Almond Cookies (page 214) or Crispy Bows (page 213).

*8 medium, sweet
    seedless oranges
1½ cups water
½ cup sugar*

**1.** Using a very sharp knife or vegetable peeler, pare very thin strips of rind from 1 orange. Cut the strips into needlelike shreds.

**2.** Put the shreds in a small saucepan and add ½ cup of the cold water or enough to cover the orange shreds. Bring to a boil, turn down the heat and simmer gently for 5 minutes. Drain and rinse the rind with cold water, then dry with paper towels to remove excess water.

**3.** Combine the remaining 1 cup water and the sugar in a small saucepan and bring to a boil. Turn down the heat, add the orange rind and simmer gently for 15 minutes or until the syrup thickens slightly.

**4.** Meanwhile, with a serrated or very sharp knife peel the remaining oranges, cutting away the white pith around the outside. Hold each orange over a bowl to catch the juices as you work. Cut each orange crosswise into 4 disks. Reconstruct the orange shape and push a toothpick through the slices to hold them together.

**5.** Arrange the oranges in a serving bowl and pour the syrup and orange-rind mixture over them, taking care to coat all of them. Chill thoroughly.

# SWEET RED BEAN PASTE

*Makes about 3 cups*

The nutritious azuki red bean is native to China, and is available in most U.S. health-food stores. The Chinese use it as a sweetened filling for pastry or steamed buns.

*½ pound dried azuki red beans*
*1 quart cold water*
*¾ cup sugar*
*¾ cup corn oil*

1. Check over the beans and discard any bad ones. Rinse several times, then drain. Put the beans in a heavy 2½-quart saucepan, add cold water and bring to a boil. Cover and cook over very low heat for about 1¾ hours, or until the beans are very soft and the water has been absorbed or has evaporated.

2. Put the beans in the bowl of a food processor and process to a smooth paste, using the metal blade. Or, if working by hand, mash the beans.

3. Return the bean paste to the saucepan and add the sugar. Place a Flame Tamer on the burner to reduce the temperature and put the saucepan on top. Turn on the heat to medium-low and, stirring occasionally to prevent the beans from sticking, cook the paste until it begins to dry. Slowly add the oil, stirring constantly until it has been absorbed. Continue to cook the paste slowly, stirring occasionally, for about 1 hour until it does not stick to the fingers when touched. Cool. It is now ready to use as a filling for desserts.

*Note:* The bean paste can be stored in the refrigerator for weeks or frozen for months. If you want to make steamed sweet buns, make the Yeast Dough (page 185) and fill the buns with the paste. Form and steam the buns following the directions for Steamed Cantonese Roast Veal Buns (page 187).

# ORANGE SPONGE CAKE

$S$erve this cake instead of the traditional Jewish honey cake. You can make it in advance and freeze it before adding the glaze. Then simply thaw the cake and add the glaze before serving.

¼ teaspoon kosher salt
1 cup sifted cake flour
6 extra-large eggs, separated and at room temperature
1 cup granulated sugar
¼ cup fresh orange juice, strained
2 teaspoons grated orange rind
Confectioner's sugar (optional)

### Glaze (optional)

4 tablespoons fresh-squeezed orange juice
1¼ teaspoons fresh-squeezed lemon juice
1¾ cups confectioner's sugar
2 tablespoons boiling water
2 teaspoons grated orange rind

1. Preheat the oven to 350° F. Add the salt to the flour and sift 2 more times. Have ready an ungreased removable-bottom 9-inch tube pan with 3½-inch sides.

2. In the bowl of an electric mixer, beat the egg yolks for 1 minute at low speed, then gradually add all but 2 tablespoons of the granulated sugar. Turn the speed to high and beat for 5 minutes. Mix in the orange juice.

3. Turn the mixer to the lowest speed and gradually add the flour. Be sure to scrape the sides of the bowl while beating and beat only until incorporated. Stir in the orange rind.

4. In a separate bowl, beat the egg whites until they form soft peaks. Add the remaining 2 tablespoons of granulated sugar and continue to beat until the egg whites are stiff but not dry.

5. Using a plastic spatula and being as gentle as possible, fold a quarter of the beaten egg white into the egg-yolk mixture. Add another quarter; do not be too thorough. Then gently fold the egg-yolk mixture into the remaining egg white, folding only until the egg white can barely be seen.

6. Gently pour the batter into the tube pan. Level the top with a plastic spatula. Bake for 55 minutes, or until the top springs back when touched.

7. Remove the pan from the oven and carefully invert over the neck of a bottle. Allow the cake

to hang until it is thoroughly cooled. To remove the cake from the pan, with a sharp knife cut around it as close to the pan as possible. Lift the cake from the bottom with the center tube. Now cut between the cake and the bottom of the pan. Cut around the center tube. Put a rack over the cake and invert both to remove the cake. Invert the cake again so that it is right side up. Sprinkle with confectioner's sugar or cover with the glaze.

**8.** If using the glaze, combine all ingredients except the orange rind. Stir until the mixture has the consistency of heavy cream. Add the orange rind and blend.

**9.** Carefully place the cake on a cake rack over wax paper. Poke holes randomly down through the cake with a metal skewer, then drizzle the glaze over the cake, allowing some to run down the sides. When the glaze has set, transfer the cake to a serving platter and serve.

# STEAMED PEARS WITH CANDIED GINGER

*Serves 4*

**4 hard pears, preferably Anjou**
**12 large pieces Candied Ginger (page 212) or store-bought**
**Few spoonfuls syrup from Candied Ginger (optional)**

**1.** Peel and core the pears, then place 2 or more pieces of ginger in the cavity of each pear. Arrange the pears on a deep heatproof dish. Add the ginger syrup if using.

**2.** Bring water in the base of a steamer to a boil and add pears. Steam for 25 to 30 minutes, or until pears are just soft. Save the juice in the dish. Chill the pears. Serve pears in individual bowls with a few spoonfuls of the steaming juice over each.

# INDEX

*P*age numbers in italics refer to recipes.

223